Management Consultancy

Many professionals are now working on a consultancy basis. *Management Consultancy: How to Win* is a practical guide for both those new to consultancy and experienced consultants seeking formal accreditation. The reader journeys through every stage of a consultancy operation, discovering what commonly needs to be achieved at each one. Every stage is supported by tables, charts, tips, and tools, which the reader may adopt or adapt to their needs. It also delves into the emerging trends in consultancy and its markets, ensuring the reader is up to date and in tune with the industry.

Yet theory will only take you so far. A key element of the book is learning from consultancy engagements and the problems common to all consultants, irrespective of the location or culture in which they work. The reader learns from real-life situations faced by consultancies from the largest international names to solopreneurs.

This is an essential guide for aspiring, junior, and mid-level career consultants, including those aiming to become Certified Management Consultants or gain the UK's Chartered Management Consultant status or equivalents elsewhere. Those on executive education programmes or studying business and management at the postgraduate levels will also value its deft mixture of theory and practice.

Peter Cross is an experienced international management consultant who advises organisations of all kinds on achieving successful change.

Management Consultancy
How to Win

Peter Cross

Routledge
Taylor & Francis Group
LONDON AND NEW YORK

Designed cover image: ©Getty Images – credit: AndreyPopov

First published 2026
by Routledge
4 Park Square, Milton Park, Abingdon, Oxon OX14 4RN

and by Routledge
605 Third Avenue, New York, NY 10158

Routledge is an imprint of the Taylor & Francis Group, an informa business

British Library Cataloguing-in-Publication Data
A catalogue record for this book is available from the British Library

ISBN: 978-1-032-79085-5 (hbk)
ISBN: 978-1-032-79083-1 (pbk)
ISBN: 978-1-003-49045-6 (ebk)

DOI: 10.4324/9781003490456

Typeset in Times New Roman
by Apex CoVantage, LLC

Contents

About the Author

Management consultancy was the end point of my career – but it didn't start that way. I began in local government, and it was there that I became known as a safe pair of hands. Being parachuted into a crisis to resolve whatever problems that particular department was facing. Excellent training for a consultant who needs to be a fast starter adept at quickly grasping the main issues. Later, I was made responsible for delivering IT and business change projects. I segued into the UK National Health Service as a regional computer auditor investigating any number of issues, even becoming the go-to expert on interrogating the largest payroll system in Western Europe.

I moved on to join a major international consultancy, where I mainly worked on IT security and IT-related change across the public and private sectors in the UK and Europe. Since then, I have worked independently with hundreds of small- and medium-sized businesses, global corporations, and governments. I have founded boutique consultancies and collaborations and have been a senior manager and director for other substantial consultancies on major projects nationally and internationally.

Management consultancy has taken me to more than a dozen countries. It has introduced me to refuse collectors, clerks, scientists, surgeons, CEOs, government ministers, and, even in one case, "Peter, I would like you to meet the next President of our country." I admit it was a very small country, but still . . .

I have also written the best guide for project managers ever: *Project Management Bootcamp: A Step-by-Step Guide*.

It has been a blast.

Acknowledgements

This book is the result of learning, support, and input from many people over more than four decades of consultancy. Among them, and in no particular order, there are multiple people called John, at least a couple of Mikes and Colins, several Ians, David, Robin, Sue, Georgie, Kay, Anne, Bob, Hugh, Jo, Paul, Jill, Hugh, and Mark. I also owe special calls out to Adam Packard for his thoughts on marketing and to everyone in the administration and support teams who are the ones who actually make the consultancy industry work. Only I know how much I am indebted to them all.

Also, thanks to my wife Jo for her support, tolerance, and corrections to my English, to my daughter Charlotte for her publishing know-how, and to Andrew Harrison, Zoe Everitt-Spence, and the team at Routledge for transforming my thoughts on management consultancy into this book.

As always, all of the credit belongs to these and many others, while I, once again, own all of the mistakes.

Introduction

The objective of this book is to share with you how to build a winning consultancy career by building on the aptitudes and skills you already have. It will take you through the step-by-step processes that will help you to create and deliver consultancy services successfully. This makes the book an ideal starting point for readers seeking to develop a winning consultancy career, either by growing their consultancy firm or by progressing towards managerial roles within a professional consulting firm.

What is a consultant, and is it different from a management consultant?

The term consultant is now widely used to describe the provision of expertise in many areas. A helpful starting point for us is the description of consultancy used by the UK's Chartered Management Institute, which includes the Institute of Consulting. It sees professional consulting as providing expertise, advice, and guidance to clients (Chartered Management Insitute, 2020). This definition identifies two elements: clients and expertise.

Clients: Invariably organisations, such as businesses of all sizes, international, national, and local governments, other public service providers and charities.

Expertise: Any skill a client may wish to purchase from a third party as an alternative to employing staff. For example, one company, ostensibly a global engineering consultancy, employs over 60,000 specialist staff, ranging from archaeologists to zoologists.

We could consider management consultancy a specialist subset of these skills, perhaps focused on corporate strategy and its implementation. However, drawing a hard line between these and other skills is difficult. For example, should we include information technology? Similarly, can we include other specialist areas such as taxation planning, human resources, and property management as management consultancy? This book adopts the simplest definition of management consultancy: providing professional expertise of any kind to the management of any organisation. This means that throughout the book, we will concentrate on how we deliver professional expertise as consultants not on the expertise itself.

Who are you?

Whatever definition we choose for our services, there is one thing that all management consultants should have in common: We are genuinely good at what we do. So good, in fact, that organisations value our skills and are prepared to pay a premium for them. What we sell to them is different, far more exciting, and lasting than mere goods or products; it is knowledge

DOI: 10.4324/9781003490456-1

and expertise in delivering change. Change that genuinely moves humanity, or at least part of it, forward. Most consultants will say that it is the changes they have helped clients make that reward them most. It could be the industry that they reformed to give the public a better service, the company whose fortunes they turned around safeguarding jobs and delivering a more secure return to investors, or the project they rescued, which delivered government services that were faster, better, and cheaper.

Consequently, being a successful management consultant requires an unusual blend of personal qualities and attributes. So, let's start with an honest self-appraisal. Please ask yourself:

Am I curious and inquiring?
Do I always want to know how things work?
Am I driven to find answers to make them work better?
Can I work with a huge variety of people of all types, levels, and abilities?
Am I able to take responsibility for organising my own work and equally able to work alone or as part of a team?

If you answer yes to all of the previous questions, you probably have the core personality traits needed to succeed personally as a consultant. In addition, ask yourself:

Can I:
Frame simple but penetrating questions?
Research, listen actively and intelligently, and learn continuously?
Synthesise information and answers into a coherent picture?
Draw valid conclusions, frame clear recommendations, and persuade others to take action?

If you answer yes to these questions, you should have the basis of the consulting skillset you will need. If not, you should already see the areas where you need to improve.

Another crucial aspect to consider is the currency of the professional skills and services the client will buy from us. Our skills are the "talent" we sell to clients to resolve their problems, and only by constantly improving and developing them can we ensure that we always offer the best service to our clients. So now ask:

Do I already possess core professional skills that will likely attract potential clients?

If you answer yes, you are ready to commence your career as a consultant, whether working for a consultancy organisation or creating a business yourself.

If, however, you have answered no to this (or any of the other questions), then your career in consultancy could be as a business leader. You will have to develop the skills and strategies needed to access and lead the talent required to deliver consultancy services.

In management consultancy, we are both the product and the shopkeeper. As the "product," whatever we do, we have to present the best version of ourselves every day. If we are "on fees," we have to deliver for our client. They are not paying for the hungover, tired, or jet-lagged version of us. Our best version of us is the one that they agreed to buy. This is especially true, and highly visible, if we work on the client's site. Similarly, if we are working on any other activity, such as marketing, promotion, and sales, which will be most of the rest of our time, we need to be at our best and deliver our top game. Being any less may result in failing to spot a client opportunity or a losing sale we should have won.

How this book could help you win?

Globally, consultancy is now an established route for organisations to acquire short-term professional expertise. If you are new to this area, this book and its pragmatic approach will help you avoid the more prominent issues that lurk in the shadows, ready to ambush the incautious or inexperienced. Of course, sometimes we can get lucky and become successful by being in the right place at the right time. However, it is surprising how often thoughtful preparation and the consistent application of proven processes like those in this book can put us in that right place at that right time.

To help you develop your thinking, the book has a theoretical case study and a reflections section in each chapter based on resolving problems you may encounter in creating, growing, and delivering a consultancy service. These reflections can be based on either the theoretical case study or an example of your choosing. They will build into a skeleton file that charts your thinking about a consultancy service from its initial definition to closing your first client engagement.

There are, however, no universally correct answers because, as in real life, successful strategies for overcoming problems depend not only upon the context of the problem but also on the environment and culture in which you are working.

Virtual excursions

In Chapter 1, we encounter a few individuals who have impacted consultancy in some way. Our other virtual site visits consider problems consultancies and their clients face. These are drawn from real-life examples and lessons learned at the coal face of delivering management consultancy for four decades. Each visit has been chosen to illustrate universal points about management consultancy. To protect the guilty (and the innocent), I have striven to ensure that the assignments, clients, and consultants are not identifiable.

As you might expect, if you work in a cultural or economic environment different from the example, you might need to consider how to transfer their lessons to your situation.

Success is not a methodology!

This book's core philosophy is that building a winning consultancy career consultancy is not about box-ticking methodologies, techniques, software tools, or artificial intelligence (although these and many others are useful in the proper context). Instead, it is based on the fundamental concept that it is our thought processes, research, creativity, and ability to influence and persuade others that are crucial to delivering successful consultancy services. This is as true for a stellar career in the most prominent global consultancies as it is for a solo consultant.

Equally, this book is agnostic about whether you should follow particular methodologies for delivering consultancy engagements (although there is a selection of more commonly encountered ones in Chapter 9). As any experienced consultant will tell you, some methodologies are helpful in some circumstances, others are not, and all wax and wane in popularity over time.

Sometimes, they are the creations of one or two particular individuals and were the basis of a successful company (see Charles Bedaux in Chapter 1); sometimes, they are commercial offers that can be licensed, and at other times, they are openly accessible.

A guidebook for the journey

Chapter by chapter, this book covers what we commonly need to achieve at each stage in our journey as consultants. It provides practical examples of actions or tools that you could use in your work as a consultant. Whether you use these tools, invent your own, or find a brilliant idea from a methodology or elsewhere is your choice.

The discussions in the following chapters are not definitive; they are starting points for your journey as a thinking consultant. Please consider each chapter as a one-to-one training course or personal coaching session. Feel free to argue with your trainer or coach for a different approach when you disagree. You can then translate your thoughts into strategies for your particular service in your geography and culture that may meet your unique combination of circumstances far better than the generic concepts in any book.

So, whatever your background, career objectives, and current situation, I hope you find something informative and thought-provoking in this book that will help you win in your life as a management consultant.

Bibliography

Chartered Management Institute. (2020). *Level 7 Professional Consulting Syllabus*. London: Chartered Management Institute.

1 Grasping the Basics

Aim of this chapter: To explore the issues around the delivery of consultancy services, including providing context through understanding the history of consultancy services, career paths for consultants, and the differences between working in a consultancy and other types of organisations.

Learning outcome: To be able to understand and confidently describe the context of delivering consultancy services to business.

A short history of management consultancy services

When did management consultancy begin? Arguably, decision-makers have always found advisers, but management consultancy, that is, formally providing expert advice to organisational leaders, started during the late nineteenth century. Its continuing development has followed the increased complexity and business specialisation in many different sectors and geographies ever since.

Today, the global consulting industry is estimated to generate over $250 billion in annual revenue and to consist of over 700,000 firms. These figures have enormous caveats. For example, many companies offer professional services other than management consultancy. Some, for example, are primarily accounting firms, while others operate outsourced service contracts alongside consultancy. Therefore, the actual level of global spending on advising management is difficult to unravel. What we can say is that it is an industry that has developed rapidly in line with the complexity of management, has few barriers to entry, and operates in a world very different from its early pioneers. But we can still learn from their success stories.

Throughout the book, we will conduct virtual site visits to see consultants and consultancies in action.

For now, we are going back in time to meet a management consultancy character.

It is a warm day, but you might want to wear your best clothes as we are going to a wedding!

It is 3 June 1937. We are standing just outside a modest chateau in the Loire region of France. Inside, a couple, friends of friends of the chateau's owners, are about to be married. If circumstances had been different, today would have been the wedding of the decade and would be taking place in London's Westminster Abbey. The groom is Great Britain's former

DOI: 10.4324/9781003490456-2

king, Edward VIII, and the bride is the divorced American socialite, Wallace Simpson, for whom he gave up his throne. The couple's photographs, taken on the front steps of the chateau, will appear on newspaper front pages and cinema newsreels around the world.

It is not the couple in whom we are interested but the chateau's owner. Although originally a poor French émigré, he is now an American citizen and one of the ten wealthiest people in America. He and his American-born wife bought the chateau a decade ago and have lavishly modernised it since.

He is Charles Eugene Bedaux, born in Paris in 1886 and, after various low-wage jobs, emigrated to America in 1906. Over the next few years, he became interested in the application of the emerging discipline of scientific management. This included applying F. W. Taylor's 1903 book Shop Management, particularly time-study practices, and Charles E. Knoeppel's writings on industrial layout and routing. Bedaux took their thinking forward and developed a system of standardised units by which manual work could be measured. Bedaux's consultancy career started around 1913, and he went on to create his own firm, the Bedaux Company, in 1916 in Cleveland. Over the next ten years, he built this into a very successful international organisation with operations throughout the United States, Europe, Africa, India, and Australia. Now, he and his wife are hosting a royal marriage.

Sorry, it looks like the security guards have spotted us; it's time to leave . . .

To complete his story, Bedaux's fall was even more spectacular than his rise to fame. On 18 February 1944, he died in prison in Miami, Florida, where he was being held and charged with treason. He had been arrested soon after the Allied invasion of North Africa in 1942, where he had been planning to build an oil pipeline across the desert for the Vichy French government and the Nazis. His death was adjudged to be suicide, but it was said that it came as a relief to many, as he knew far too much about the connections between American industrialists and Nazi Germany.

The firm he had created survived him, and its successor, the International Bedaux Institute, although no longer delivering consultancy, is focused on developing learning around process improvement.

Since its first emergence, management consultancy has followed leading-edge thinking, from the early principles of scientific management to the application of artificial intelligence. Its history is probably best reflected through examples of companies stretching back over 175 years to the mid-nineteenth century. We can examine this history by examining how some of the industry's large players started and have grown into the universal professional services companies of the twenty-first century. Like the Bedaux organisation, they were all started by entrepreneurial individuals, and many still carry their founders' imprint.

Arthur D. Little

The management consultancy industry has grown from multiple sources. In 1886, in Boston, Arthur D. Little started a company specialising in industrial research, initially in cellulose and paper making. It made notable advances over the following decades, including weaving the first commercial textile fibre from cellulose acetate, synthesising the first "anti-knock" compound for vehicle engines, and developing the oxygen masks used by the pilots of high-altitude warplanes. Alongside this research work, under the slogan "other people's troubles are our business," it developed a management consultancy that undertook an increasingly wide range of work, including setting up research labs and advising on developing natural resources in Canada and economic development in Puerto Rico.

In 1949, the company pioneered the application of military operations research to business. This approach was initially trialled to improve Sears Roebuck's catalogue operations. In 1951, it was used to improve logistics operations in the Johnson and Johnson Baby Products division, and then to create the SABRE booking system for American Airlines.

The story of Arthur D. Little is not one, however, of uninterrupted growth and success. After a period of poor management in 2002, the company filed for Chapter 11 bankruptcy. Tiax LLC acquired the USA assets and staff. Altran acquired the name and European assets. In 2011, the Altran directors led a management buyout and reformed Arthur D Little as a partnership. Today, Arthur D. Little operates across the Americas, Asia, Europe, and the Middle East, with offices in 32 countries in a wide range of sectors, stretching from aerospace and automotive to energy, finance, healthcare, and public services to transportation.

Little's company provides a model of how many organisations still active in management consultancy today developed their general advisory arms from a specialist base.

PricewaterhouseCoopers

Another source of management consultancy firms, again starting in the late nineteenth century, was the growing financial audit practices. Companies were used to purchasing the required independent audits of their accounts from such partnerships, which gradually broadened their service offer to include a range of advisory services. One example of such a firm is PricewaterhouseCoopers (pwc is a brand name, not the company), now with 360,000 staff in 151 countries. It started as a sole practitioner accountancy in 1849 when Samuel Price set up in Gresham Street in the City of London. Five years later, William Cooper established a similar practice – becoming Cooper Brothers seven years later. Samuel Price was joined by William Hoyland, who persuaded a colleague from his existing firm, Edwin Waterhouse,[1] to join as well. After Hoyland left, the partnership changed its name in 1874 to Price, Waterhouse & Co.[2] In 1890, the company opened its first overseas office in New York.

The spate of mergers and acquisitions in the financial professional services sector in the second half of the twentieth century led Coopers to merge with several other firms. In 1998, it finally merged with Price Waterhouse to form the current company as a federation of country-based partnerships. For many years, regulators were concerned that auditors providing consulting services to audit clients may not correctly report any audit issues to safeguard valuable management consultancy contracts. In this climate, in 2002, the pwc partners sold their management consultancy arm to IBM for a reported \$3.5 billion. Over the following years, however, pwc re-entered the sector and now offers services in areas such as finance, technology, strategy, operations, human resources, and transformation consulting.

McKinsey & Company

James O. McKinsey was born in 1889; after a career that included groundbreaking work in accounting education and becoming President of the American Accounting Association, he changed his focus to management. In 1926, he was appointed professor of business policy at the University of Chicago, where he started his own management consultancy business. In 1944, when opening its third office, the firm rejected the concept of a loose network of geographic offices and permanently committed to a structure based on a single firm with shared resources and a single mission. It is now led by a Shareholders Council, essentially an elected board of 30 directors and the managing partner.

As early as the 1920s, McKinsey advised the USA government on the organisation of government departments, which it has continued to do since. In the 1950s, it introduced corporate planning to companies such as Ford and AT&T. During the 1980s, the company introduced the Six Sigma methodology to General Electric, and in the 1990s, it championed Operational Excellence based on the work of Tom Peters and others. Post 2000, it has grown a significant interest in helping clients with issues around sustainability. As of 2023, McKinsey reported employing approximately 45,000 staff based in 130 offices in 65 countries.

It is time for a second virtual site visit to meet another management consultancy character.

This time, we are going to visit a Friday night cattle auction in Texarkana, Texas, so dress appropriately. It is a hot Friday night in 1940.

You need to look out for a 10-year-old boy who is closely observing the auctioneer selling cattle, mules, and horses. Look again, and you will see that he and his father are also buying and selling inexpensive bridles. From his father, he is learning how to focus on profit margins, buy low and sell high, hone his negotiation skills, and follow his one rule: Never take anything home at the end of the night.

Let us pick up our budding entrepreneur again on 27 June 1957, his twenty-seventh birthday. He has come out of the USA Navy and is joining IBM as a salesperson back in Texas. His negotiation skills from that Texarkana barn will be put to very good use, and by 1962, he will make his entire annual sales target in just 19 days. He suggests to IBM that instead of just selling hardware, they sell the complete package of hardware, software, and consultancy services to their customers. They decline and so on his thirty-second birthday, 27 June 1962, Ross Perot sets up EDS – Electronic Data Services with a borrowed $1,000.

Starting by processing data for hard-pressed companies, EDS grew to such an extent that by the early 1980s, when looking to improve its internal systems, General Motors bought EDS for $2.5 billion, more than had ever been paid for a computer services company. The entrepreneur soon reemerged, and in 1986, with his son and associates, he founded Perot Systems. His son took over as chair and CEO in 2004, and in 2009, they sold the company to the computer manufacturer Dell for nearly $4 billion. Dell later sold Perot to Japan's NTT for about $3 billion.

Of course, Ross Perot's story was not confined to IT and consultancy services. In 1992, he became the most successful third candidate in a USA Presidential election since 1912. Perot gained 19% of the public vote. Running again in 1996, he still secured an 8% vote.

The development of management consultancy from very small beginnings to today's global industry can be summarised as follows:

- **Late nineteenth century**: Firms looked to their audit firms for broader financial advice and support as the impact of legislation and company ownership became more complex.
- **Early twentieth century**: New firms, often started by a single individual, appeared to help support the drive for operational efficiency and the employment of scientific management principles. This service area has spawned many different performance improvement approaches and methodologies, creating an alphabet soup of acronyms.
- **Mid-twentieth century**: Clients sought advice on developing corporate strategy, improving the organisational structures that would deliver it, and driving service improvements through different models.
- **1980s onwards**: The driving force has been supporting clients through technological change, especially information technology. This information technology revolution has driven an increase in the range of services offered by existing consultancies and led to the creation of entirely new information technology consultancies. Some of these are an adjunct to other professional services, for example, when computer giant IBM bought pwc's consulting arm, or as a commercialisation of internal services from large companies, for example, Tata Consultancy Services, which grew from Tata's IT department.

The stories of the consultancy pioneers and similar backstories of leading firms across today's management consultancy industry show that they have grown, often from single-person businesses, by extending their range of consultancy services to meet increasing client demands. While these new services are frequently provided by existing players, the market's growing demands also create opportunities for new entrants. Over time, some of these new entrants have expanded their service offerings, but others have remained focused on a single service niche.

Today, the management consultancy market is characterised by segmentation into many different service lines. The scope of these still grows and changes as a result of three factors that have always impelled the growth of consultancy services:

- Increasing complexity of issues facing organisations.
- Increasing pace of change.
- Shortage of specialists able to advise organisations.

Career paths for consultants

Consider the first results (of over 2,000) of a search for management consultancy vacancies on a major job site.

IT Risk Management Consultant Estimated $108K–$136K a year: *Cybersecurity and risk management experience. Identify risk remediation activities and create action plans for our clients with . . .*

General Management Consultant $73,100–$166,000 a year: *Whether standing up a new organisation, transforming an existing one, or transitioning an organisation, including a merger or split-up, our clients need a . . .*

Innovation Consultant $140,000–$180,000 a year: *Knowledge of innovation management or strategy. 2–4 years of project management experience. 3–6 years of client management/consulting/SaaS experience.*

Management Consultant $145,000–$165,000 a year: *Work with client leaders in sales, marketing, finance, and human resources to solve sales management issues and grow revenue.*

Senior State HR Management Consultant (HR Consultant 2) $6,901–$10,161 a month: *Eight years of professional-level human resource experience in workforce management, investigations for clients, and implementing human resource management principles and practices.*

Disability Management Consultant $78,800–$175,000 a year: *Must have strong relationship management, interpersonal, collaborative, and organisational skills, with the ability to ask thoughtful questions to . . .*

Change Management Consultant $111,000–$141,000 a year: *The Change Management consultant will use change management principles and practices to help clients plan, implement, and integrate change and user adoption initiatives . . .*

The salary ranges indicate that employers may expect applicants with different experience levels. The breadth of skills listed shows that consultancy now covers the broadest range of industries and management skills. However, these roles in consultancy firms represent only one of three management consultancy career paths; the others are independent and internal consultancy. These are not separate career paths, and many consultants will switch between them during their careers.

The employed route

Consulting firms are usually hierarchical and typically have a four- or five-level career pyramid. This structure is seen across the United States, the UK, India, Europe, and Australia. Firms often have different naming conventions for their roles and grades, and there is some variation between different geographies. The following types of roles are encountered in most major consultancies, but smaller firms may have a much flatter structure. However, they may also focus on hiring only more experienced staff:

- **Intern roles**: Usually, fixed-term posts offered to college students, possibly vacation roles or more extended periods of work experience. Most interns will be providing support to other consultants. Not all companies offer internships, and there may be intense competition for those in leading consultancies. It may also be worth searching for a recruitment agency specialising in internships and approaching mid-level and niche consultancies.
- **Consultant/analyst**: Typically filled by recent graduates or new entrants to consultancy. They may handle small workstreams or engagements under the supervision of more senior staff.
- **Senior consultants**: Expected to have three years of relevant experience. They will handle larger, more important workstreams and complex engagements.

- **Manager/managing consultant**: Typically having eight to ten years of experience in consulting or may be brought in as experienced hires with management experience in a key area. They are responsible for managing the day-to-day activities of more significant engagements, supervising the quality of work, and potentially leading sales initiatives or defined business areas.
- **Partner/director**: May lead an area of the overall practice, be in charge of selling consulting projects to clients, and act as owners of individual projects.[3]

Promotion between levels is typically based on aptitude and experience, which are assessed regularly, often every six months. The assessment will consider the progress demonstrated by the work undertaken on individual engagements and may include feedback from colleagues, engagement managers, and clients.

Up or out

Many consultancies have a pyramid staffing structure; Accenture, for example, has over 774,000 staff and an executive leadership team of 30 (2024 figures). McKinsey's has 2,700 partners and around 45,000 staff (2022 figures). In many companies where a staff member fails to achieve promotion between grades, they may be "managed" out, creating headroom for promotions of employees on a lower level. This is not a universal policy adopted across all consultancies; alternative approaches to "Up or Out" include the following:

- **Dual career track**: This system allows employees to choose between two career paths: one leading to a management position and another to a senior technical one. This system allows employees to choose a career path that aligns with their interests and strengths.
- **Rank and tenure**: Employees are given a rank based on their performance and are granted tenure after a certain number of years. This system provides job security and allows employees to focus on their work without worrying about being "let go."

Even where an "Up or Out" policy is not adopted, career success usually depends upon maintaining a successful track record of profitable completed client engagements. Continued employment is at risk if the individual or the broader company fails to maintain demonstrable profitability. In 2023, for example, the big four accountancy firms were reported as shedding 9,000 management consultants to pivot their focus onto other services.

The prospects of a continuing consultancy career for those not being accelerated to partner/director status are still buoyant. The training, experience, and qualifications gained, especially in brand-leading consultancies, are still desirable attributes. Many consultants will successfully switch employers during their careers, potentially gaining promotion to higher levels more quickly or may move into independent consultancy.

The independent consultant route

Individuals becoming independent consultants usually fall into one of two groups:

- **Established professionals**: Having a track record of delivering specialist services who feel they can successfully provide similar services to multiple clients rather than supporting one organisation.
- **Experienced consultants**: Those leaving a consultancy organisation and striking out on their own, possibly due to being "managed out."

When deciding to follow the independent route, we should be aware that countries have different rules on setting up businesses and taxation regimes. We also need to consider different procurement regimes and practices that can adversely affect newly created and small consultancies.

The general business pressures on independent consultants are a microcosm of those of all other consultancy businesses:

- Maximum total income is always the outcome of the number of chargeable days available to provide services and the amount the market is willing to pay for those services (stock × sales price).
- Time spent on marketing, sales, and management is at the expense of chargeable work.[4]

Larger consultancy businesses can average these factors over many consultants. Therefore, they have more resilience than the solo consultant, who is locked in a cycle of chargeable delivery absorbing all available time, followed by intense sales and marketing and very little delivery.

Internal consultancy

Some larger organisations maintain internal consultancy teams, which are free from these general business pressures. Compared to the overall size of the consultancy industry, these represent a relatively small number of career opportunities. Some companies see them as a stepping stone into management roles rather than a separate career stream. There may be less travel as an internal consultant than an external one, which may be an advantage for some consultants. However, not having a wider range of exposure to different clients and industries or access to the training programmes of large consultancies are career disadvantages.

Culture shock – the transition to consultancy

Anyone entering a large consultancy from education will find they are included in a cohort of new entrants. Their cohort embarks together on a programme designed to equip them with the tools and skills that they will require at every stage of their career. These programmes typically mix training, on-the-job experience, coaching, and mentoring. As "first jobbers," they face the same challenges as everyone leaving education and entering work.

Experienced hires from industry will not only find themselves undertaking similar training programmes but also see significant differences from employment in other types of organisations:

- **Loss of status**: Many will have been line managers or internal company experts. Now, they will be team members, valued for the experience they can bring to clients but with little or no responsibility for the management of the business. In previous life, they may have achieved the sought-after corner office with a team responsible for meeting their every need. As consultants, they will have a laptop, a phone, and perhaps a hot desk if they can find one!
- **Time is money (1)**: Every minute of their contracted hours must be recorded accurately.

- **Time is money (2)**: Client consultancy assignments are usually delivered against a contracted budget and timeframe. The consultant is pressured to ensure that their contribution is delivered within that budget and timeframe.
- **Travel**: The opportunity to travel is often seen as one of the main attractions of a career in consultancy. However, the reality of a relentless travel schedule to work on client sites, attend internal meetings and conferences, or give sales presentations disrupts personal life. All too frequently, travel time is extra to "normal" working hours.[5]

The consultancy cycle

Consultancy is often referred to as a cycle and is shown as having five typical stages:

1. Entry and contracting.
2. Data collection and diagnosis.
3. Feedback and the decision to act.
4. Implementation.
5. Extension, recycling, or termination.

This is a massive oversimplification. The delivery of management consultancy services is a series of two interrelated, repeating processes, each of which consists of five or six distinct steps:

1. Sales.
2. Engagement.

For many consultancy companies, obtaining a follow-on contract from an advisory engagement to deliver or manage an implementation project is a key sales objective. Implementation project delivery is far more closely allied to project management than engagement delivery and is outside the scope of this book.[6]

Figure 1.1 shows how the two primary cycles interact.

In terms of the impact on the consultant, it should be noted that each cycle tends to operate with different timelines and dynamics. The two cycles covered in this book are those covering sales and engagements. The sales element of the process tends to be driven by clients, engagement timescales are agreed upon between the client and the consultancy, and implementation deadlines are identified by the consultant and ratified by the client.

There is another cycle that overlays these intercutting client and serviced focus cycles: the consultancy business cycle. This cycle deals with a business organisation's creation, maintenance, and growth. While it applies to all businesses, it has many distinct flavours for consultancies, which are covered in the following chapters.

Management consultancy and ethics

Management consultancy is an industry producing no physical product against which a client can apply measurements and standards. Instead, clients trust that we will work in their best interests to deliver a professionally competent service in accordance with proposals made and

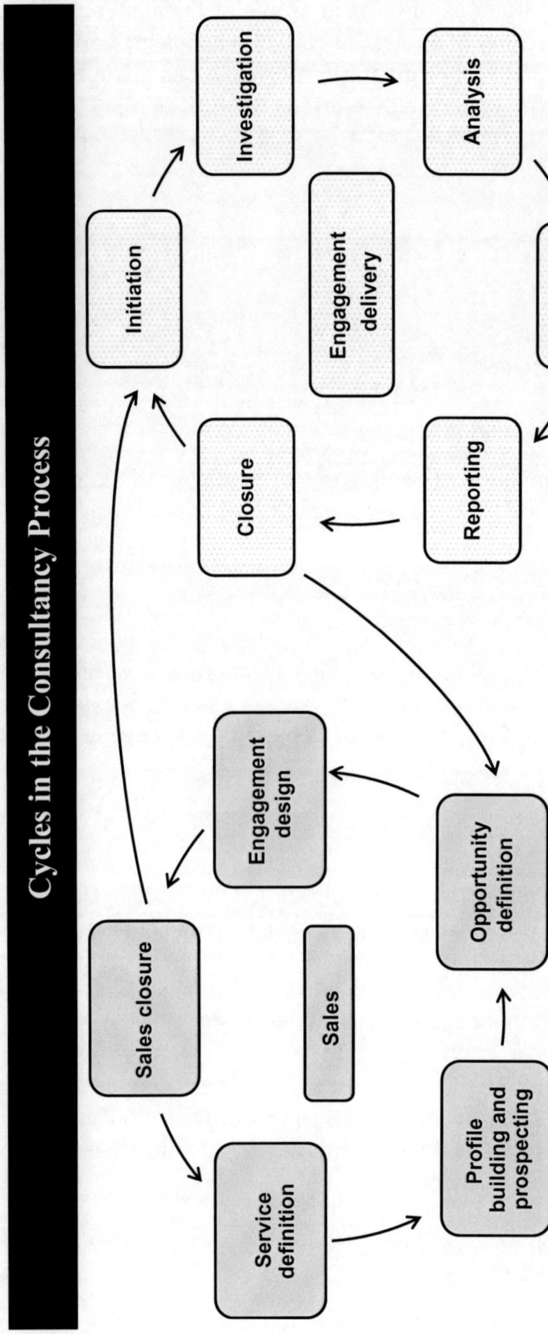

Figure 1.1 Cycles in the Consultancy Process.

It's time for another site visit, the first to our continuing case study.

You literally are in the hot seat.

PNX Consultancy Services is a newish regional company aiming to grow its reputation for high-value consulting and client base quickly. A recruitment consultant approached you and encouraged you to jump into consultancy from your role as a business technology manager in an insurance company. Previously, you were a junior manager in their marketing team, specialising in online channels.

PNX wants you to develop new consultancy service lines to draw out the "best-of-breed" technologies and operating methods from financial services and introduce them into other sectors. You started this morning. A senior manager arranged for your building pass, IT, and telephone. They have shown you around and introduced you to those of the team who happened to be in the office. Now, they have deposited you outside the partner's office to whom you will report. This was not the partner who interviewed you; they have left to spend more time with their money.

You knock and go in.

Partner: "Welcome [insert your name here]. I know we have not met before, but I have been fully briefed on your capabilities, and I have been looking forward to you starting. We are keen to use your expertise in technology exploitation to develop new services across our client base. You should know that all managers and partners follow a twin-track approach to our work. The first track is fundamental to our business model; we all undertake sufficient billable work to cover our personal costs to the firm: our salary, pensions, and benefits. My first boss referred to this as 'wiping your face.' I must admit I didn't understand the phrase then, and I don't now! The second track is that the company invests the rest of our time in other activities such as service development, sales, training, and mentoring. At this point, I always have to explain to starters coming new to consultancy from what I like to call an inside role that we depend on effective and immediate time recording. This is the time you have spent and the time you plan to spend. Do stop me and ask questions."

You: "OK, I would like to ask one question. I understand that time spent has to be billed to clients, but why is planned time so important?"

Partner: "Time represents our stock. I have a forward-looking weekly timeline representing chargeable time booked, non-chargeable time allocated – that's holidays, training, sales, etc. – and the balance of time available. It really is the last one that I have to be most concerned about; it is the "stock" that we still have to sell. This brings me neatly to you."

You: "Me? I thought I was here to develop and lead a new service offering."

Partner: "Yes, you are. That is your track two, and I will come to that in a minute, but I wanted to ask for your help on another matter first. This is track one, and it is more immediate. I met with a client yesterday. There are difficulties with an assignment, and I need to bring in someone first for an impartial view of how we might rectify the situation to rebuild client trust and then to oversee the resolution process. I will get the job manager to give you all the gory details and to set up the necessary meetings. The fundamental issues are as follows: We are halfway through the engagement and nowhere close to delivering, but we have spent 90% of the budget, and the client is close to starting legal action."

You, diplomatically not sharing your actual thoughts: "Well, that's something client-related to get my teeth into straight away. Now, about my track two?"

Partner: "I want to keep in close touch with you over this problem. Turning to track two, by the end of the month, can you please work up a short paper with your overall vision of what a full service would look like, say in one, two, and three years, and a high-level plan to get there? The third thing you will be doing in that time is undergoing our manager induction programme, and you will now be taken down to meet our HR team, who are organising that for you. They will also show you the hot desk area. Please call me on Friday morning to let me know how you are progressing with track one."

At that, he beckons to an HR intern who has been waiting outside, and you are led away.

So, it's baptism by fire, and later, as you go back into the open-plan main office to fight for a desk, your thoughts turn to the quiet life, the personal assistant, and that corner office that you had until just last week . . . .

contracts agreed upon. This trust is, therefore, the basis on which we can sell our services. It is hard-won and easily destroyed, which means that maintaining an ethical approach to our work and our clients is essential to our continued success.

Time for another site visit.

This time, we are going to observe a meeting between Jack, an independent IT consultant, and Jill, the local manager for a hardware supplier responsible for the small business sector. There is no need for a coat; we will be inside.

The meeting is taking place in one of those nondescript modern office buildings in an out-of-town business park. Jack subcontracts to a company run by one of his old bosses. It has a call-off contract with a government body to help small businesses develop strategies to modernise their computer systems. Only a couple of manufacturers are interested in supporting the small business market, and Jack has been talking to them about hardware solutions for various clients for some months. Jill has requested the meeting.

After discussing the pressing needs of three of Jack's clients over coffee in the office cafeteria, Jill invites Jack into a private meeting room and closes the door.

"Jack, I want you to know that we are very grateful to you for the clients that have come to us as a result of your work."

Jack nods.

Jill continues: "We want to recognise the importance of our continued relationship by offering you an agency agreement. Nothing between us would change, and nothing between you and your clients would change. You will continue to do your investigations and make recommendations. We will continue to specify the solutions to the client needs you bring to us, and we will offer you a standard 10% commission on all sales we make to your clients. What do you think?"

How should Jack respond?

Before considering the issues, this example raises, we should consider the guidance on ethical standards applicable to management consultancy that have been drawn up to promote trust and confidence in the industry. The International Council of the Management Consulting Industries has published a Code of Conduct for Certified Management Consultants that categorises the required behaviours as serving the interests of:

- Clients.
- Society.
- Those I work with.
- The consultancy profession.

(International Council for Management Consulting Institutes, 2024)

By contrast, the International Standards Organisation (ISO) analyses the code of ethics required of management consultants differently under the following headings:

- **Responsibility to the public:**
  - Efficiency.
  - Sustainability.
  - Responsibility.
  - Legal.
  - Public confidence.
- **Responsibility to the profession:**
  - Respect for the profession
  - Integrity and professionalism.

(International Standards Organisation, 2017)

Our code of ethics, however, should be more than a set of policies to comply with recommended national or international guidelines. It should embody the core values of our consultancy, inform its every action, and against which both it and the individuals within it should be judged.

The example code of ethics for our hypothetical consultancy firm, PNX, covers the main requirements of professional bodies and the ISO and communicates key responsibilities to staff, clients, and stakeholders.

PNX Consultancy Services

CODE OF ETHICS

Introduction

PNX Consultancy Services is a professional service provider that supports its clients through high-quality and value-adding services in dealing with issues such as strategy development, innovation, management of change, and performance improvement.

This Code of Ethics sets out our core values of integrity, independence, objectivity, and responsibility that guide the behaviour and actions of PNX, its directors, managers, consultants, staff, subcontractors, and associates. It also sets out the expectations and obligations that PNX has towards its clients, the public, and the profession.

Integrity

PNX acts honestly, transparently, and fairly in all dealings with clients, stakeholders, and the public.

It will avoid any conduct that might compromise or damage its integrity or reputation.

It will disclose and mitigate any conflicts of interest or potential conflicts of interest that might arise during its assignments.

Confidentiality

PNX respects the confidentiality, privacy, and security of its clients and other parties' information, data, and intellectual property and will use them only for the purposes authorised by its clients or the law.

PNX ensures that its consultants and staff understand the importance of confidentiality and provides them with the necessary training, guidance, equipment, and support to maintain it.

Professionalism

PNX provides its clients with high-quality, value-adding services that meet their needs and expectations, and it maintains the professional competence of its staff.

PNX complies with all laws, regulations, and ethical standards and promotes the adoption of best practices and standards in the management consultancy profession.

Health: Safety and Welfare

PNX complies with all laws, regulations, and standards related to health and safety, including those required by clients when operating on their premises or on their behalf, and promotes the adoption of best practices and standards in these areas.

Efficiency

PNX has a systematic and structured approach to its assignments and applies relevant methodologies or techniques to ensure that its services are effective and efficient.

PNX monitors and evaluates the progress and outcomes of its assignments and takes any appropriate actions to ensure that client requirements and expectations are met.

PNX provides clear, accurate, and timely reports, feedback, and recommendations to clients and ensures that these are based on professional analysis, judgement, and reasoning.

Transparency

PNX provides clients with clear, accurate, and timely information about its services, fees, and terms of engagement. It ensures that both parties understand and agree upon them.

PNX raises any necessary changes to or deviations from the agreed-upon scope, objectives, deliverables, or fees of the assignment as early as possible and seeks client authority before proceeding.

Offers of Employment

PNX will not accept applications from, engage in any discussions or negotiations with, or offer employment to a client's employees or contractors without the client's prior consent for a period of not less than six months following the completion of a client engagement.

Sustainability

PNX considers the social, economic, environmental, and ethical implications of any assignment and will recommend actions to its clients to minimise any negative impacts or risks that may arise.

Legal

PNX will not engage directly or indirectly in any activity that might contribute to corruption, bribery, fraud, or other forms of unethical or illegal behaviour.

PNX will take appropriate measures to prevent, detect, and report any suspected or actual illegal behaviour.

Public Confidence

PNX will avoid any actions or omissions that might harm or damage public confidence in the management consultancy profession.

PNX communicates honestly, accurately, and transparently with the public and avoids making false or misleading claims or representations.

Respect for the Profession

PNX respects the rights of other management consultancies and avoids any conduct that might harm or damage their reputation or interests.

PNX contributes to developing and advancing the management consultancy profession and actively participates in relevant professional bodies and associations.

Workplace Diversity: Equality and Inclusion

PNX values the diversity of its clients, consultants, and staff and promotes a culture of diversity, equality, inclusion, and respect within our organisation and with clients.

PNX has a zero-tolerance approach to discrimination or harassment based on race, gender, age, religion, nationality, sexual orientation, or any other personal characteristic and will maintain robust measures to address such behaviour.

PNX considers the diversity implications of its assignments and will recommend actions to its clients to minimise any negative impacts or risks that may arise.

Reporting and Whistleblowing

PNX encourages its consultants and staff to report any concerns, issues, or violations of this code of ethics or any other ethical standards as early as possible, either to line managers, nominated senior managers, or such bodies as may be appropriate.

Using the end-of-chapter reflections

In the reflections section at the end of each chapter, please draw on your experience or current situation or use the theoretical case study. There are no correct answers or crib sheets at the back of the book – the reflections are here solely to help focus your thinking on the topics raised in each chapter.

Creating notes in response to each question and sticking with a single case study throughout the book will constitute a record of how you choose to think through building and delivering a service from its inception to its successful operation.

Theoretical case study

Our background for the theoretical case study is simple. You are the newly engaged consultancy manager in PNX Consultancy Services in the site visit. Your background is in marketing, technology, and management in the insurance industry. Your brief is to develop and market a range of services to the public and service sectors based on expertise drawn from insurance and broader financial services. You will create and lead a team of high-performing consultants to sell and deliver the services. You have been told that you will have a direct route to a partnership if you meet your financial targets.

Currently, the firm has strategy, IT, and process improvement experts and a sales and marketing support team working mainly in financial services and manufacturing but with little experience with public bodies or the broader service sector. The management team has given you three months to prepare a strategy, an implementation plan, and an operating model for the new service.

The reflection sections in the following chapters will help you consider the issues involved in creating and managing such a service.

If you have no knowledge of the sectors nominated, this case study presents you with the opportunity to sharpen your research skills. These are essential for a consultancy career where you may have to switch to clients in different industries or sectors immediately.[7]

Reflections

- List three lessons from the history of management consultancy that may be useful in developing and delivering successful consultancy services.
- Briefly set out the vision for a new consultancy service and how it may be justified in business terms.
- Prepare a draft of a code of ethics for the new service.

Notes

1 The Waterhouses were a power family of the Victorian era. Edwin became president of the UK Institute of Chartered Accountants from 1892 to 1894. Alfred was a famous architect who, among other buildings, designed London's Natural History Museum and was President of the Royal Institute of British Architects (as was his son Paul and grandson Michael). Theodore was a lawyer and founder of the legal firm Waterhouse, which merged with Fieldfisher in 1989. Waterhouse was only dropped from that company name in 2014.

2 The comma in the name was dropped during World War II. It was joked that the printing ink saved was the company's main contribution to the war effort!

3 One partner in a global consulting practice was known for checking a printed draft of every report for spelling and grammar. They used a postcard to obscure the remainder of the text, so they were not distracted by meaning. They insisted that this was because their personal reputation was at stake as they would be signing the final report.

4 Or sleep.

5 Such as completing a full-on day with one client and travelling in the late evening/night to be ready for a client breakfast meeting at 8.00 am the following day. This is fine until the plane develops a fault, is delayed by 2 hours, and the seats behind you are occupied by two overtired, bored, and screaming children, who should have been in bed hours ago, and by their frazzled mother who is definitely not sitting between them to stop them fighting, nor is their father who is sitting three rows back, dozing and pretending that he has nothing to do with them! Did I mention the change of time zones, so we lost an hour as well?

6 Guidance on implementation support is covered in books concerned with project management.

7 For example, as part of an assignment to improve a local authority's performance, I spent Thursday observing processes by riding around the countryside on a refuse collection vehicle. On Sunday evening, as one of the team selecting an accounting system for the world's largest information services company, I had to welcome its country finance directors from South and East Asia, Australia, and New Zealand to the UK.

Bibliography

International Council for Management Consulting Institutes. (2024, January 31). *Certified Management Consultant*. CMC-Global. Retrieved from https://www.cmc-global.org//sites/default/files/public/icmci_cmc003_code_of_conduct_4.0.pdf

International Standards Organisation. (2017). *ISO 20700 Guidelines for Management Consultancy Services 2017-06*. Geneva: International Standards Organisation.

2 Creating a Consultancy Service

Aim of this chapter: To introduce the concepts and processes involved in consultancy service creation.

Learning outcome: To design and justify a new consultancy service and prepare business and implementation plans for its successful creation and launch.

We encounter similar business problems and need a similar systematic approach, whether we are developing new consultancy services within an existing business or launching a new consultancy. The differences are in the levels of justification and decision-making required and the availability of supporting expertise. It is easier for us as solopreneurs to reach a decision as the finance director, marketing director, and CEO are all rolled into one. However, it seems that defining a new service in a larger company requires endless meetings, discussions, and presentations before a decision is reached.

Time for a site visit.

Defining a service is not easy, and launching it can be fraught with obstacles.

We will eavesdrop on a planning meeting in a major accounting firm's consultancy arm. This is an upmarket office with ten directors and equity partners sitting around the table.

Managing consultant Jay has presented a plan to use existing staff to deliver a new service: reviewing the health and security of hospital information systems. After many frustrating months of discussion, other providers have entered the market, and Jay believes that they are losing their prime mover advantage.

We have reached the last decision – how to promote the service to potential clients and the most senior partner present is speaking.

"Well, Jay, we approve of the service concept and think the content for the website is first-class. It all tells a very persuasive story. We thought the text of the letter that you propose is succinct and to the point. The target recipients for your letter are 250 target hospital directors. Each of these is already assigned to one of 25 partners, and our policy is that all such letters to a client must be signed personally by the nominated partner. Experience dictates that each of these partners will have views on wording to be used, prospects for the service, its attractiveness, or not, to their clients and the risk that selling short-term consultancy engagements will have for their existing audit relationships. They even each have the right not to send the letter at all. So, your next step is to meet with each of them and discuss the whole idea."

DOI: 10.4324/9781003490456-3

How would you suggest that Jay progresses?

To complete the story, due to internal changes, the partner for whom Jay worked was asked to leave the partnership. Half of their team, including Jay, were released, and the company never sent the letter.

The following month, as a newly independent solopreneur, Jay mailed a letter with identical wording to the same 250 target recipients. From this small start, they created a thriving business.

Every service requires a unique approach because it addresses different client needs and markets and originates from consultancies with various processes, market positions, and business cultures. At one extreme, an individual consultant might decide to jump straight in and promote an idea to potential clients. The dangers here are that time may be wasted on an unattractive service, higher-value market opportunities may be missed without proper analysis, or the service may become locked into a low-day rate perception. At the other extreme, as in our site visit, we can reach virtual paralysis and potentially miss our market opportunity.

Figure 2.1 shows a model step-by-step process designed as a general guide to help develop new consultancy services which:

- Provide services that clients recognise as addressing their needs economically.
- Help ensure that the service meets the consultancy's aspirations.
- Manage risks inherent in developing consultancy services.

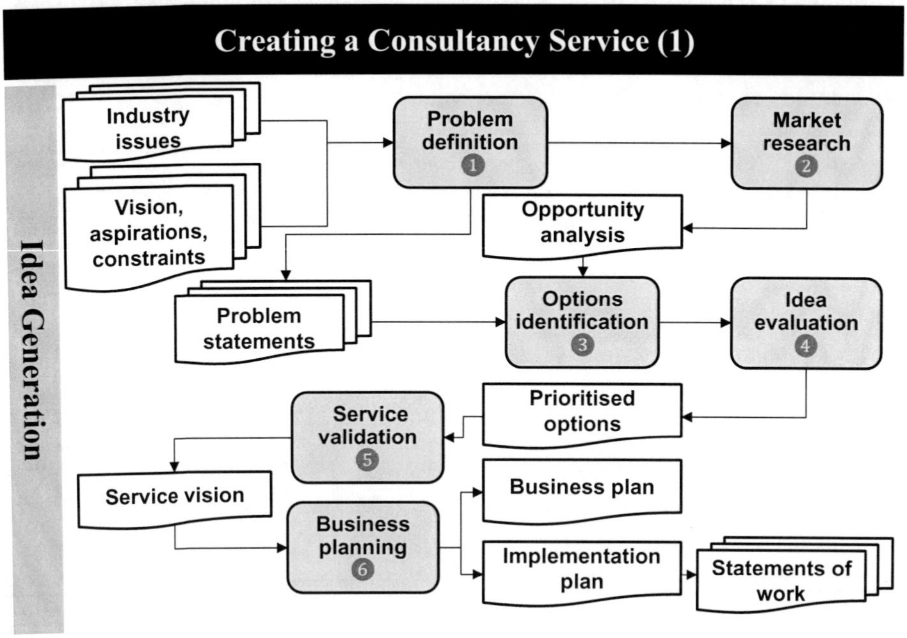

Figure 2.1 Creating a Consultancy Service (1).

Each process step builds ideas by extending and deepening thinking and documentation produced earlier. These steps should be seen as a starting point for creating a bespoke solution to meet individual situations as we need to adapt each of our processes due to:

- Variations in types of service being developed.
- Nature of the organisations developing them.
- Range of geographies in which services will be delivered.

We aim to follow a systematic, repeatable process to harness the excitement generated by developing new ideas. The output of this process is a well-planned, highly likely-to-succeed new service.

In following the step-by-step processes, throughout this book, we will be turning our management consultancy toolset on our most demanding client – ourselves. As ever, the key to this is our own skill set, and so it is worth bearing in mind our four self-assessment questions as we work through the different steps of creating our consultancy service:

Can we:

- *Frame simple but penetrating questions?*
- *Research, listen, and learn intelligently?*
- *Synthesise information and answers into a coherent picture?*
- *Draw valid conclusions, frame clear recommendations, and persuade others to take action?*

Step 1: Problem definition

At this step, our inputs fall into two categories: the issues and problems arising from the industry and the vision, aspirations, and constraints arising from the consultancy. An excellent technique for exploring these is creating groups of interested parties that can work together in facilitated discovery sessions. Such group formation may be a challenge for smaller consultancies. Still, it is worthwhile as following these steps creates a firm foundation upon which the service creation process can build, whatever the size of the consultancy.

Discovery sessions that operate as open group discussions or unstructured idea-generation sessions have drawbacks. One is that the most senior or loudest voices can dominate or skew the debate; however, if we use structured facilitation techniques, we can prevent such domination and ensure that all views are heard.

It's time to put you back in the hot seat at PNX.

Over the last week, you have identified eight people with health or technology expertise who could help you start working through the process of developing the new service. You have booked the best meeting room, ordered coffee and biscuits, and arranged for Chris, a trained facilitator, to lead the meeting. You are going to be a participant.

You: "Welcome to this problem discovery session. I have emailed or spoken on the phone to most of you over the last few days, but for those of you that I haven't met yet, I am [insert your name here]. I started at PNX just over a week ago, and our partner has asked me to leverage my knowledge of information systems and processes in the financial services sector to develop a new offer for our clients elsewhere. Our aspiration is that this will be a major area for revenue growth and will deliver high-quality, high-value, and high-profile engagements that benefit our clients. Over five years, we plan to grow this fintech transfer to other sectors to be at least 10% of overall fee income. Today is an initial session to help define our thoughts on future service offerings. Chris will explain the process and lead us through it."

Chris: "Hi, I know most of you. I'm your facilitator today, and I'm here to help explore the problems preventing fintech from driving other service sectors forward and identify how PNX can help clients overcome them. You are here because of your knowledge of either the sectors or the exploitation of leading-edge technologies elsewhere. First, as part of our health and safety policy, you all know that we start every meeting with a brief safety moment. Please raise your hand if you spotted the trip hazard I deliberately placed in this room."

We can fast forward and rejoin as Chris starts his introduction to the main work of the meeting.

"Our stance as a company is that better use of information technology is vital for delivering high-quality, integrated services. We know that achieving this has many challenges and barriers, including sharing information effectively and securely. This affects the quality, safety, and efficiency of services and the satisfaction and trust of clients, citizens, and professionals.

To better understand the problems we may encounter and quantify their impact, we will undertake five exercises, each designed to help us gain a different perspective and insight into them. Our time today is only the start of a process, and our answers will be refined as we proceed with future steps in the design and validation of the new services.

In this process, it is easy to think about ourselves and lose our proper focus: our clients. So, in everything that you do today, please put yourselves in the shoes of clients by answering two questions:

> *'How will this delight our clients?'*
> *'How will this turn them from our clients into our ambassadors?'*

The four exercises are:

- ***Problem statement**: To define the problems we are trying to solve clearly and concisely, we'll use the format: 'How might we (goal) for (users) in (context)?' For example, 'How might we leverage information technology to facilitate knowledge sharing for public sector staff drawn from different organisations but working in integrated service teams?' or 'How could we exploit artificial intelligence-based technologies to support a risk-based approach to delivering planned logistics services?' We'll also identify those problems that are most likely to be the basis for our services.*
- ***User research**: To work through the questions, we need to ask the users to understand their needs, pain points, and expectations regarding each problem. For example, What information do you need to provide or receive services? How do you access, share, and store information? What are the benefits and challenges of information sharing?*

We'll prioritise and refine the questions and assign responsibilities for conducting user research. Today, we are working at a high level, so I envisage we will also need to talk to those with access to current information later. Then, we can plan and schedule any further research activities, such as interviews, surveys, observations, etc., that we may need to plug any information gaps.

- ***Data analysis**: We will identify how we will analyse the research data using qualitative and quantitative methods, such as coding, categorising, sorting, clustering, measuring, etc. We'll identify the key themes, insights, and patterns from the data and how we might visualise them using charts, graphs, or diagrams. We'll also discuss the roles of interpreting and drawing conclusions from the data.*
- ***Solution ideation**: We will generate ideas for potential solutions to the problem using creative and divergent thinking techniques, such as mind mapping, sketching, prototyping, etc. We will be imaginative and innovative and consider different perspectives and scenarios. We will also evaluate and shortlist the most feasible solutions using criteria such as impact, cost, time, risk, etc.*

These exercises will help us design a high-quality, evidence-based management consultancy service for our clients. We'll also have to show the net benefit to them, their stakeholders, and, of course, their customers.

I hope you're excited and ready to start our discovery session.

Let's begin with the problem statement."

Chris then hands out a series of different coloured sticky notes.

"Take your sticky notes and a pen, and write five problem statements, one per note. Remember the format is: 'How might we (goal) for (users) in (context)?' When you're done, please stick your notes on the board. We'll have 20 minutes for this exercise."

Table 2.1 summarises a different PNX discovery session for a service focusing on delivering AI-related consultancy in healthcare organisations. It shows how the individual thoughts, group discussions, and exercises were combined into a series of problem statements, which are primary inputs to the next step in our process.

Table 2.2 suggests a simple format for tracking not only the successful problem statements passed forward for further work but also those being paused or dropped, allowing us to revisit them later if necessary.

Engagement is not consultation

Fully engaging from the start with those people who will help deliver our new service fosters their ownership of the problem and their support of the eventual solution. The time and effort they have invested also help drive the change forward, which is a far stronger effect than achieved through a mere consultation process. However, with this engagement comes a risk, especially where new information conflicts with previously held views and assumptions, when we must be cautious about the objectivity of evaluations. This is because there is a natural tendency to overvalue that which supports previous decisions and undervalue that which does not. This is called continuation bias and not acknowledging it could lead to wasting resources on ideas and services that either are not viable or should have a lower priority.

Table 2.1 PNX Consultancy Services Application of Advanced AI in Healthcare Agreed Problem Statements

PNX Consultancy Services Application of Advanced AI in Healthcare Agreed Problem Statements						
Problem Area	**Description**	**Potential AI Solutions**	**Constraints**	**Stakeholders**	**Research Needed**	**Data Analysis Method**
1. Data Management	The health sector processes large volumes of data, which are challenging to manage/analyse	Efficient data management, predictive analysis, real-time decision-making	Data privacy regulations, interoperability between systems, quality of data	Healthcare providers, patients, software supplies, regulatory bodies	Best practices for data management in healthcare, latest AI techniques for data analysis	Statistical analysis, machine learning algorithms
2. Patient Diagnosis	Accurate and timely diagnosis is critical in healthcare. Manual diagnosis can be time consuming and prone to errors	Analysing data and images for quicker, accurate diagnoses, proactively identify and assess patients with "at-risk" prognosis from profiled data	Acceptance of AI decisions, integration with existing diagnostic processes	Doctors, patients, hospital management research bodies, professional bodies	AI models for medical diagnosis, validation studies	Deep learning for image analysis, natural language processing for clinical notes
3. Treatment Personalisation	Every patient is unique and may respond differently to the same treatment	Personalising treatment plans based on patient data	Complexity of human biology, long-term validation of AI	Doctors, patients, pharmaceutical companies, funding bodies	AI models for the prediction of treatment outcomes	Machine learning for prediction models, data mining for discovering patterns
4. Operational Efficiency	Health sector operations are complex, possibly inefficient	Streamline operations, automate routine tasks, improve efficiency	Change management, training of staff to use AI tools	Hospital management, funding bodies, staff	AI in healthcare operations, successful implementation case studies	Process mining for understanding workflows, AI for optimising resource allocation
5. Research and Development	R&D in the health sector can be slow and expensive	Accelerate R&D by identifying patterns and insights from large datasets	High investment costs, need for multidisciplinary expertise	Researchers, pharmaceutical companies, funding bodies	Research on AI in drug discovery, clinical trials	Data mining for hypothesis generation, AI for simulation and modelling

Table 2.2 PNX Consultancy Services Application of Advanced AI in Healthcare Problem Statement Summary

PNX Consultancy Services Application of Advanced AI in Healthcare Problem Statement Summary		
Resolved	**Unresolved**	**Closed archive**
Problem statements with reference numbers and supporting information that are closed because an agreement has been reached that they should be carried to the next stage	*Problem statements with reference numbers require more discussion because agreement was not achieved or the discussion revealed new items that needed further research or consideration*	*Problem statements with reference numbers that are closed because the discussion has revealed them as not helpful or not required*
2. Patient diagnosis 3. Treatment personalisation 4. Operational efficiency	1. Data management	5. Research and development
Next steps		
Suggestions for future actvivity. Complete market research proposals for problem statements 2, 3, and 4. Arrange for further discussion to examine problem statement 1 data management. No further action is required for problem statement 5 as it was felt that this might be an area for potential future development.		
Prepared by	**Date**	

Step 2: Market research

Having defined a set of potential problem areas around which we could build new services, we need to understand which ones could be viable and in which markets they might be most attractive to clients. This means we have to gather sufficient data to build a picture of the viability of each service in each potential market. We may already have identified some of the key information required, data sources, and contacts while developing our problem statements; if so, we need to revisit and update them before proceeding.

The data required will naturally vary for each idea generation exercise but should include elements of the following:

- **Competitor analysis**: To help us position our services, we need to analyse our potential competitors and understand their strategies, strengths, weaknesses, service offerings, pricing, reputation, client base, and market share.
- **Willingness to pay**: Before developing a competitive (but profitable) pricing strategy, we will need to assess potential clients' willingness to pay for our services using surveys, interviews, or other market research.
- **Market demand**: We need to assess potential growth rates, technological, economic, and other factors that influence our market (see Chapter 9 PESTLE) influencing our markets.

- **Client needs and expectations**: Shaping our proposed services to meet client needs will give us a competitive edge. To do this, we need to research what potential clients are looking for from a consultancy service, including identifying current and future pain points. We must also assess how well potential clients understand how our service would ameliorate their problems.
- **Regulatory environment**: We need to investigate their regulatory environments, including any licensing requirements, data protection laws, and industry-specific regulations in each of the markets which we might wish to target.
- **Market segmentation**: To target our services more effectively, we must identify different market segments based on factors such as industry, company size, and location.
- **Marketing and promotion strategies**: We should analyse different marketing and promotion strategies used in our target markets to help us determine which are the most effective ways of communicating with our potential clients and promoting our services.
- **Service differentiation**: Differentiating our services from those of our competitors is key to standing out in a competitive market and setting effective pricing strategies.

The output from the market research stage is an analysis of the areas of opportunity for services segmented by market sector and tailored for each problem statement. Our analysis should be concise and contain sufficient detail to inform the next step in the process: options identification. The following is a sample of how the market analysis for one of the PNX team's ideas looks.

PNX Consultancy Services

Opportunity Analysis

Management Consultancy Services for AI-based Predictive Patient Assessments

1. Competitor Analysis

We have not discovered boutique or local consultancies offering AI-related services in healthcare in any market. In all markets, most healthcare AI software providers offer implementation services. These are being discounted as they cannot provide clients with either unbiased strategy or procurement support. Our main competitors, therefore, will usually be established leading consultancies.

USA: Leading competitors include ABC and DCE consulting groups, which have a combined market share of 35%. Their strengths are extensive experience, a wide service range, and strong brand recognition. Our flat structure, lower-cost base, and lower target margins allow us to offer lower fee rates, which will be significant advantages for us.

Canada: The key players are FGH and IJK, with a combined market share of 35%. Their strengths are brand reputation and a range of services. They lack our tight focus on healthcare AI. Our flat structure, lower-cost base, and lower target margins allow us to offer lower fee rates, which will be a significant advantage for us.

UK: LMO and PNQR are dominant, with a combined market share of 40%. They have very robust service offers and a high level of brand recognition. However, they are not as agile as smaller, more specialised consultancies like ourselves. Our flat structure, lower-cost base, and lower target margins allow us to offer lower fee rates, which will be a significant advantage for us.

Europe: STU and VWX are dominant players in many countries. Each has a strong regional presence but lacks the global reach of some competitors. Our flat structure, lower-cost base, and lower target margins allow us to offer lower fee rates, which will be a significant advantage for us.

India: YZA and BCD are the major competitors. They have a strong understanding of the local market and a massive IT systems presence. Their services are competitively priced, but they have little experience in AI implementation in healthcare.

Australia: EFG and HIJK have a significant presence in healthcare and strong brand recognition but limited exposure to AI. There is potential competition from new boutique firms focusing on AI in healthcare. Our flat structure, lower-cost base, and lower target margins allow us to offer lower fee rates, which will be a significant advantage for us.

In summary, our advantages over competitors are that we offer a more competitive offer because of a sharp and unbiased focus on AI in healthcare and competitive fee rates.

2. Willingness to Pay

USA and Canada: Clients pay a premium for expert services, with an average day rate of $X,XXX for AI-focused healthcare consultancy.

UK and Europe: Prices are sensitive due to competition, and the maximum acceptable day rate is likely to be $W,WWW.

India: The market is highly price sensitive, with an average day rate of $V,VVV, but there is a high demand for consultancy services.

Australia: Clients are highly willing to pay for quality services, with an average day rate of $U,UUU.

3. Market Demand

USA and Canada: The growing adoption of AI in healthcare is generating high demand for strategy and implementation consultancy. Annual growth is predicted to be above 20%.

UK: The market is being driven by a slower digital transformation in healthcare than in the United States. However, the UK government has now committed to using AI to revolutionise the National Health Service despite a poor success rate of national IT projects in health. Centralised public sector procurements, opposition to using consultants, and a lack of genuine benefit realisation may make the market more difficult to penetrate. Annual growth is predicted to be between 15% and 20%.

Europe: The market is driven by an accelerating digital transformation in healthcare. Annual growth is predicted to be above 15%.

India: Rapid digitisation in healthcare means that this is a high-growth market. Annual growth is predicted to be above 25%.

Australia: Steady market. The annual growth rate is predicted to be 10%.

4. Client Needs and Expectations

Clients across all markets seek reliable, effective, and user-friendly AI solutions that can integrate with their existing systems. They perceive they need help defining an AI strategy and support selecting the right system supplier. They also need comprehensive after-sales support and training.

5. Regulatory Environment

AI solutions must meet stringent regulatory standards in all markets. Additionally, each market may have regulatory considerations and variations, for example, data privacy (GDPR in Europe, HIPAA in the United States, etc.).

6. Market Segmentation

The market can be segmented by the size of the healthcare provider (small clinics to large hospitals), region, and provider type – private, public, or charity. We will tailor our services to each segment to better meet their needs.

7. Marketing and Promotion Strategies

Using online marketing tools with high-value content will effectively reach decision-makers across all markets. Partnerships with healthcare associations and presence at industry events will increase visibility. Key influencers will be identified as thought leaders in each market.

8. Service Differentiation

Having analysed potential competition in each market, we have identified that the main differentiators that we will stress in our promotion campaigns are our focus on AI in healthcare, provision of unbiased advice, and comprehensive suite of services, from AI readiness assessments to strategy definition, AI implementation, and long-term support.

Our Key Market Opportunities

1. **USA**: Clients show a high willingness to pay, and growing demand makes this a lucrative market.
2. **India**: Rapid digitisation in healthcare and a lack of specialised competitors present a significant opportunity, although willingness to pay may be an issue.
3. **Europe**: The digital transformation in healthcare and the stringent regulatory environment call for expert consultancy services. However, client willingness to pay is tempered by the need to demonstrate high levels of added value for our services.
4. **Australia**: High willingness to pay and low levels of competition present a market opportunity.
5. **Canada**: As in the USA, the growing demand for AI in healthcare and the high willingness to pay offer a solid market opportunity.
6. **UK**: Lack of willingness to pay for outside consultancy services and slower uptake of leading-edge technologies.

Step 3: Options identification

This step aims to develop the thinking from the problem statement and combine it with market information contained in the opportunity analysis to identify how we might build a service offer.

As in the problem definition step, we can use a facilitated workshop to bring together the thoughts of a range of people. As always, the agenda for such a discovery workshop will depend upon the previous outputs and the organisation's size. Again, the solopreneur may have to work through the issues covered alone or with a close confidant or mentor.

It's time to drop in on our second workshop.

You: "I see that we mostly have familiar faces and a few new ones. Thank you all for coming and freeing up the time from everything else you are doing. We appreciate it. Before we start today, I want to update you on what has happened since we last met. I have put our problem statements from the first workshop and the opportunity analysis to a panel of partners charged with validating new services against our corporate strategy. They want me to compliment you on the work that we have done. We prepared ten problem statements, of which we decided to park two and not pursue another. They have shortlisted five ideas from the remaining seven for us to pursue for now."

"Our first task is creating a prioritised list. We will select the top two and progress them to the next stage. Our other ideas are not dead; they are just held back for now to allow us to focus on those we think will be most successful. Once again, we have engaged Chris to run the workshop. So, it's over to you, Chris."

Chris: "Today, we will build on the problem statements and the evaluation of market opportunities. We will develop our ideas of what our services could look like and how we could deliver them. We will also document any advantages and disadvantages that we identify. We are not making judgements just yet, but I cannot overemphasise the importance of the work we will do today for the company's future growth and the quality of the services we will offer our clients.

Over the next 6 hours, we will undertake a series of facilitation exercises, the output of which will build upon each other. First, we will focus on the five problem statements selected by the partners and the associated market opportunity analyses emailed at the start of the week. The following exercises will be:

1. ***Brainwriting**: I will give you each one of the five problem statements. You write down your ideas on service delivery to meet the problem in a single sentence. Then you pass it on to the next person who builds upon those ideas and then passes it on for a second time, and we repeat the process until everyone has commented on each idea. We will then come together and prepare a consolidated outline of the services that we will be discussing during the rest of the day*
2. ***Mind mapping**: To help organise the information generated from the first exercise, we will split into five groups, each considering one problem statement. I'll take you through it when we get there, but it is a visual tool that helps structure information. We start from a central idea, branch out into new thoughts, and then branch out again. Ending up with a concept for one or more new services.*

3. ***Starbursting**: We will focus on generating questions about each service concept in your groups. I will explain in detail later. Each group will be drawing a lovely six-pointed star, putting our idea in the middle, and asking multiple levels of questions based on 'who, why, what, when, where, and how' I should add that we also ought to include 'how much' in some form. What we don't do yet is to answer them.*
4. ***Stakeholder mapping**: We will identify the key stakeholders involved, such as partners, clients, regulators, staff, and client shareholders. We'll analyse stakeholders' interest levels and the degree of influence on our service for each of the service concepts we have identified.*
5. ***Facilitated discussion**: We come back together for a structured debate during which we will finalise the design of our service ideas and prepare a SWOT Analysis – a tabulation of Strengths, Weaknesses, Opportunities, and Threats for each. Now, we start to answer our previous questions. There will be two rounds of discussion on each service, and we will follow some straightforward rules, which I will rigorously enforce to make sure we collect and give equal weight to everyone's views:*
   - *In the first round, you will have up to 2 minutes to state your views. Ideally, you should write this down first before we start the round. You then read it aloud so that we hear your opinions without being influenced by anyone else.*
   - *In the second round, you will have 1 minute to speak, and you should adjust your views as necessary, bearing in mind the points made by other speakers.*
   - *Interruptions and cross-table discussions are not permitted.*

Please note that I will be picking the speakers in both rounds in a random order.

At the end of the workshop, I will prepare a summary and circulate it to you all.

I saw that you all came into the room in groups and seem to have sat together. So before we start the brainwriting exercise, I am going to mix you all up. . ."

The success of such a discovery workshop heavily depends on the active participation of all attendees, so it is essential that we create an open and inclusive environment that encourages non-judgemental idea sharing. Experience shows that adopting specific techniques can help increase the quality of the outcome, and these could include the following:

- **Movement**: Creating a reason for attendees to move at regular intervals lessens the chance of them zoning out during a session. This might be as simple as calling a refreshment break, breaking up into smaller teams, or calling an attendee to the front of the group. If space permits, encouraging standing by using cards placed on the floor, for example, for synthesising views rather than the ubiquitous use of sticky notes placed on a wall, introduces movement and informality.
- **Diverse groups**: During the site visit, immediately after introducing the tasks, Chris broke up existing groups of attendees into fresh, diverse teams. This helps ensure that a wide range of views are brought to each team exercise, lessening the risk of answers being based on one perspective, for example, from the accounts department or the marketing group. Sometimes, it may be helpful to bring in outsiders to widen views even further. These could be outside experts or established clients.
- **Unpredictability**: During the site visit, Chris said that speakers would be picked in random order. This avoids "creeping death syndrome," where attendees can see their turn to speak gradually getting closer, and their concentration on the current speaker often lessens proportionately.

Table 2.3 PNX Consultancy Services Application of Advanced AI in Healthcare Brain Writing Exercise

PNX Consultancy Services Application of Advanced AI in Healthcare Brain Writing Exercise	
No.	**Sentence**
1.	The service should be global and led through regional centres of excellence, which are charged with developing thought leadership, sales and delivery methodologies, and training courses
2.	Services should be part of local sales and delivery infrastructure reporting to local partners, not a globally led and marketed service
3.	We need to seek partnerships with both national sector expert consultancies and general AI software suppliers
4.	A shared service centre could support smaller healthcare providers with a full range of services, including software, hardware, and consultancy.
5.	The consultancy offer should include a variety of services, from an opening, low-cost readiness review through strategy definition, procurement, and implementation support to post-implementation effectiveness audits and benefits reviews
6.	We should consider leveraging our existing client base in health insurance
7.	This service could be an ideal way to enter geographies where we have no or limited presence

- **Equality**: Controls are needed, so senior attendees cannot unduly influence, lead, or dominate facilitated or break-out team discussions. It is usually best to call on them towards the end of a discussion round, which is much easier if we have established that speakers will be called in an unpredictable order.
- **Control**: Part of ensuring that we obtain everyone's views is controlling each speaker so they cannot dominate the discussion. We are very strict over the imposition of the agreed time limits – a bell or gong is helpful. We can also say, "Do you have a final point that you want to make?" or, "That's a very interesting topic you have raised. Let's note it for now and come back to it later." The other aspect of control is preventing cross-table discussions, over which we need to be very firm. Usually, cutting across the debate with a simple "ZZ, you will have your opportunity to speak in a moment; please let XX finish" is sufficient.

The following are sample outputs from a discovery workshop for our PNX Consultancy case study. They show how they build on each other through the discovery workshop. Table 2.3 shows the sentences' output from a brainwriting exercise. Figure 2.2 is a simple mind map that has captured a series of ideas for the service. This service is carried forward into the example Starburst diagram in Figure 2.3 and the sample SWOT analysis in Table 2.4.

Stakeholder mapping is an essential tool to help us focus our communication and engagement activities. We analyse stakeholders on two axes: their degree of influence (or power) over our proposed service and their level of interest in it. The result is a simple two-by-two matrix, as shown in Figure 2.4, which groups stakeholders by the type of relationship we will need to have with them. These relationships will each require different communications and engagement goals and activities.

When using stakeholder mapping in a client situation, we can go a step further by assigning scores to the different stakeholders' degrees of influence and levels of interest and using these to plot a detailed heat map.

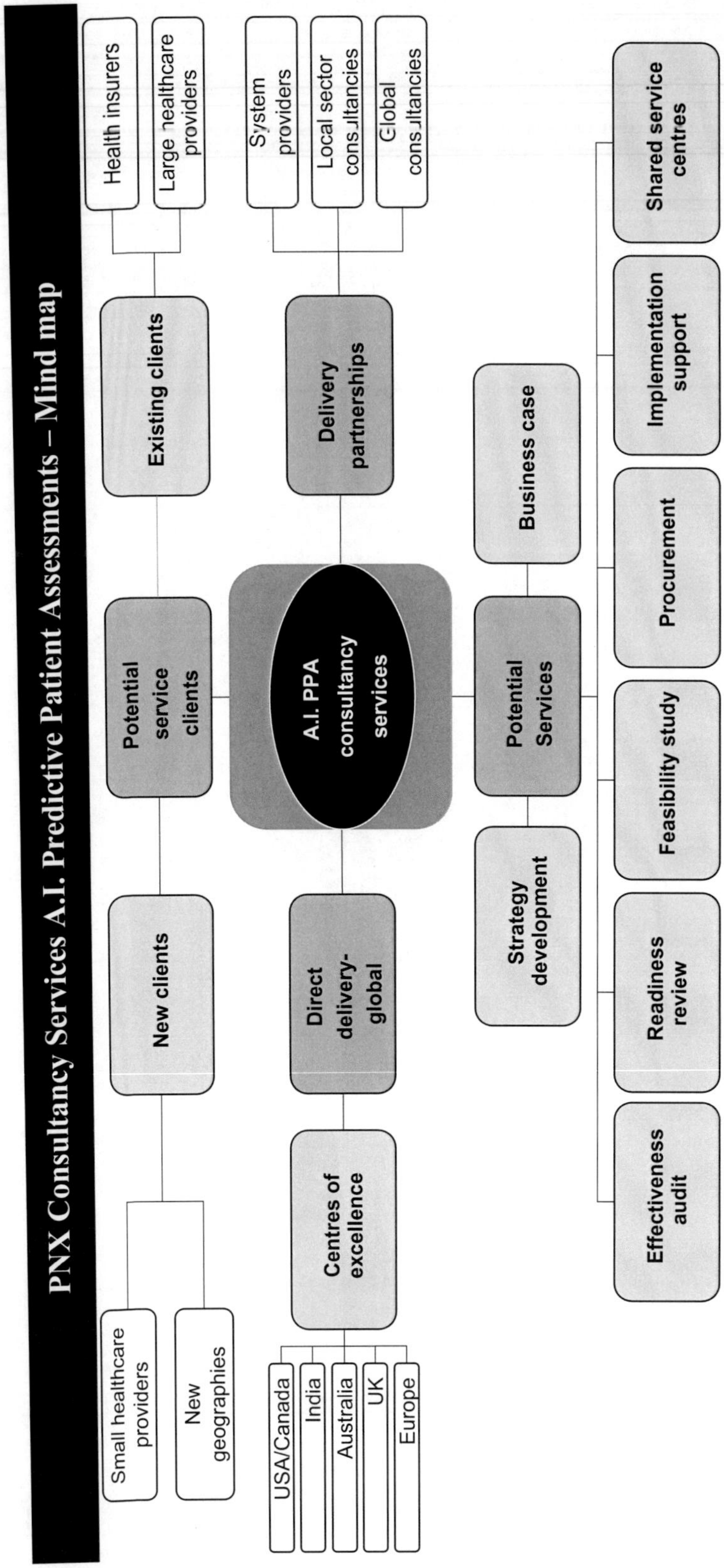

Figure 2.2 PNX Consultancy AI Predictive Patient Assessments – Mind map.

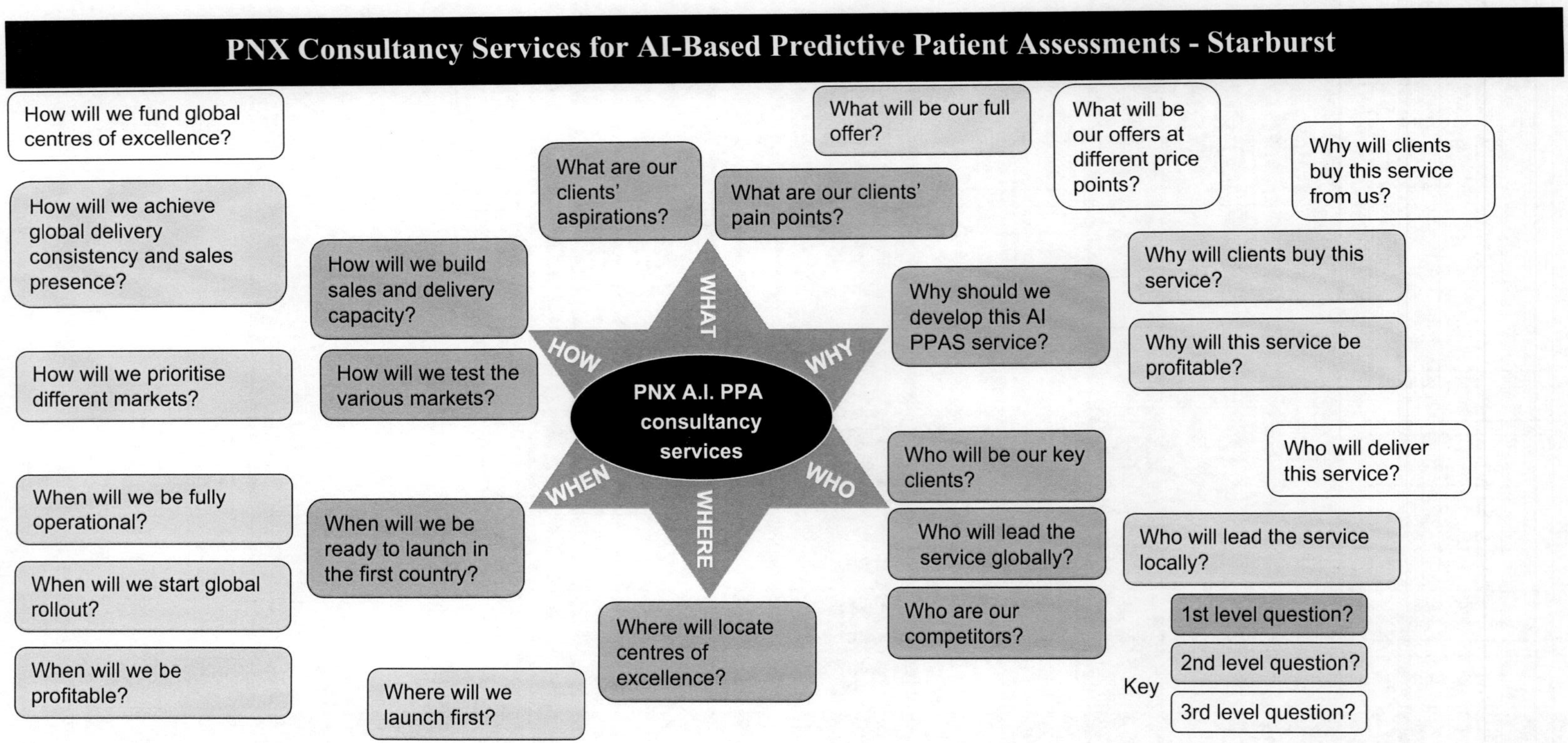

Figure 2.3 PNX Consultancy Services for AI-Based Predictive Patient Assessments – Starburst.

Table 2.4 PNX Consultancy Services Application of Advanced AI in Healthcare SWOT Analysis

PNX Consultancy Services Application of Advanced AI in Healthcare SWOT Analysis	
Positive	**Negative**
Strengths *Features of the service that give it an advantage over other projects.*	**Weaknesses** *Features of the service that would place it at a disadvantage relative to other projects.*
1. Maximises the use of expertise from other sectors and is counter-cyclical	1. There is currently little available specialist AI staff with healthcare-specific knowledge to support the proposed service
2. Can utilise existing client and contact base in large healthcare providers and insurers	2. Will require establishing local centres of excellence to drive the service in different geographies
3. Increases the company's profile in the healthcare sector, supporting our existing practice	3. Coordination and resource sharing across different regions run counter to current distributed partnership organisation and financial reporting
4. Enables the company to establish thought leadership in an emerging technology	4. Attacking multiple markets may stretch marketing and sales resources too thinly
	5. Heavy investment in either specialist training or recruitment and induction of new specialists will be required
Opportunities *Positive elements in the external environment of which the service could turn to its advantage*	**Threats** *Negative elements in the external environment which could adversely impact the service*
1. First mover advantages, including premium pricing	1. Few barriers to entry for global consultancies – although they will also find staffing difficulties
2. Shared service centres could provide services for smaller providers more cost-effectively than dedicated internal systems and processes	2. Software suppliers currently provide implementation services and may look to expand their consultancy offer
3. Lack of competition in most markets	3. Economic pressures in some markets will restrict clients' ability to buy our services

Step 4: Idea evaluation

We have now reached the stage where we have to evaluate our ideas critically and start choosing between them. We could make a single subjective judgement as:

> *I prefer service A to service B.*

However, our judgement will be more balanced by looking at how service A compares to service B on a range of different criteria and state our judgement as:

> *Service A is preferred because it is likely to perform better than Service B in terms of X, Y, and Z.*

Our judgements about X, Y, and Z are often subjective. Essentially, we are attempting to improve our overall decision by structuring our subjectivity and, where possible, adding any (frequently incomplete) data available to help us.

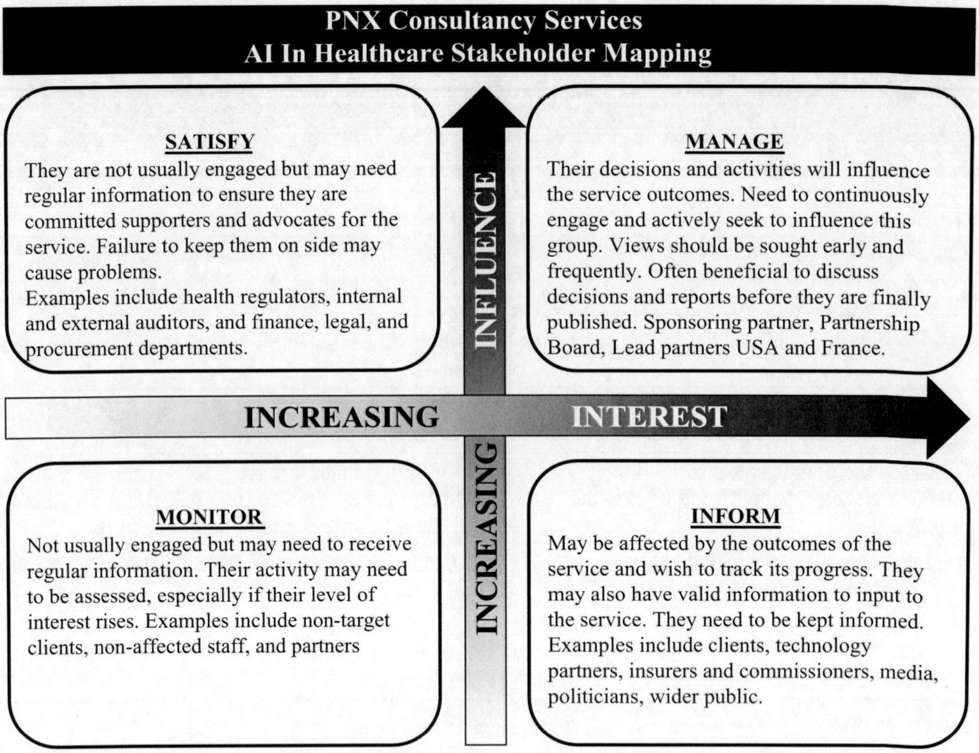

Figure 2.4 PNX AI In Healthcare Stakeholder Mapping.

Various techniques can help us evaluate any list of options and support our recommendations for action. These are useful in client contexts, for example, shortlisting options, assessing risks, or evaluating supplier tenders.

Our first task is to draw up a list of critical success factors (CSFs).

Back to Chris

"Welcome to session three, which is about developing our consultancy service offer. The output from the previous sessions has been outstanding. Your creativity has given us a clear view of what we could do. We cannot, however, do it all. So today is all about prioritising our ideas into a list upon which we can all agree.

What we are going to do first is to identify the parameters against which we will be evaluating the different options that we have. Eventually, these parameters will build into the SMART goals we will set for our service. As a check on learning, do you all understand what I mean by SMART goals?"

Most heads nod, although some are a bit too hesitant. Chris has no option but to explain.

"Nowadays, SMART is taken as standing for Specific, Measurable, Achievable, Relevant, and Time-bound. However, when the acronym was first coined in 1981 by George T Doran,

it was subtly different: Specific, Measurable, Assignable, Realistic and Time-related. I prefer his original idea that we have to assign responsibility, and our goals should be realistic rather than merely relevant.

Now, we will use a high-technology approach to setting our parameters. Ten sticky notes are in front of you, and I would like you to please take 10 minutes to write an end to this sentence on each one.

This service will succeed if . . .

Please include a quantifiable test for each one if you can identify one. After that, we will gather all our views, establish a consensus on the most critical success factors, and document any comments we have on each one.

At the end of the session, the output from the group for year three goals was as follows:

1. ***Current and future profitability**: 'This service will succeed if it generates additional revenue at a margin ten per cent higher than the averages currently achieved.'*

   Understanding the sector's current and future profitability is crucial. This includes assessing revenue streams, cost structures, and profit margins and analysing trends and growth rates.
2. ***Market demand**: 'This service will succeed if it delivers thirty engagements annually in response to new demands in the services sector.'*

   Before launching a new service, it's vital to assess demand. This involves understanding potential client needs and preferences for the service.
3. ***Availability of skills**: 'This service will succeed if it maximises the use of current staff in delivering higher margin work measured by an increase in utilisation rates of five per cent and supports the growth in staff numbers of five per cent.'*

   The firm must evaluate whether it has the necessary skills and expertise to provide the new service. If not, we may need to invest in training and recruit new hires.
4. ***Ethical principles**: 'This service will succeed if it meets all of the principles laid out in the firm's Code of Ethics with no client complaints of code breaches each year.'*

   This includes maintaining patient confidentiality and providing unbiased advice.
5. ***Organisational structure**: 'This service will succeed if it can be delivered with zero change to our current organisational and financial framework.'*

   This consideration could involve integrating with global reporting lines, team structures, business processes, fees, and cost-sharing.
6. ***Corporate social responsibility (CSR)**: 'This service will succeed if it can positively contribute to meeting our CSR goals for each country of operation each year.'*

   The new service should align with our CSR goals and assist in meeting them.
7. ***Global profile**: 'This service will succeed if it contributes to raising our profile as a leader in service sector technology exploitation, including artificial intelligence, thereby creating opportunities for further growth.'*

   This could involve supporting our strategies for international expansion and brand recognition.
8. ***Regulatory environment**: 'This service will succeed if it can be developed flexibly to ensure that it meets all regulations for each country where we intend to operate.'*

This could require engaging advisors with local knowledge of each country."

Next, we have to decide how significant each critical success factor is to us. Two methods are very useful for facilitating groups' views of relative desirability:

- **Ranking a list of options**: There are alternative ways of scoring options to produce a ranked list that reflects the group's combined views. We could ask all participants to produce a ranking individually and incorporate them into an overall list. Participants, however, frequently struggle with accurately reflecting their views when ranking multiple options, which requires multiple decisions about their preferences. If we use a paired comparison analysis instead, it lets participants determine their opinions of the options and allows us to build a group view quickly. The easiest way to do this is to list all the options to be considered and assign each a letter. For every possible pair of options, participants answer the simple question:

  Do I prefer A to B?

  Table 2.5 shows all the possible preference pairs in the PNX case study workshop output. In practice, for each possible pairing, our panel members consider the following question:

  Do I prefer the option in the column or the option in the row?

  The panel member enters the answer into a simple table for each possible pair. If they have no preference, they leave the cell blank. Table 2.6 shows one person's answers. After the table is

Table 2.5 PNX Consultancy Services Application of Advanced AI in Healthcare Paired Comparison Analysis

PNX Consultancy Services Application of Advanced AI in Healthcare Paired Comparison Analysis								
Critical Success Factor	A. Profitability	B. Market demand	C. Availability of Skills	D. Ethical Principles	E. Organisation	F. CSR	G. Global Profile	H. Regulatory
A. Market demand		BA	CA	DA	EA	FA	GA	HA
B. Profitability			CB	DB	EB	FB	GB	HB
C. Availability of skills				DC	EC	FC	GC	HC
D. Ethical principles					ED	FD	GD	HD
E. Organisational structure						FE	GE	HE
F. CSR							GF	HF
G. Global profile								HG
H. Regulatory environment								

Table 2.6 PNX Consultancy Services Application of Advanced AI in Healthcare Paired Ranking Analysis

PNX Consultancy Services Application of Advanced AI in Healthcare Paired Ranking Analysis								
Critical Success Factor	A. Profitability	B. Market Demand	C. Skills	D. Ethical Principles	E. Organisation	F. CSR	G. Global Profile	H. Regulatory
A. Market demand		A	A	E	A	G	A	A
B. Profitability			B	B	B	B	B	B
C. Availability of skills				E	C	C	H	C
D. Ethical principles					D	D	H	D
E. Organisational structure						G	E	E
F. CSR							H	F
G. Global profile								G
H. Regulatory environment								
Count	**5**	**6**	**3**	**3**	**4**	**1**	**3**	**3**
Rank	**2**	**1**	**4**	**4**	**3**	**8**	**4**	**4**

completed, we ask the panel member (or sometimes their neighbour) to count the number of appearances of each option in the whole table and enter the number into the score column.

We total the participants' scores for each option and rank them to synthesise the panel's view. This can be done by passing the scored tables to the facilitator for calculation. However, the session is more dynamic and engages the participants more if we run the totalling of the scores as an interactive session, with group members calling out their own, or possibly their neighbour's, scores. Another team member records these on a flipchart and does the arithmetic for us.

- **Weighted list**: Quite often, and certainly, when developing services, we need to move beyond ranking in order of desirability and recognise that each critical success factor can have a markedly different impact beyond its numerical rank. So, instead of asking participants to indicate which of the pair of factors they prefer, we ask them to answer a subtly different question:

By how much do I prefer the option selected?

The participant's answer is in the format B3, where B is the preferred option, and 3 is the preference factor.

Table 2.7 uses a preference factor of 1, 2, or 3 (maximum). If there is no preference, the cell is left blank. We could allow a greater range of preference factors, say one to ten, which

Table 2.7 PNX Consultancy Services Application of Advanced AI in Healthcare Weighted List of Priorities

PNX Consultancy Services Application of Advanced AI in Healthcare Weighted List of Priorities								
Critical Success Factor	**A. Profitability**	**B. Market Demand**	**C. Skills**	**D. Ethical Principles**	**E. Organisation**	**F. CSR**	**G. Global Profile**	**H. Regulatory**
A. Market demand		B1	A2	A1	E3	A2	G1	A2
B. Profitability			C2	B2	B3	B1	B1	B2
C. Availability of skills				C3	E1	C2	C2	H1
D. Ethical principles					E1	D2	D3	H2
E. Organisational structure						F2	G1	E3
F. CSR							F1	H2
G. Global profile								G3
H. Regulatory environment								
Score	**7**	**10**	**9**	**5**	**8**	**3**	**5**	**5**
Calculated %age weight	**13.5%**	**19.2%**	**17.3%**	**9.6%**	**15.4%**	**5.8%**	**9.6%**	**9.6%**

should give a more graduated result, but the increased choice can also make our participants' decisions more difficult.

The table is completed with weighting percentages calculated as each critical success factor's preference factor score as a percentage of total preference factor scores. For simplicity, the example shows how weightings are calculated based on the sample scoresheet. We then do the sums and produce the final result.[1]

Back to the PNX workshop.

Chris is about to explain how the group will tackle prioritising the five areas selected by the panel of partners.

"In making our final prioritised list, we need to take into account two variables:

First, the importance of the critical success factor to the firm, which is our weighted list of priorities.

Second, the degree to which we consider that the proposed service will meet the critical success factor. Again, this is often a subjective judgement as hard factual data is frequently not available."

"We will go through three steps:

1. *You score each idea against every critical success factor based on what you believe its performance is likely to be.*
2. *In your teams, you discuss the scores you have given and agree on a team view of the score.*
3. *We will come together and discuss each team's results and come to a group view."*

"We will still not know the final result until we multiply each score by the agreed weight and total the score for the idea. I will do that while you have a coffee break.

I am now distributing a series of score sheets to you. Please write down your scores without discussing them. Use zero for failure to meet the CSF at all and ten for completely meeting it.

You have 20 minutes before I want you to meet in your teams.

Please appoint a spokesperson to chair your discussions and lead your reporting back. We will meet back here in one hour."

Table 2.8 shows the results obtained at the end of the session.

A final sense check

Whatever method we have chosen to prepare our prioritised list, having a final sense check is always helpful. Closing our workshop with a short, facilitated discussion to confirm that views were captured correctly requires running a single round of 1-minute facilitated discussions with participants individually asked to answer one of two simple questions:

If we have used a paired comparison analysis to prepare a ranked list:

> *If you could move just one item in the list up to two places, which one would it be and why?*

Or if we have prepared a weighted list:

> *If you could increase the score of just one of the options by three points, which one would it be and why?*

These are positive questions because the participants should finish positively whenever we ask for closing comments in a discovery session or interview process.

We can now answer two key control questions:

- *Have we avoided an utterly ridiculous answer?*
- *Will this result be acceptable to the decision-makers we have to report to?*

If the answer to either of these is yes, we need to state why the answer was yes and lead a facilitated discussion to resolve the issue.

Table 2.8 PNX Consultancy Services Application of Advanced AI in Healthcare Weighted Scoring Matrix

PNX Consultancy Services Application of Advanced AI in Healthcare Weighted Scoring Matrix											
		Service 1		**Service 2**		**Service 3**		**Service 4**		**Service 5**	
	Weight (a)	**Score (b)**	**Weighted Score (a × b)**	**Score (b)**	**Weighted Score (a × b)**	**Score (b)**	**Weighted Score (a × b)**	**Score (b)**	**Weighted Score (a × b)**	**Score (b)**	**Weighted Score (a × b)**
A. Market demand	13.50%	30	4.05	45	6.08	25	3.38	40	5.40	35	4.73
B. Profitability	19.20%	45	8.64	50	9.60	35	6.72	40	7.68	45	8.64
C. Availability of skills	17.30%	25	4.33	30	5.19	45	7.79	35	6.06	40	6.92
D. Ethical principles	9.60%	50	4.80	50	4.80	40	3.84	50	4.80	40	3.84
E. Organisational structure	15.40%	45	6.93	35	5.39	35	5.39	50	7.70	35	5.39
F. CSR	5.80%	35	2.03	45	2.61	25	1.45	20	1.16	15	0.87
G. Global profile	9.60%	40	3.84	45	4.32	35	3.36	30	2.88	30	2.88
H. Regulatory environment	9.60%	50	4.80	50	4.80	40	3.84	40	3.84	40	3.84
Total score	**100.00%**		**39.42**		**42.79**		**35.76**		**39.52**		**37.11**
Rank			**3**		**1**		**5**		**2**		**4**

Step 5: Service validation

Some people would avoid a service validation step altogether and move straight into piloting delivery. This approach is expressed as "Running it up the flagpole and seeing who salutes." However, this approach risks wasting time and resources on a service proposition that is not well adapted to clients' needs, in a market not ready to accept it, or aimed at clients not willing to pay an economic price.

Service validation builds on our previous outputs and aims to establish a vision of our proposed service's viability in each of our target markets, including a broad view of how it might be priced. How we do this, and the contacts with whom we engage depend on the service and the current status of our network. If we are already established in a market, we will have a network of trusted clients and respected contacts. If, however, the market is new to us, we need to build such a network. This includes taking advantage of every opportunity to build our profile as a credible player in our target market space.

Our tactics will need tailoring to every situation, but those commonly used include the following:

- **Competitor analysis**: Updating our evaluation of existing consultancies and others offering services similar to the proposal. Analysing their strengths, weaknesses, and market share to differentiate our offering effectively.
- **Define and survey our niche and target audience**: Setting limits around the range of potential clients that we might wish to contact with regard to our service. We also need to identify the best method of assessing their views we could use various techniques for this including surveys (online, face-to-face, telephone, by post), personal interviews, focus groups, and round-table discussions.
- **Expert validation**: Forming an advisory panel of professionals or leading academics also enables us to gain their insights (and perhaps their endorsements) which help refine our ideas and may expand our potential client network.
- **Targeted outreach**: Identifying key decision-makers and personalising our outreach based on their needs. Working with them to understand how our services could address their issues.
- **Partnerships**: Exploring potential partnerships with other providers, governments, academic institutions, and other bodies. These can provide a detailed understanding of current and future client needs to map against our service proposals.

Based on the results of the above, we can adapt service proposals to each target market to reflect local regulations, systems, and the roles of key bodies in each target area.

Going public

There is a balance between reaching out to a market to understand its needs and potential and raising our profile in relation to our service proposals. Openly promoting our ideas early can help us find new contacts to assist us in our research. However, it can also open our ideas to scrutiny before they are entirely formed and alert potential competitors to our interest in a service area.

When we decide to "go public," to any extent, we should also consider how and when we undertake the following marketing-related actions:

- **Digital presence**: Creating a quality website which reflects our service and our values and developing the social media profiles of the company and key individuals that we wish to promote as thought leaders.

- **Content marketing**: Publishing white papers, blog posts, and case studies to showcase our expertise and establish thought leadership.
- **Attend industry events**: Actively participating in relevant conferences and proactively using them to network with potential clients and gain visibility.

Table 2.9 shows how this approach could be used for the PNX AI case study. It also extends the approach by capturing valuable data for each potential market, such as professional bodies, conferences, websites, and publications.

Table 2.9 PNX Consultancy Services Application of Advanced AI in Healthcare Validation Approaches

PNX Consultancy Services Application of Advanced AI Healthcare Validation Approaches	
Define and survey target audience	Target specific healthcare verticals In each market, work with hospitals, clinics, pharmaceutical companies, or other players within the healthcare system Focus on sub-sectors within healthcare where AI has the most significant potential for transformation
Competitor analysis	Evaluate existing consultancies offering similar services Analyse their strengths, weaknesses, and market share to differentiate our offering effectively
Build case studies	Develop hypothetical case studies to illustrate the potential benefits of AI and our services Demonstrate tangible outcomes and quantifiable metrics highlighting the AI-driven improvements our service would bring to efficiency, cost savings, and patient outcomes
Ethical AI framework	Develop and demonstrate a robust ethical AI framework outlining our commitment to responsible AI use, addressing bias, transparency, and patient privacy. This will be critical for building trust
Multidisciplinary team	Assemble an initial team with expertise in healthcare, AI, data science, change management, and regulatory compliance specific to each target market to lead our market engagement
Expert validation	Form an advisory panel of healthcare and AI professionals from each market. Their insights and endorsements will enhance our credibility and attract potential clients
Targeted outreach	Identify key healthcare decision-makers Personalise our outreach based on their specific needs and how our services address them
Understand local market dynamics.	Research the unique reimbursement models, healthcare delivery systems, and cultural nuances of each target market and adapt our approach accordingly
Partnerships	Explore potential partnerships with AI solution providers, healthcare associations, or leading academic institutions to expand our reach and build trust
Thought leadership	Publish white papers, blog posts, video posts, and case studies to showcase our expertise

(*Continued*)

Table 2.9 (Continued)

PNX Consultancy Services Application of Advanced AI Healthcare Validation Approaches	
Targeted webinars	Host webinars showcasing our expertise in AI solutions, tailoring them to the pain points of healthcare providers in specific markets and establishing how services could be adapted to meet perceived needs
Digital presence	Create a professional website and maintain active social media profiles to attract clients and connect with industry leaders Engage with key members of the AI and healthcare communities stakeholders active in each market on social media platforms like LinkedIn and X
Attend industry events	Build visibility and connect with potential clients at each region's most significant AI in healthcare conferences
Tailored approach	Adapt our strategies to each market Understand local regulations, healthcare systems, and the roles of key professional bodies in each region
Market-specific data	
North America	
Conferences	HIMSS, HLTH, Connected Health Conference, AI in Healthcare Summit
Publications	Modern Healthcare, Health Affairs, Healthcare IT News, Becker's Hospital Review, Politico (Healthcare section)
Websites	Centers for Medicare & Medicaid Services (www.cms.gov/), Health Resources and Services Administration (www.hrsa.gov/)
Professional bodies	American Medical Association, American Hospital Association, American College of Healthcare Executives
AI organisations	American Board of Artificial Intelligence in Medicine, American Medical Informatics Association
Europe	
Conferences	European Health Forum Gastein, World Health Summit, Digital Health World Congress, HIMSS Europe
Publications	European Journal of Public Health, Health Policy
Websites	European Commission (Directorate General for Health and Food Safety), European Medicines Agency
Professional bodies	European Federation of National Associations of Physicians, the Standing Committee of European Doctors (*Comité Permanent des Médecins Européens*), European Healthcare Management Association
AI organisations	European Association for Artificial Intelligence
The UK	
Conferences	Digital Health Rewired, NHS Confed Expo
Publications	The BMJ, Health Service Journal (HSJ), The Lancet
Websites	National Health Service (NHS.uk https//www.nhs.uk/)
Professional bodies	The Royal Colleges, General Medical Council (GMC), British Medical Association (BMA)
AI organisations	Alan Turing Institute, UK Office for Artificial Intelligence

(*Continued*)

Table 2.9 (Continued)

PNX Consultancy Services Application of Advanced AI Healthcare Validation Approaches	
India	
Conferences	Global Digital Health Summit, Healthcare Leaders' Summit
Publications	The Economic Times, Express Healthcare, Financial Express (Healthcare section)
Websites	Ministry of Health and Family Welfare (https//mohfw.gov.in/), National Health Authority (https//nha.gov.in/)
Professional bodies	Indian Medical Association (IMA), Medical Council of India
AI organisations	Centre for Development of Advanced Computing (C-DAC), NASSCOM
Australia	
Conferences	Australian Healthcare Week, Health Informatics Conference
Publications	Australian Journal of General Practice, Medical Journal of Australia
Websites	Australian Government Department of Health, e-Health (https//www.digitalhealth.gov.au/)
Professional bodies	Royal Australasian College of Physicians (RACP), Australian Medical Association (AMA)
AI organisations	CSIRO Data61, Australian AI Council

Our level of investment of time and funds needed for service validation can vary significantly depending on several factors, including the following:

- **Market maturity**: More mature markets may have more readily available data. Here, a validation process might take a few weeks. Emerging markets with less readily available data may require more primary research and take several months to validate thoroughly.
- **Depth of validation**: At a basic level, designing and conducting a market research survey and analysing potential client feedback might take two to three months. A more comprehensive approach might require building partnerships, conducting pilot projects, refining our service offering, and retesting the changed service, which could take several times longer.
- **Resource and expertise availability**: Building a focused team with experience in our target market and service area accelerates the validation process. Having a team instead with limited expertise in the market or service area or limited time available for the validation will inevitably extend the validation phase.

There is a significant risk of loss of impetus in undertaking service validation. Engaging with individuals and organisations outside our direct control will often require a considerable period. This results from the time our initial contact building and networking will take and the sheer pressure on our contacts' time. We must accept that when we ask others to undertake commitments in addition to their regular workload, while it is our top priority, it is unlikely to be theirs.

In fast-moving markets, we need to put in place monitoring arrangements so that once we have sufficient information to justify a decision, we can close the service validation step and move on. Of course, we can carry over our relationships to provide additional information to refine our service offer and keep our contact network engaged.

Step 6: Business planning

Our business planning step produces two outputs: the business plan and a detailed implementation plan. In some organisations, both are required before submission for approval. In others, the business plan may be sufficient for approval. A solo consultant may not prepare a formal business plan at all. However, we should always prepare an implementation plan. This is our working document, which establishes the detailed tasks required to deliver a project to create and launch our new consultancy service.

The business plan

Our business plan is a high-level overview of the service's delivery that will enable a final decision on whether or not to launch it. Different organisations will have their views on what constitutes a sufficiently detailed business plan. Some may require a document many pages long; others merely a summary and the confidence that a body of work supports the case being made.

Back in the hot seat again.

You are returning from the partner's difficult client later on Friday evening. It's been a hard week, working long hours with the client to get the project back on track, restraining your staff, and dealing with the client's capricious project manager. Your evenings have been spent reviewing all of the information from the service validation exercises, trying to untangle how you can best modify the service vision.

Your phone rings as you arrive home, looking forward to a long hot bath and a quiet weekend. It's the partner.

Partner: "I'm so glad I managed to reach you. We had a partner's weekly meeting on Wednesday, and they want to discuss your business plan for the new service. Can you get me a draft to look at on Monday and take to the next meeting?"

You note that the last sentence was not really a question and that today is Friday and you could have got this call two days ago.

You calmly say: "OK, I was finishing the service vision. Can you email me a copy this evening of a business plan they approved before? That way, I'll follow a format that they like. I'll get you something later on Monday."

At least you'll get time for that long hot bath while the partner sorts out a previous document, but what will your business plan look like?

Take a few moments and jot down some main headings of a business plan.

When writing our business plan, at least some of its readers may know nothing of our proposed service. Consequently, we must identify previous activities and explain the service vision in detail. An executive summary will give all our readers a brief overview of the current situation, with the opportunity to dive deeper into those sections that interest them.

It is also best for us not to present such a document unseen to a meeting but to circulate a draft to the meeting members and discuss it with them individually first. This allows us to identify any weaknesses they perceive in our plan and discuss how they would wish us to overcome them. This way, we gather support and are more likely to obtain approval or at least acquiescence in the decision process.

We can use the six question types from the Starburst exercise to inform our business plan (see Figure 2.3). These six question types were drawn up initially by Rudyard Kipling in a poem which starts:

> I keep six honest serving-men;
> (They taught me all I knew);
> Their names are What and, Why and When
> And How, and Where, and Who.
>
> (Kipling 1902)

We need to answer questions such as:

- **What** are we going to deliver?
- **Why** are we doing this? For example, market need, profile, or profit potential.
- **When** will it be delivered?
- **How** will it be marketed?
- **Where** will it be delivered markets (clients) and locations (staff)?
- **Who** will deliver it: management, staff, administration, and business partnerships?

There is a seventh question, which the poet missed: How much?

In our continuing case study, PNX Consultancy Services' policy is that the business plan should be a summary document up to 2,000 words in length, supported by a detailed interview with the proposing manager and responsible partner.

PNX Consultancy Services

Three-Year Business Plan

AI in Healthcare Consultancy

Executive Summary

This business plan outlines the launch and growth strategy for a management consultancy service focused on helping healthcare providers in North America and Europe leverage artificial intelligence (AI) solutions.

Service Description

PNX will offer a comprehensive suite of AI-related healthcare services focusing initially on the delivery of systems to identify high-risk patients for early intervention:

- **Readiness reviews**: Assessing the ability of an organisation to profit from AI and the changes that may be required.
- **Strategic consulting**: Developing AI-driven strategies and developing business justifications and plans for its implementation.

- **Implementation support**: Project management, procurement support, and technical leadership and support for AI implementation.
- **Change management**: Facilitating smooth adoption and user training.
- **Data governance and security**: Ensuring data privacy, security, and ethical AI practices.

Market Analysis

The global AI in healthcare market will reach $67.6 billion by 2025, with North America and Europe holding significant market share due to established healthcare infrastructure and growing digital adoption.

Target Market

Our primary target markets are hospitals, financial institutions, and health service providers wishing to invest in the successful implementation of AI solutions.

Competitive Advantage

- **Combined expertise**: An interdisciplinary team who are seen as industry thought leaders in healthcare and AI, combined with business development knowledge of key clients.
- **Tailored solutions**: Customised consultancy services designed to address specific client challenges and regional regulations.
- **Client-centric approach**: Collaborative partnerships focusing on long-term client success.

Marketing and Sales Strategy

We have built a thought leadership profile and established networks of respected individuals in both targeted regions through our engagement with key players during the service validation stage. We will continue to develop this profile and these networks through the following:

- **Targeted content marketing**: Publishing white papers and articles and attending industry events to establish thought leadership.
- **Strategic partnerships**: Collaborating with key healthcare and technology stakeholders.
- **Direct sales approach**: Building relationships with prospective clients through targeted outreach and personalised meetings.

We also plan to seek opportunities to work with government partners to establish publicly funded exemplar projects in different countries.

Financial Arrangements and Projections

The service will operate as a unified cost centre with funding and profit contributions split 60/40 initially between the North American and European Partnerships, each serving as a single profit centre. This split will be revised based on performance and updated plans in future years. The following table summarises the financial projections for the next three years.

Year	Objective for # Client Engagements	Total Fee Income (USD Million)	Staff Costs (USD Million)	Other Costs (USD Million)	Profit/Loss Objective (USD Million)	Objective % Profit (rounded)
1	30	4.1	3.5	0.1	0.5	12%
2	65	8.8	5.5	0.25	3.0	34%
3	80	10.8	6.5	0.3	4.0	37%

Assumptions

The following projections use our average costs and income targets across the two regions for current staff and show mid-range forecasts for growth in size.

- The average fee per engagement is $135,000. We expect to undertake a variety of engagements, with between $25,000 for readiness reviews and $200,000 for strategy preparation and procurement support.
- Average annual staff cost per employee is $100,000.
- Projected staff growths are Year 1 (40), Year 2 (50), and Year 3 (65).
- Reallocated corporate costs are in Year 1 ($0.1 million), Year 2 ($0.25 million), and Year 3 ($0.3 million).
- Business split 60% of business in North America and 40% in Europe.

Financial Justification

The number of client engagements progressively increases year-on-year, reflecting successful marketing efforts and growing demand.

The total fee income steadily rises due to increased client engagements and project complexity.

Staff costs rise per the planned staff growth.

Other costs are projected to increase modestly due to additional resources needed for office space, equipment, and marketing activities.

The projected profit/loss statement demonstrates an increasing profit margin over the three years, indicating a sustainable business model.

Action Plan

Year 1: Implementation

- Establish New York and Paris-based Centres of Excellence
- Recruit core team members (months 1–6)
- Complete recruitment (months 7–12)
- Develop and refine service offerings
- Establish marketing and sales channels
- Secure first client engagements

Year 2: Consolidation and Expansion

- Expand team size and expertise as required by the growth in client engagements
- Strengthen brand awareness and market presence
- Secure larger and more complex client engagements
- Refine service offerings based on client feedback

Year 3: Continuing Improvement and Growth

- Further expand team and geographical footprint
- Secure long-term partnerships with key stakeholders
- Develop new service offerings based on market trends
- Continuously improve operational efficiency and client satisfaction

Management Team

The PNX Consultancy Services AI team in North America and Europe will be led by experienced professionals with proven track records in healthcare, technology, and business management. Partner leadership will be provided by one partner from each region selected by the partnership management board, who will report directly to it.

Risk Management

The market is not, however, risk free. The following risks have been identified:

- **Slow market adoption of AI in healthcare:** Mitigation – Continuous market research and education highlighting the benefits of AI for healthcare providers. We will also assess the willingness of different types of clients to pay for our services and focus our attention on appropriate areas
- **High competition from established consultancies:** Mitigation – We will differentiate ourselves through stressing our deep domain expertise in AI and healthcare, focusing on customised solutions and offering highly competitive pricing models.
- **Difficulty attracting and retaining top talent:** Mitigation – We will offer competitive compensation packages, stress our positive work culture, including our commitment to work–life balance, and highlight our commitment to providing ongoing professional development opportunities.

Other potential risks include technological advances and regulatory changes. The company will mitigate these risks through continuous market research, monitoring industry trends, and proactively adapting its service offerings to comply with evolving regulations. We will seek to engage leading academics to provide staff development to help maintain a leading-edge advantage in the services being delivered.

Future Strategy

The long-term goal is to establish PNX Consultancy Services as a leading provider of AI in healthcare consultancy services. Assuming significant market share and profitability are achieved, it is expected to become the leading supplier of specialist

AI in health services in North America and Europe, with future expansion to Australia, India, and the UK.

Conclusion

This business plan outlines a path for establishing a successful consultancy service catering to the growing demand for AI implementation in healthcare. By combining a comprehensive service offering, targeted marketing strategies, and a strong management team, PNX is well positioned to capitalise on this market's vast potential.

The implementation plan

Preparing an effective implementation plan is the first critical step in transforming our ideas into a fully operational service. In the business plan, we included a high-level action plan for launching our service during Year 1. Now, we build this into a detailed series of tasks and link these together in a logical sequence.

This is how the PNX implementation plan looks:

PNX Consultancy Services

B2B AI in Healthcare Implementation Plan (Months 1–12)

Executive Summary:

This document outlines a comprehensive 12-month launch plan for PNX's AI in healthcare consultancy services in North America and Europe. The plan details the activities to be undertaken to support Year 1 of the Business Plan, that is:

- Recruit core team members.
- Develop and refine service offerings.
- Establish marketing and sales channels.
- Secure first client engagements.

Months 1–3:

1.1. **Market Research and Legal Establishment:**

- **1.1.1.** Conduct initial market research to refine our service offerings and adjust them to meet regional regulations and needs.
- **1.1.2.** Establish any necessary separate legal entities in the USA and France, ensuring compliance with all local regulations.

1.2. **Centre of Excellence Development:**

1.2.1. Secure New York and Paris office space, considering accessibility, collaboration-friendly layouts, and scalability.
1.2.2. Appoint global coordinating partners and lead partners for Centres of Excellence.
1.2.3. Recruit leadership teams in both locations of experienced professionals with expertise in business development in healthcare or AI.
1.2.4. Hire and train/transfer administrative staff to provide operational support.

1.3. **Service Development and Marketing:**

1.3.1. Create local visions for services for our strategic consulting, implementation support, change management, and data governance and security in North America and Europe.
1.3.2. Develop our new range of marketing materials in US English and French, focusing on our high-value proposition.
1.3.3. Create user-friendly websites and social media platforms for brand awareness in US English and French.
1.3.4. Research existing key local players to expand reach and credibility.

Months 4–6:

2.1. **Market Activation and Lead Generation:**

2.1.1. Implement a targeted content marketing strategy to illustrate the benefits of strategy development in partnership with PNX's experts. This includes commissioning thought leadership articles, white papers, and industry presentations based on hypothetical case studies.
2.1.2. Research and participate in industry events and conferences to connect with potential clients and build brand recognition.
2.1.3. Work through existing PNX contact networks to extend our reach and build relationships with key decision-makers in target clients.
2.1.4. Review existing contract frameworks and establish if they are potential vehicles for generating client engagements.
2.1.5. Develop our contact and support strategies in healthcare markets to elevate leads towards client engagements.

2.2. **Sales and Client Acquisition:**

2.2.1. Train existing and new sales personnel on PNX's unique services and value proposition, emphasising client-centricity, high-added value, and customised solutions.
2.2.2. Create a new sales support information pack for all staff engaged in any client contact.
2.2.3. Implement a structured sales process, including lead qualification, personalised proposals, and effective negotiation strategies.
2.2.4. Secure our first client engagements and use these to demonstrate a track record in each market.

Months 7–12:

3.1. **Project Delivery and Client Satisfaction:**

- **3.1.1.** Manage and deliver client projects to client satisfaction within agreed timelines and fee budgets.
- **3.1.2.** Gather client feedback to support improved service offerings and ensure that they meet evolving client needs.
- **3.1.2.** Request clients to provide testimonials and referrals, and assess willingness to participate in promotional activities.

3.2. **Team Expansion and Development:**

- **3.2.1.** Grow the team in both locations, focusing on recruiting top talent with diverse AI, healthcare, and consulting expertise.
- **3.2.2.** Maintain training and development programmes to increase team members' skills and expertise and maintain our industry-leading knowledge.

3.3. **Long-Term Strategies and Growth:**

- **3.3.1.** Conduct market research to identify new service opportunities and adapt offerings to address evolving industry trends.
- **3.3.2.** Explore further partnerships and monitor development in markets in Australia, the UK, and India.
- **3.3.3.** Maintain a risk management plan and monitor and mitigate emerging risks.

The controlled execution of the tasks in our implementation plan will deliver our new business service. Consequently, each planned task has to be supported by a detailed statement of the work to be done, including a timeframe, necessary resources, funding, quality requirements, and, most importantly, the individual responsible for delivery.

Theoretical case study – reprise

You have already made some progress as a newly engaged consultancy manager. Your brief is to develop and market a range of services to the public and service sectors based on expertise drawn from insurance and broader financial services. You will go on to create and lead a team of high-performing consultants to sell and deliver the services. You have prepared and agreed to a vision for a new consultancy service and set out how it may be justified in business terms. You have also drafted your new service's code of ethics.

Reflections

As a reminder, please draw on your personal experience or your current situation or use the theoretical case study.

- Prepare problem statements for three potential consultancy services.
- Set out how you would move from these to consider the most suitable option for progressing to the next stage.

- Select one of the options and draft a three-year business plan for its creation and delivery as a profitable service.
- Draft a high-level task list covering the first 12 months of the business and prepare statements of work for three of the tasks.

Note

1 Doing the arithmetic always takes some time. Consequently, we do this while the participants have a refreshment break. So, here's a little facilitator's trick. Order the coffee for about 10 minutes before the end of the exercise. Leave the team pondering their views, nip out of the room, and grab a coffee and one or two of the best biscuits. Then, come in, coffee in hand, and announce the end of the exercise. Otherwise, if we do manage to finish the maths before the end of the break, the coffee is usually all gone and only the rubbish biscuits are left.

Bibliography

Kipling, R. (1902). *Just so Stories*. London: Macmillan.

3 Developing a Consultancy Service Offer

Aim of this chapter: To show how we create viable consultancy service offerings to the market.

Learning outcome: To be able to define and launch one or more consultancy services and to be able to monitor and control delivery success.

Previously, we looked broadly at our target market and the ideas that could underlie the services we could viably deliver. Now, we are concerned with moving our previous work forward and focusing on preparing for a successful delivery stage. This requires a more detailed consideration of service definition, the outputs we require, and all the steps we need to take to bring our ideas to market successfully.

At this point, many, if not most, businesses, including management consultancies, start by asking and answering the simple question:

What are we going to sell to the market?

This is a serious and possibly catastrophic mistake because it wrongly focuses on:

US, the provider.
Whereas it should focus on:
YOU, our customer.

We will often encounter this difference in perspective on our journey to delivering an effective consultancy service. Remember, we always put ourselves in the customer's place. So here is the key takeaway message from this whole book: It deserves to be on the home screen of your phone and laptop, written on the cover of your notebook, and even tattooed on your wrist:

*It's not about **US**. It's about **YOU**.*

As a result of our preparatory work, we already have a fair idea about a whole raft of answers to questions that we should ask instead of, "What are we going to sell to the market?" These questions include:

Who is our ideal customer?
Where can we find further information about them?
What do we know about their pain points?
How can we help them to define their problems clearly?
Why might they buy this service?
Why would they buy from us?
When in their strategy and budget cycles can they commit to purchasing a new service?

DOI: 10.4324/9781003490456-4

What limitations does our buyer have on their powers to purchase?
How much would they be prepared to pay for it?

(Have you noticed a common theme in our questioning? If not, turn back to Chapter 2 and review the starbursting technique.)

There is another concept that may be missed. Up to this point, our attention has been focused internally, but from now on, the balance shifts, and most of our activities will be externally focused. Whether we are recruiting staff, arranging office accommodation, or overtly marketing, every external contact is an opportunity to tell the story of the service we are developing. Consequently, we need to create and understand that narrative now. This means that from now on, we need to fully understand the strengths of our service offer and be able to communicate its benefits clearly to contacts and potential clients.

Time for a site visit.

A hat, coat, scarf, possibly gloves and sensible, waterproof shoes are required.

We are in a small European country's capital city, indeed the only actual city. It is a cold, grey morning towards the end of winter. It has rained heavily overnight, and the morning is very foggy. We can see three people standing in an abandoned leaking supermarket. The floor is mainly covered by a huge puddle. Even from a distance, we can see their breath hanging in the air. The electricity is off; the only light comes from the distant, grimy windows. It is as if the fog has crept in and taken over the inside of the building. It is a genuinely desolate sight.

We approach the group, skirting the puddle as much as possible (you were warned about the shoes). We see that they are an odd assortment: a young, stocky man with a large moustache and an overly loud check jacket, a tall, stooping older man looking out of place in a sombre business suit and overcoat, and a third very striking man who is speaking and whose voice shows his south London roots. He is introducing the reason for the on-site meeting to the tall man.

"I am Tom, and this," he gesticulates, "is where we intend to put our contact centre. Forty agents at first on two floors, plus four managers. Stav here will be the director in overall charge." He nods towards the younger man.

"As our proposal shows, this will be a showpiece and an important piece of economic regeneration. We plan for this to be the national telephone and internet contact centre. It will handle multiple services such as booking health appointments, providing telephone directory enquiries, and outsourced services across all government and private sectors.

The centre will be government-owned but run on a commercial basis. Profits will be channelled to developing national sports capabilities from grassroots clubs to our elite and Olympic athletes. My role is advising on marketing the services over the first three years of operation."

Stav nods in agreement. Our interest, however, is in neither the speaker nor Stav nor their scheme but in the taller man. We need to know why he is here, why he has been taking notes so intently, and what led to today's meeting. As the meeting ends, we quietly ask him for a private conversation. He agrees and later in the day, we meet in a local coffee shop.

Over a pastry and a double expresso, he explains what he is doing here.

"I am Jon. Actually, I am a management consultant, and I work with a specialist telecommunications consultancy in London. An international bank has been asked to fund the project, and I am here on a due diligence exercise. We are providing technical advice to the accountancy firm assessing the project's financial viability and risk for the bank. I am assessing the soundness of the technical and business approach being proposed. There should have been two of us here today: Serge, the firm's accountants, and myself. Bizarrely, he went on a similar site visit last week to another country, and at the moment, he can't get to the airport because there is a coup in progress. I believe he is currently in his hotel basement, and men with submachine guns are periodically blasting away outside. Still, it's much safer here.[1]

You asked about how I got here. Back in the company, my job is developing a new business area, assessing the effectiveness of customer-facing services, especially of contact centres. Unusually, there is a straight line from these activities to that empty supermarket this morning. We knew anecdotally that there was poor service in many contact centres. In order to raise our profile as industry experts, we wanted to tell a strong story about the scope for improvement. I commissioned some research on contact centre performance. Its results included sixty per cent of customers dissatisfied with some aspect of the service they received from contact centres.

Working with a marketing and public relations consultancy, we exploited this information in a press release. I also developed a direct engagement campaign targeting about 50 large retail companies, which the press coverage would back. Anyway, the marketing people sent out the press release. I should add that they also engaged a company to track wherever it was mentioned. We got coverage one hundred and four times, including the UK's Financial Times. That is the direct link to today. The responsible partner in the accountants read the article in the Financial Times and called me immediately. We hadn't fully sorted out our story on benefits or collateral, but here I am. It is not the sort of work we would have ever thought about chasing, either. But it's very profitable and high profile, and it's now part of our story of being the 'go-to' experts in contact centre optimisation.

The press release also received coverage in Australia's Sydney Morning Herald and Ireland's Cork-based Examiner. No leads have come from there yet, and Australia certainly is not a target market. However, it does show the reach that a strong story can have."

As in Jon's case, we may only just be starting to be able to communicate the benefits of our service and build that confidence and trust in us and our service by our target clients when the phone rings and something unexpected happens. Jon's story also reminds us that clients will seek us out once we have started establishing our profile as experts in a field. This type of contact is usually to help them resolve the problems they perceive they are facing rather than for our perception of the market's issues. Like Jon, being flexible in meeting our clients' needs is an essential component of our success.

In our business plan (see Chapter 2), we developed an outline of the service as the foundation upon which we will build our detailed offer. This offer may have many titles in many different organisations, but for the sake of simplicity, we will refer to this as our service proposition. Our objective during this stage is to develop, test, and bring this service proposition to market.

Figure 3.1 centres on the main elements we should address in building our new service. This process is iterative, and the service proposition will grow and change as we follow each of the

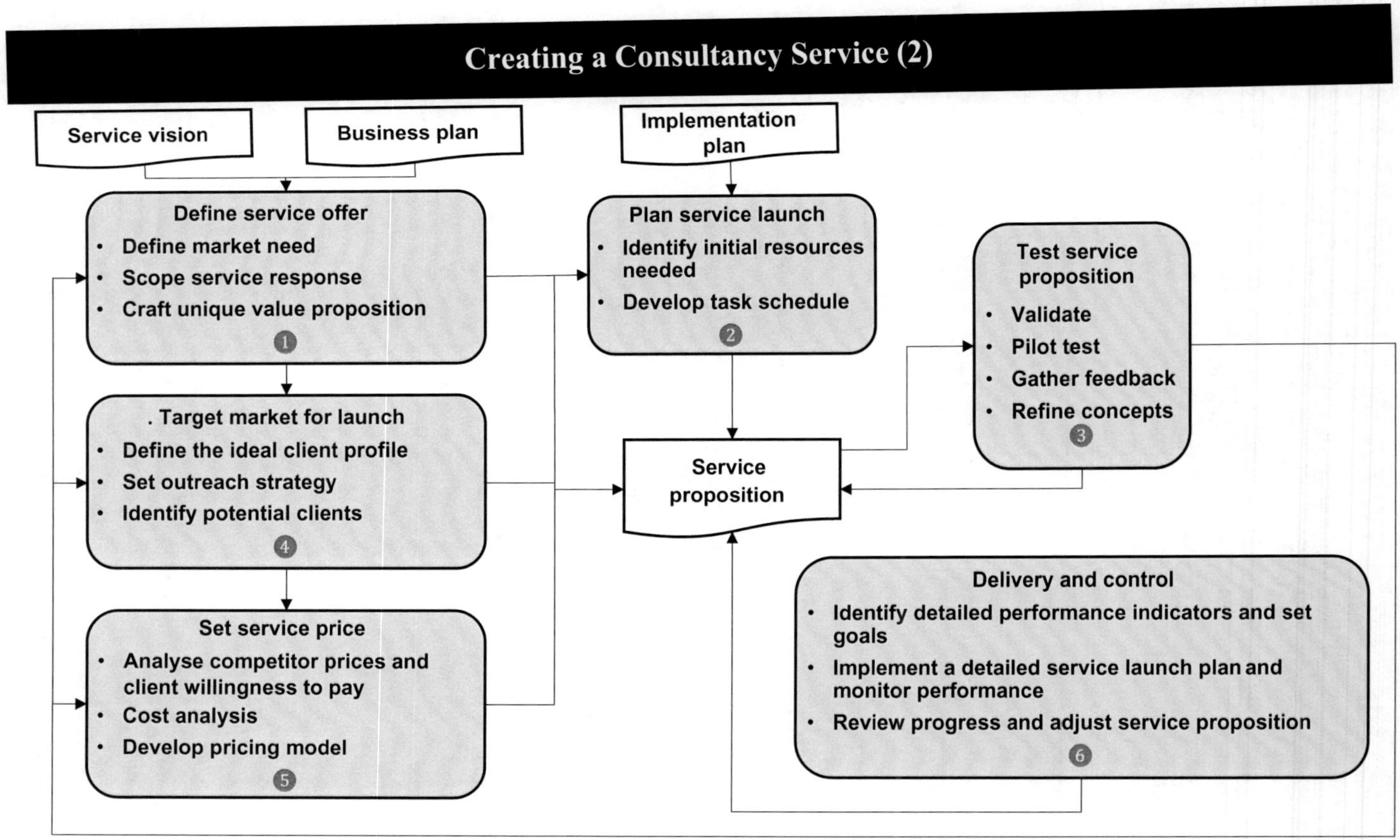

Figure 3.1 Creating a Consultancy Service (2).

steps outlined. Once again, these steps form a core process that will often need to be adapted to meet individual circumstances.

Step 1: Define the service offer

The service offering draws on our previous market research, which we should also consider updating, particularly when changes in an industry are fast moving, or the decision to proceed with the service has taken a long time. The service offer needs to pull data from our agreed business plan (see Chapter 2) and modify it in two ways. First, we need to be highly specific in terms of both clients and services. Second, we must develop a client-benefit focus in our service offer.

It is now you back in focus.

It took the whole weekend to finish the business plan and you finally sent it to the partner and got to bed until 3:00 am on Monday morning. Sadly, the partner called you at 7:00 am to discuss it. But that's consultancy, and at least you met the hastily imposed deadline.

It's 1.30 pm on Wednesday, and the partner rings you.

"[Insert your name here] It's great news. The board was extremely enthusiastic about your ideas and asked to see a detailed service proposition for next month's meeting. That gives you three weeks as the papers for the meeting have to go out one week in advance. Could you come back to me at the end of next week with a draft outline of the document for us to discuss?"

Again, it didn't seem so much like a question the partner was asking, much more like a direct instruction.

Please pause for a moment and list the main headings that you would need to include in such a service proposition.

As you have never seen a detailed service proposition for a consultancy service before, you call Chris, who is now rapidly becoming a combination of your best friend forever and workplace mentor.

Chris explains: "The short service description in the business plan needs to be expanded to become a much fuller explanation of the service. Think of it as a detailed narrative for briefing everyone who will be engaged in promoting, buying, supporting, delivering, or making decisions about the service.

The Partnership Board is a very busy group of individuals concentrating on running their own operations. They need to be given clear, succinct information on which to make decisions. In fact, if any document for them is over five pages, I recommend starting with an executive summary.

So, let's think about how you might build this narrative about the service in manageable chunks. The trick is focusing our thinking on answers to a series of key questions that we might be asked. I prefer to group these questions around the following areas, which are pretty generic but seem to fit most consultancy operations.

1. *Client focus and target market.*
2. *Service offer.*
3. *Team and expertise.*
4. *Engagement management.*
5. *Business operations.*
6. *Growth and sustainability.*

This is an iterative process, not a list to work down. For example, you might start by defining clients and services but have to modify these when you have looked at expertise and growth. For now, I propose we identify detailed questions on the first two issues for you to take away. I know we already have answers to some of these in our earlier work, but remember two things:

- *It will have various readers as an audience, including people who have not seen the previous work.*
- *It acts as an update and a reinforcement for those already familiar with it.*

The client-focused questions that I feel we need to address include:

- ***Target industry**: Who will we specialise in serving, e.g., retailing, healthcare, non-profit, service sector, public services?*
- ***Size**: Will we focus on small businesses, large enterprises, or a mix?*
- ***Needs**: what specific management challenges will we address, e.g., strategy, customer operations, HR?*
- ***Desired benefits**: Will we help clients increase efficiency, improve customer service, restrain costs, increase profitability, or achieve other goals? Do they vary between different clients?*

There are equally several key questions we need to answer about the service itself.

- ***Breadth and depth**: Will we provide broad consulting or specialise in a specific area, such as digital transformation or supply chain? Will we be focused on strategic advice or detailed tactical and implementation support?*
- ***Commercial basis**: Will our service be project-based, ongoing retainer, shared risk and reward, or a combination?*
- ***Deliverables**: What tangible outputs will clients receive, e.g. reports, implementation plans, and implementation support training?*
- ***Methodology**: What tools will we use to analyse and solve client problems?*

That's a lot for you to get your head around, so let's take a break now. But first, I want to add another area for you to consider before we meet again: your Unique Value Proposition. This should become the driver of everything that we are doing. It should summarise why the client must buy this service and why they should buy it from us. It has to be clear and concise, benefit-oriented, and unique. Ideally, in one sentence but maybe two – short ones.

Let's get back together at the beginning of next week and work through the next part of the service proposition. Oh, and by the way, do you have a code for me to charge this time against?"

Chapter 2 described the service proposed in our continuing PNX case study as follows:

PNX will offer a comprehensive suite of AI-related healthcare services, focusing initially on the delivery of systems to identify high-risk patients for early intervention:

- *Strategic consulting, assisting healthcare organisations in developing and implementing AI-driven strategies.*
- *Implementation support, managing the technical and operational aspects of AI integration.*
- *Change management, facilitating smooth adoption and user training.*
- *Data governance and security, ensuring data privacy, security, and ethical AI practices.*

These aspirations are reflected in PNX's AI in Healthcare Service Proposition, which answers the detailed questions posed during our last site visit. Although it is presented here as a document for approval by PNX management, what is important is thinking about our service and recording answers for future use rather than the format.

PNX Consultancy Services

AI in Healthcare Service Proposition

Part 1 Service Description

Understanding the Client's Unique Challenges

The healthcare industry in Europe and North America is a complex mix of needs and priorities. Clients require reliable and effective AI-powered solutions that integrate with existing systems. They perceive a need for help defining an AI strategy and further support selecting the best systems and suppliers. They will also need comprehensive training and implementation assistance.

We will create a team combining deep AI specialists, transformation leaders, and healthcare experts who will use leading-edge thinking to develop value-added, unique methodologies. Our clients will benefit from a service designed to empower them to achieve transformation in service delivery, effectiveness, and cost management that would be otherwise impossible.

We will tailor our services to the needs of different sectors in the healthcare industry.

Sector Hospitals and Health Systems (Europe, Canada, the USA)

Define the Advantages of AI Implementation

We will work in a structured way with each organisation to:

- Identify their strategic and tactical opportunities to benefit from the use of AI-powered systems.
- Assess their state of readiness.
- Develop milestone-based transformation plans.

Early Detection of High-Risk Patients

We will concentrate on deploying and customising AI systems that analyse vast datasets, including electronic health records and lab results, to predict the potential for chronic diseases. This will enable clients to intervene proactively to personalise preventative care plans, improve long-term patient outcomes, and reduce overall healthcare costs.

Optimising Resource Allocation

We will create systems for clients that leverage AI to analyse historical data and predict patient demand for specific services. Such systems will enable hospitals to schedule and plan resources more efficiently. The benefits will be shorter waiting times, increased patient satisfaction, and a more even flow of patients.

Reducing Readmission Rates

We will develop and deploy AI models that identify patients at risk of rapid readmission after discharge. This will benefit our clients by allowing them to create personalised post-discharge care and support plans, improving patient adherence and recovery rates and reducing the costs of early readmissions.

Sector Health Maintenance Organisations (HMOs) (USA, Canada)

Define the Advantages of AI Implementation

We will work in a structured way with each organisation to:

- Identify their strategic and tactical opportunities to benefit from the use of AI-powered systems.
- Analyse the organisation's readiness to implement AI.
- Create transformation plans with clear achievement milestones.

Proactive Disease Management

We will develop updated client systems and processes to maximise the benefits of AI-powered tools to improve the analysis of member data. This will enable clients to proactively identify individuals at risk of chronic illnesses, allowing them to shift from reactive to proactive healthcare delivery. HMOs will be able to personalise preventative care programmes, intervene before the onset of serious health conditions, improve member health outcomes, and potentially lower long-term healthcare costs.

Targeted Wellness Campaign

We will create bespoke processes to use AI to analyse HMO member data and identify groups at risk of specific health conditions like obesity, diabetes, or mental health issues. This will allow HMOs to develop targeted wellness campaigns that promote healthy habits and preventative measures, leading to a healthier membership base and potentially lower future healthcare claims.

Fraud Detection and Cost Management

We will implement AI systems for clients to analyse claims data and detect potential fraud or billing errors. This helps HMOs ensure accurate claims processing, optimise healthcare spending, and protect valuable resources that can be reinvested in member care.

Sector Insurance Companies (Europe, USA, Canada)

Define the Advantages of AI Implementation

We will work in a structured way with each organisation to:

- Identify their strategic and tactical opportunities to benefit from the use of AI-powered systems
- Analyse the organisation's readiness to implement AI.
- Create transformation plans with clear achievement milestones.

Risk Stratification and Personalised Premiums

We will leverage AI functionality to analyse datasets and assess patient risk profiles accurately. Companies will be able to use individual risk profiles to tailor premiums and risk reduction programmes more to each patient. This will reduce overall healthcare costs by enabling personalised preventative measures and allowing the company to offer competitive premiums for the patient.

Medical Claims Processing Automation

We will design and implement solutions which streamline client administrative processes, including medical claims processing. This will benefit our clients by increasing accuracy, expediting payouts for policyholders, and reducing transaction costs and staffing required for routine tasks.

Fraudulent Claims Detection

We will develop tailored AI models that analyse claims data and identify and deter fraudulent activity. Such fraud reduction will benefit insurance companies by safeguarding their financial resources, allowing them to maintain competitive premiums for honest policyholders.

Beyond Technology: Ensuring Sustainable Transformation

Core to our service proposition is our understanding that successful AI integration to deliver cost and service benefits goes beyond simply deploying cutting-edge technology. Our comprehensive service suite ensures that our clients experience a smooth transition and long-term success. This includes the following:

- **Change management**: People are key to adoption, and we will engage with them before, during, and after the transition to AI-driven processes. We implement robust early engagement and training programmes tailored to user roles and needs and clear communication plans to address concerns and build trust in AI solutions. This will foster understanding, user buy-in, and smooth adoption of AI across our clients. After implementation, we will continue to provide expert support and effectiveness reviews to ensure that the benefits of the transition to AI are fully experienced.

- **Data governance and security**: We will protect sensitive patient information and foster trust in our client's commitment to data security by adhering to the highest data privacy compliance standards (HIPAA, GDPR, etc.).
- **Ethical considerations**: We will build trust in clients' AI-powered solutions by adhering to ethical principles throughout AI development, deployment, and use.

Commercial Basis

Our AI consultancy services will typically be provided on a negotiated fixed fee per engagement basis. In certain circumstances, we will share a daily rate table with clients, which will be used to agree on contract extensions. We do not propose entering risk-sharing contracts in the first three years of the service's operation.

Engagement Deliverables

Due to the broad scope of services offered, sector and market deliverables for each engagement will be individually agreed upon with each client at the time of contract negotiation.

Methodology-Based Approaches

We recognise that utilising established methodologies reassures clients that we have a structured approach to supporting them and enables us to introduce a degree of repeatability into our work. However, we also recognise that different approaches are relevant in various sectors and geographies. We have identified three methodologies that we will draw on to ensure a comprehensive and user-centred approach to change tailored to each client situation:

1. **ADKAR model (Prosci methodology)**: We will apply this method to deliver a step-by-step process to create a knowledgeable and supportive community for change in healthcare, including the following:
    1. **Awareness**: Educating all stakeholders, including patients, managers, medical, nursing, and admin staff, so that they understand the potential benefits of AI to them.
    2. **Desire**: Highlighting the improvement that AI systems can bring to patient care and organisational goals to build enthusiasm for the changes required.
    3. **Knowledge**: Delivering training programmes to enable managers and users to fully understand the new insights that AI can bring to their roles.
    4. **Ability**: Enhancing the skills of all staff to enable them to use AI solutions most effectively.
    5. **Reinforcement**: A supportive environment needs to be created to reinforce user experiences and skills post-implementation. Our objective is to ensure that when users have any concerns remaining, there are ways to address them, which supports long-term adoption and prevents reversion to old ways.

2. **Kotter's eight-step change model**: We will use this model to help build an understanding of the change process and to foster support for it when implementing AI in healthcare. We will adapt Kotter's steps as follows:

    1. **Create a sense of urgency**: Highlight the increasing costs of reactive care and the potential for AI to improve healthcare outcomes and efficiency.
    2. **Form a powerful guiding coalition**: To champion AI adoption, assemble a team with strong leadership and representation from all key stakeholder groups, including patients, professionals, medical professionals, and other staff and funding agencies, where appropriate.
    3. **Develop a vision and strategy**: Develop a compelling vision that clearly explains to all parties how implementing AI-driven solutions across the client organisation will transform the delivery of healthcare services and prepare an overview plan for their implementation.
    4. **Communicate the change vision**: Prepare a communication programme that addresses the needs of all stakeholders, including staff and patients, by addressing their concerns and using language, channels, and styles appropriate to them, which promotes their understanding of potential benefits and the route to achieving them.
    5. **Empower broad-based action**: Provide opportunities for all staff members to participate in the change process and, through their engagement, contribute to the successful integration of AI across our client's services.
    6. **Generate short-term wins**: Create an implementation process designed to deliver early demonstrable successes from implementing AI-facilitated services. Use these success stories to develop momentum in the programme and build stakeholder confidence in the achievability of the long-term vision.
    7. **Consolidate gains and produce more change**: Utilise initial successes to refine the AI strategy and address ongoing challenges.
    8. **Anchor new approaches in the client's organisational culture**: By embedding the use of AI solutions to real problems into the fabric of the healthcare organisation, we will ensure the long-term sustainability of AI as a route to meeting client objectives.

3. **Appreciative inquiry (AI) approach**: This methodology is a slightly different focus from the other two and helps to inform our consultancy interactions with the client stakeholders. It concentrates on identifying and building upon the client organisation's strengths and positive experiences. In the context of AI in healthcare,

    1. **Discover**: We will hold facilitated discussions with staff and other stakeholders about positive experiences with technology in healthcare. Using these experiences and case studies, we will build enthusiasm for using AI for service transformation.
    2. **Dream**: In this stage, we build on our previous work and engage stakeholders in creative thinking sessions. Our objective is for them to develop a vision of AI as a means to transform their work and improve healthcare delivery for patients and staff. At the end of this process, we also prioritise the areas in which AI is perceived to have the greatest impact and the earliest visible benefit.
    3. **Design**: Still working closely with stakeholders, we develop a detailed implementation plan for the AI system that reflects the organisation's priorities and takes the most cost-effective implementation route.
    4. **Destiny**: We develop post-implementation processes by which the client can collate user feedback, map its evolving needs, and use these to refine the implemented AI systems.

Unique Value Proposition

Unlocking the potential benefit of AI in healthcare.

We will be the only genuinely independent advisers working right across healthcare AI. PNX will be the one-stop shop for unlocking the power of AI for our clients. We will deliver technology and a transformative journey towards a more economical, efficient, effective, and ethical healthcare system that improves patient outcomes and leads to a more sustainable future for our clients.

Step 2: Plan the service launch

Although we developed a high-level view of the implementation for the approval process, we need to define in greater detail how the service will be created and launched. At this point, we need to define these identified tasks, logically connect them into an actionable delivery timeline, and develop detailed work statements for each. We can define each task more closely by referencing our standard set of questions of who, why, what, where, when, how, and, of course, how much. Table 3.1 is an example of how our answers can be recorded in a task datasheet.

Table 3.1 Task Datasheet

Task Datasheet			
Part 1 Basic task data			
Task reference			
Task name			
Inputs			
Activities			
Outputs			
Quality standards			
Resources needed			
Predecessor tasks			
Successor tasks			
Part 2 Planning data			
Effort (Days)		**Start date**	
Daily rate		**Duration (Elapsed days)**	
Budget		**End date**	

Note the inclusion of a daily rate box and a budget. This allows us to include internal resource costs that we must charge for our service development project. Table 3.2 shows how a task data sheet might be completed for one of PNX Consultancy's identified tasks.

The final step is to prepare an updated delivery timeline, usually in a Gantt chart. While project management software packages, such as Microsoft Project, will assist in preparing a Gantt chart,

Table 3.2 PNX Consultancy Services Application of Advanced AI in Healthcare Completed Task Datasheet

PNX Consultancy Services Application of Advanced AI in Healthcare Completed Task Datasheet			
Part 1 Basic task data			
Task reference	1.3.2.		
Task name	Marketing material development		
Inputs	Service propositions		
Activities	Develop high-quality marketing materials showcasing PNX's unique value proposition tailored to each target region		
Outputs	Two flyers, conference banners, and white papers on each of AI in health insurance and AI in healthcare delivery		
Quality standards	All marketing materials must comply with corporate guidelines and be available initially in American English and French versions		
Resources needed	Publications require a specialist designer and a writer. Their allocation to the team is to be agreed upon with corporate marketing Practice lead partner to provide briefings and draft content for white papers Translator		
Predecessor tasks	1.3.1 Finalise service packages		
Successor tasks	3.1 Sales and Client Acquisition stream		
Part 2 Planning data			
Effort (Days)	**15**	**Start date**	Week 8
Daily rate	**n/a**	**Duration (Elapsed days)**	10
Budget	**$10,000**	**End date**	Week 10 close

there are freely available templates in MS Office that help prepare a suitable chart. Figure 3.2 shows the implementation plan for PNX Consultancy using Excel.

Step 3: Proposition testing

This is another iterative step, building on our previous research and using the contact network that we have established. The difference is that we now have a firm service proposition to test. Proposition testing has two clear objectives for engaging with the market to validate a service proposition: First, the coherence of the proposed service and the ability of the customer to engage with it must be tested; and second, to assess the value of the benefits that a client would achieve from the service and inform our service pricing strategy.

Client recruitment

There are several strategies that we can follow when seeking to find suitable and willing clients to engage with our testing process:

- **Incentive programmes**: Before asking clients to work with us on the testing programme, we need to consider how we would reward their participation. Offering attractive incentives may encourage them to do so. This could include providing the service we are testing free or with a heavy discount, offering discounts on future services, or providing free access to other intellectual property or training.

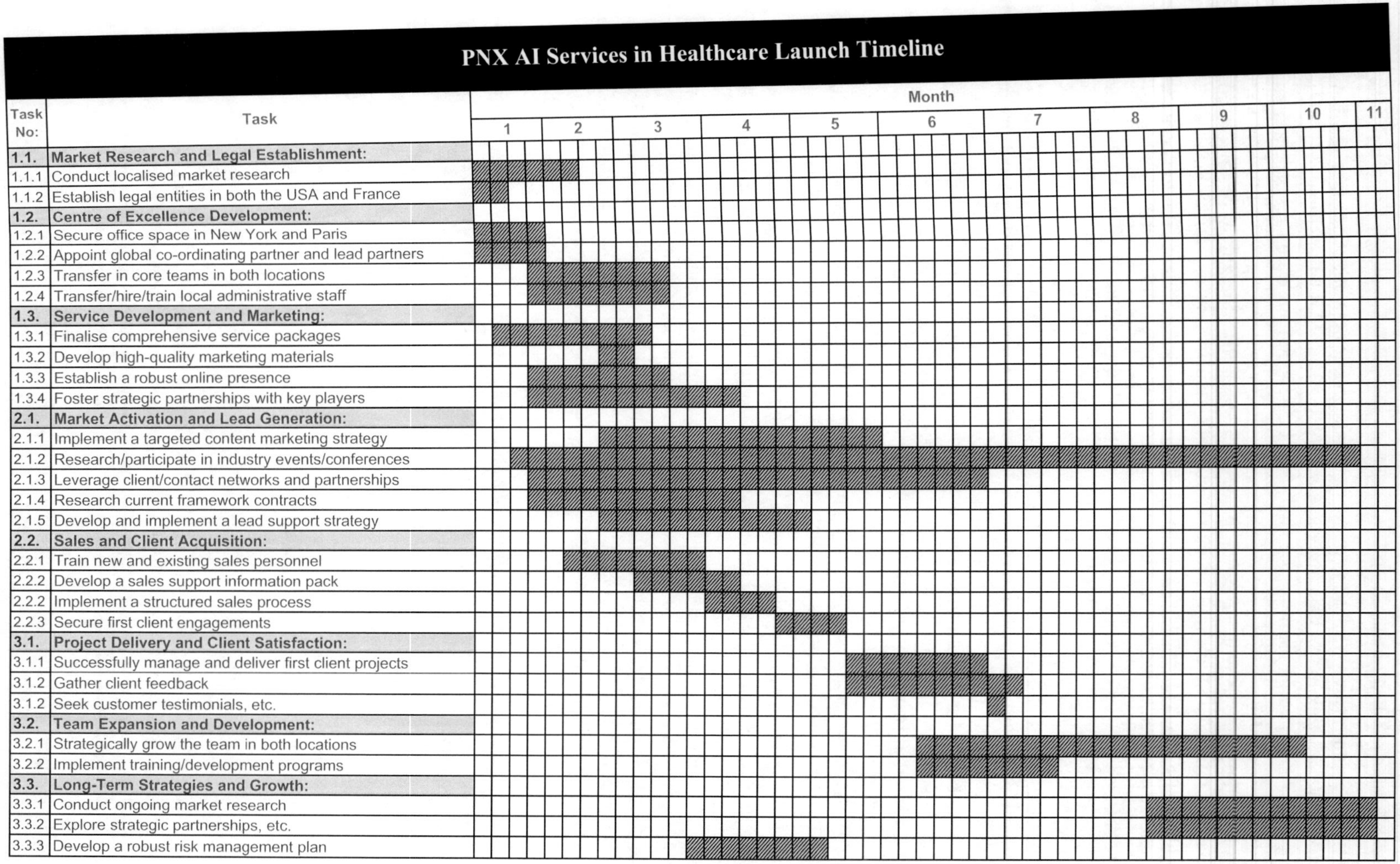

Figure 3.2 PNX AI Services in Healthcare Launch Timeline.

- **Network exploitation**: We need to understand who in our network of contacts is in our target market. We are seeking to make the most of existing trusted relationships, and whilst these may be with client organisations, they may also be between our team members and individuals in the target market. Even if contacts decline to participate in our testing, we should ask if they will provide us with a referral to another organisation that might be interested.
- **Targeted outreach**: We should seek to leverage industry events, conferences, and online communities relevant to our targets. It is worth considering whether attending such events should be elevated to include seeking speaking opportunities and conference stands.
- **Partnerships**: We can seek to collaborate with industry associations, chambers of commerce, or relevant non-profit organisations to reach businesses and organisations that would be prepared to cooperate with us.
- **Requests for tenders**: Public sector procurement rules mean that government bodies often issue tender requests. We should scan these to determine whether our proposed service could be amended to align with their requirements. To find such requests easily, it may be necessary to subscribe to an online platform that lists them. Winning such a tender will enable us to secure an opportunity to pilot our ideas and probably a case study.
- **Professional networks**: Senior individuals working with potential clients in our target market may use platforms like LinkedIn. If that is the case, we may be able to connect with them, engage in discussions, share insights related to our proposed service area, and highlight the benefits of participating in our pilot testing programme.

Alongside our test client recruitment process, we should develop a minimum viable service. Creating a restricted version of our full service allows us to gather feedback and test core functionalities in the field with reduced investment. For example, PNX Consultancy could offer a free or low-cost "AI maturity assessment" to validate their assumptions about an AI transformation service for health industry sectors in different jurisdictions. Discussing and refining this minimum service concept with contacts early during the client recruitment process may be beneficial. We should also clearly articulate the specific challenges the proposed service will address and how the testing will operate, including timings, feedback mechanisms, commercial arrangements, and discounts, if applicable. This can then be discussed with the target clients being recruited.

Once we have assembled a panel of persons interested in cooperating with our testing and piloting approach, we must undertake a series of tasks to help evolve our service proposition to reflect the market's perceptions. They are as follows:

- **Conduct targeted interviews**: In Chapter 2, we engaged in broader research to help define our service. We can interview targeted potential clients to understand their pain points, decision-making processes, and budget constraints. It may also be worthwhile to interview thought leaders and respected professionals. The results of these interviews will allow us to refine our proposition test to ensure that our service more fully addresses the identified need.
- **Recruit test pilots**: The next sub-step is to identify a small group from our panel of potential clients willing to try our minimum viable service in exchange for their feedback. The key to selecting clients will be timing, as we need to respect their workloads and, at the same time, balance these with our availability to undertake the test and our planned timeline. It is also worth asking if the recruits would be willing to be identified subsequently in marketing material, such as case studies and white papers, and potentially to collaborate in speaking events.
- **Conduct pilot tests and gather feedback**: While the management of the client may understand the concept of a pilot test, this may not have been discussed with staff. As we wish to gain feedback from all levels, commencing a pilot study with a briefing session for all engaged staff will often be helpful. During this briefing, they should be introduced to a nominated contact to whom they can submit their thoughts and concerns during the pilot.

Regular review meetings with client management are also advisable to ensure that problems are addressed as early as possible during the pilot. The period between such meetings will depend on the length of the pilot. For example, it would be advisable to speak daily for a one-week study, but for a one-month study, a weekly meeting may be sufficient. At the end of the pilot, we should seek formal feedback through surveys, structured interviews, and user review sessions. This feedback should be open and frank, as our objective is to identify areas for improvement and confirm if our service resonates with the target market.

- **Analyse results and refine the service proposition**: Pilot testing feedback lets us refine our service proposition based on client needs and preferences. We should also gain insight into the added value of our service as perceived by the client to inform our marketing strategy and pricing decisions.

Step 4: Targeting our launch

At this point, we should review our previous evaluation in light of the testing of our refined service proposition and identify where and how we will initially launch our service. While launching to the broadest market is tempting, a more selective approach is advisable given that our resources, including staff and time, are always limited. Fortunately, as a result of our initial market research and pilot testing, we should already have a firm understanding of our market, a network to talk to, and we may even have some warm contacts to follow up.

However, always be prepared to evaluate opportunities that may arise from continuing to scan requests for proposals or be entirely unexpected, as in our earlier site visit to that soggy ex-supermarket.

Define our ideal client profile

Our first task in targeting our launch is to identify our ideal client and ideal client contact point by considering the following:

- **Industry**: The industries or sectors within an industry where we believe that our proposed service will address critical or endemic pain points and offer a significant advantage over other approaches. For example, PNX argues that their service offers advice independent of that from large system suppliers and integrators.
- **Organisation size**: Size is a poor indicator of readiness for change, and we should consider whether an organisation falls within a range that matches the scale and complexity of our service proposition. For example, PNX may view its AI in healthcare proposition as more suited to large general hospitals than small specialist clinics.
- **Decision-making hierarchy**: A key to success is identifying the level within any target organisation with the authority to purchase our service. This could be at the chief officer level, department heads, or specific teams. Understanding different levels of authority to incur expenditure may also influence how we can price and sell services. For example, gaining financial approval for a lower-cost entry level service may often occur at a lower level in the hierarchy than for our complete services. This is especially true of public sector bodies where rules about competitive supply also have a significant impact. Using our panel of interested clients, it is worth considering whether we should conduct short interviews to gain first-hand insights into their decision-making processes.
- **Challenges and needs**: Having identified the industry, company size, and target contact points, we should clearly define the challenges that our service meets and the needs that it fulfils for each.

Identify our outreach targets

We now have a narrowly defined target area and need to consider how we will research and approach the individuals within that target area. Our first task is to continue speaking to the network built to help us with the pilot test. They will all have knowledge of the industry and the players within it. Consequently, conversations with them will help identify our first list of prospects. We can then update our contact information and repeat the targeted outreach used to recruit parties for the pilot test. If, however, no customer relationship management system is already in place, it is useful now to formally start recording information manually about our contacts. Table 3.3 provides a simple format for collecting valuable information.

Table 3.3 Target Profile

Target Profile			
Company/ Organisation			
Primary Contact		**Title**	
Primary contact details			
Email	**Address**	**Office number**	
		Mobile number	
Preferred contact methods			
Influence over purchase decisions/ outcomes			**Influence score (0–8 highest)**
Interest in purchase decisions/Outcomes			**Interest score (0–8 highest)**
Contact category	**Decision-maker/influencer** (delete as appropriate)		
Summary of known initial opinions/views on the proposed service			
Desirable changes of views on the proposed service			
Proposed communications/ engagement plan			
Actions taken	**Action**	**Date**	**By**
Created (date)	**Created by**	**Reviewed (date)**	**Reviewed by**

A word of caution

The profiling data we collect can be personal to an individual and represent a judgement of them. Consequently, any information we collect may be covered by data protection legislation in each jurisdiction in which we operate. We should, therefore, assure ourselves that we are operating with due respect to all our legal obligations. Even with no legal restrictions, our professional and ethical responsibility is to keep our data relating to identifiable individuals secure.

Additionally, when we note any information about an individual's views, capability, or influence, we should consider whether our notes are soundly based and use moderate language. We may privately think that the attention span of the CEO of a potential major client compares unfavourably with an IQ-challenged goldfish or is more interested in betting success on horse racing than ensuring the success of their company. Still, we should be more measured in the information we record. Data is not always secure, and it will probably not help the sales process, the success of our marketing campaign, or our career if a very adverse and intemperately worded profile is leaked.

At this stage, our outreach strategy should be "bottom-up" based on a summary of the information we have recorded for each target client. For example, there is no point in attending, displaying, or seeking speaking slots at a conference the target clients have not said they attend. However, preparing an article for a magazine they commonly read would be appropriate, especially teamed with a contact campaign saying, "I thought that you might find our article in this month's XYZ Industry Monthly of interest."

Step 5: Set service price

Setting a price level for market entry involves considering multiple factors, which often pull in different directions. Our chosen price needs to find a "sweet spot" that balances these competing forces. We should also recognise that we could fall victim to cautiousness and set a service price that is too low for long-term sustainability.

The two most important factors to consider first are as follows:

- **Value to the client of the service**: This is the foundation of our pricing strategy. We have to clearly and realistically define what unique benefit we offer clients. Whilst some of these benefits may be intangible, such as "improved customer service," we need to quantify the financial impact we can have on their bottom line, probably over a number of years. This is because, at some point, the Chief Financial Officer, or their equivalent, will ask a version of "How can we afford this?" We need to identify how we can help them increase revenue by X% or reduce costs by Y%. We can then frame our pricing around the value we deliver, making it easier to justify a premium rate.
- **Cost to us to deliver the service**: We have to be equally clear about our break-even point and know how much it will cost us to deliver the proposed service. We need to consider not only the full hourly or daily costs of staff deployed to the client and management time but also all overhead costs, such as office space, software subscriptions, marketing expenses, training, and IT. Expenses are always an issue; do we wrap them into the price or recharge them separately?[2] We must also factor in our desired profit margin for a sustainable daily rate, project fee, or retainer amount. This ensures that our pricing allows us to cover costs and generate a planned profit.

We have now established a range within which our service can be priced, that is, between the minimum price that we require, based on our costs, and the maximum potential customer value. However, there are other factors that we can take into account:

- **Early adopter strategy**: In order to build our credibility and track record, we can offer a launch discount, but this can be a double-edged sword. Although it helps attract initial clients and contributes to overcoming our lack of testimonials and case studies, starting with a price that's too low can set market expectations of a price that is difficult to overcome later. We should also recognise that early adopters might require more hand-holding, which would increase our costs. If we offer a launch discount, we should regard these as part of the service proposition development costs. Setting a fixed time limit for the discount will also create a sense of urgency and minimise the risk of creating unrealistic client pricing expectations.
- **Competitor pricing**: We should attempt to research established consultants in our niche and understand their pricing models. We should not offer a lower price; instead, we need to redouble our focus on offering competitive value. If our expertise is highly specialised, we should consider offering a premium service package with a higher price tag that reflects the additional benefits we deliver.
- **Client budget**: Understanding our target client's typical budget range helps us price realistically. We will have already established some information during the pilot testing. Still, we must also research industry benchmarks and competitor packages to see what our ideal clients are willing to pay. Later, when offering the full range of related services, we should consider offering tiered service packages with varying levels of service complexity and price points to cater to different budget constraints.
- **Long-term sustainability**: Our launch price needs to be set at a level that allows us to grow and reinvest in our business and avoids locking us into a pricing model that is unsustainable in the long run. We will also need to factor in inflation and the potential need to raise prices in the future to maintain our profit margins.
- **Pricing model selection**: There's no one-size-fits-all approach. The best model for us will depend on our service offering, project predictability, and the preferred relationship style by both ourselves and the client. The most commonly encountered pricing models all have plus and minus points to consider; they include:
  - Hourly or daily rate:
    - \+ Simple and transparent for both us and the client.
    - \+ Flexible for unpredictable project scopes.
    - – Clients might perceive time-based billing as expensive, potentially incentivising us to work additional time instead of optimising efficiency.
    - – In certain tax regimes, it may be seen as employment and taxed differently.
    - – Clients perceive our value as being in the time spent by consultants rather than the actual value delivered. This includes comparing offers from different consultancies based on day rates.
  - Engagement-based fees:
    - \+ Provide predictable income and encourages us to work efficiently to complete the engagement within the agreed timeframe.
    - – Require accurate upfront scoping, which can be challenging.
    - – Clients might hesitate to commit to a significant upfront cost.

- Retainer agreements:
  - + Recurring revenue stream which supports long-term client relationships.
  - – Less flexibility for the consultant and the client.
  - – Requires the client to commission work consistently to justify the retainer fee, even when it is not required in a particular period.
  - – There is a risk of scope creep.
  - – The consultancy's overreliance on a few significant retainer agreements introduces real commercial risk if the client fails to renew.
- Shared risk and reward:
  - + Strong incentive for delivering successful outcomes, which builds trust with clients.
  - – Requires careful risk management.
  - – Relies heavily on delivering quantifiable results over an agreed period.

Step 6: Service launch – delivery and control

Now for another phone call from the partner at an inconvenient time . . .

It's 7:30 on Friday night, and you are just settling down at home with your preferred beverage to watch the lead-up to a big game on a cable sports channel. It is your reward for a hard week. Buzz – your mobile is on silent, but you glance at it anyway and can see that it's the partner. You wish that you knew a stronger word than bother! Still, you should immediately be glad you can now pause live TV. You take a deep breath and answer.

"Hi [insert your name here], I am happy I caught you; we haven't seen much of each other lately." No apology for disturbing your game, you note. "We are off to a corporate weekend early tomorrow. It's a bit of a jolly game of golf in the afternoon, a dinner, and more golf the following morning. But I am going to be asked how you are getting on. Could you wing me a note on your progress before I leave in the morning, say by around ten o'clock?."

Another one of those questions that looks remarkably like an instruction.

"That's OK. I have been keeping track of everything. I need to fire up my laptop and send you a report. I will get it to you within the hour." Of course, this allows you to earn maximum points from the partner and still leave sending it until half-time!

But what would you include in such a report? Please take a few moments to jot down the main headings.

Performance indicators

Our first task is to identify and, if necessary, agree on detailed performance indicators and target achievement levels. We have generated a large amount of data about our service proposition, the business results it should achieve, and the performance expected from each engagement. Although we have researched, tested, and validated each class of data item at this stage, they are still only assumptions. We will need to review our real-world performance against them and show how they will support the SMART business goals and our business justification. We also need to set a timetable for formal progress reviews.

Our SMART goals are still relatively high level, and we should turn our assumptions and planned activities into lower-level or more immediate key performance indicators (KPIs) for set goals for each of them. Chapter 8 covers performance monitoring in more detail.

In the service launch phase, we should monitor metrics such as sales and marketing effectiveness, engagement delivery, client satisfaction, and financial performance. Together, these can give us a comprehensive picture of our progress against our plan and business justification.

- **Sales and marketing effectiveness**: Sales and marketing measures are early cycle indicators that will show our service proposition launch phase's early success or otherwise. Before defining our indicators, we must consider our sales and marketing process, including different routes to acquiring a paying client. We can then determine the indicators required to analyse the effectiveness of the various marketing and sales channels we will use (e.g. social media, content marketing, requests for proposals). The measured results we achieve will show if we need to adjust our launch marketing strategy and will inform our sales and marketing beyond the launch period. Possible indicators to consider include the following:
    - Lead generation rate by channel: The number of qualified leads generated through our marketing efforts (e.g. website forms, referrals).
    - Conversion rates at different stages of our sales process: For example, website visitors to enquiries to qualified leads and leads to paying clients.
    - Client acquisition efficiency: This is the average cost of acquiring a new client. These costs include marketing, sales staff, and any discounts offered. We should also monitor our client acquisition costs alongside our average engagement value to ensure that our marketing efforts are sustainable. A high client acquisition cost compared to project value can be acceptable at our launch stage, for example, from initial discounting. If the high-cost situation continues, it could indicate the need to refine our target audience, adjust marketing strategies, or reconsider our pricing.

- **Engagement delivery performance**: There is often a mismatch between the engagement resources scoped during the sales process and those consumed by the delivery process. We can track the percentage of engagements delivered within our proposed timeframe and budget, and monitor their variance from expectations. This assessment of completion rates on time and on budget measures the effective management of our engagements and the accuracy of our scope estimations during the sales process. Where there are variances, we must investigate further to identify their causes and target areas for improvement.
- **Client satisfaction**: At all stages of our service delivery, we should monitor customer satisfaction. During the launch phase, when we are still seeking to fine-tune our service offer and how it is delivered, such monitoring is critical. We should conduct regular surveys to gather client feedback and ask about consultants' expertise, communication effectiveness, service quality, and overall satisfaction. It is better to collect this information through a client meeting wherever possible. While the engagement manager can do this, a better result may be obtained if it is conducted by an independent surveyor or by a senior consultant not involved in the engagement. However, the feedback survey is undertaken, and it is always helpful to conclude with three questions, in this order:
    1. Please could you identify three things that we need to do better?
    2. Please could you identify three things that went well and that we should do more of?
    3. On a scale of one to ten, how likely would you be to recommend our service? This is called the net promoter score, which provides valuable insight into client satisfaction and

promotes brand advocacy. A high NPS score indicates that satisfied clients will likely recommend our services to others, driving organic growth through referrals. A word of caution: Inferring a score may be better than asking the client directly if the interview raises various adverse issues and comments.

- **Financial performance monitoring**: In our business plan for the service proposition, we set certain expectations for our financial performance – and detailed several assumptions on which those performance figures were based. During the launch phase, we need to understand that there can be limitations and timing issues with data from some financial systems we have to use for performance monitoring; for example, purchases may only be shown when the invoice is paid or staff costs attributed to the engagement after the monthly payroll has run. We may need, therefore, not only to separately track costs and income from each engagement but to prepare forward projections on an engagement and a team basis. This will enable us to identify potential cost overruns much earlier and allow delivery adjustments to maintain our profitability and utilisation targets.

Our service launch involves spending resources on tasks to achieve specific outcomes. Consequently, we can borrow from established project management concepts to control its delivery. The primary project management concept we should employ is simple to say but not always easy to do. The agreed plan should be the sole focus of all our activities. There are two techniques that we can use to help us to keep this focus on the plan. At the end of each day, spend a few quiet moments noting down what has been achieved today that contributes to achieving the plan, listing today's difficulties that still need resolution, and reviewing tomorrow's activities.

The second technique is progress monitoring and reporting on our implementation plan. The discipline of formally reviewing and recording progress ensures that all tasks are reviewed, any tasks encountering problems are identified, and mitigation measures are prepared. In some instances, a weekly review is necessary; in others, a more extended period is acceptable. The rule should be that the shorter or more intense the implementation plan, the more frequent the progress report. The format in Table 3.4 includes most of the information needed to demonstrate progress and to show whether the implementation is on track. A handy way of assessing any status is against a traffic light system of RED, AMBER, and GREEN, usually abbreviated to RAG status. A simplified use of this technique is as follows:

GREEN: If any task has been completed, or we believe it will be completed, on or before the scheduled completion date, it gets a GREEN status.

RED: Any task to be completed late that may delay other tasks or the planned overall completion date automatically switches to a RED status. A task should similarly get a RED status if it will force us to run over our budget. A RED flag means that we must put in place strategies to mitigate the impacts that such a delay or cost overrun is likely to have. We may also have to escalate this as an issue if decisions are required that will alter our implementation plan.

AMBER: This includes tasks currently running late that should not adversely impact other tasks or tasks that may run over budget. These tasks might call for more judgement. Their default status should be AMBER, but we should also consider whether there may possibly be an impact on the overall project delivery dates or costs and whether we need a mitigation strategy.

Table 3.4 Implementation Plan Progress Report

Implementation Plan Progress Report				
Report Period		**To**		
Original plan completion date		**Forecast date**		
Reason for variance in completion date				
Current delivery RAG status		**Red**	**Amber**	**Green**
Prior delivery RAG status		**Red**	**Amber**	**Green**

Escalated Decisions

Milestones in Period

Ref:	**Progress**	**RAG status**		
		Red	**Amber**	**Green**
		Red	**Amber**	**Green**
		Red	**Amber**	**Green**
		Red	**Amber**	**Green**
		Red	**Amber**	**Green**

Current Tasks Update

Task delivery status		**Red**	**Amber**	**Green**
Ref:	**Progress**	**RAG status**		
		Red	**Amber**	**Green**
		Red	**Amber**	**Green**
		Red	**Amber**	**Green**
		Red	**Amber**	**Green**
		Red	**Amber**	**Green**

Deliverables

Deliverables status	**Red**	**Amber**	**Green**
Completed in period		**Date complete**	
Due in next period		**Due date**	

A periodic review of our progress against our business plan is a valuable tool for ourselves as well as for reporting to our stakeholders. Unlike the highly task-focused implementation plan progress report, it considers how well we are meeting the aspirations set out in our business plan. It should also review the business plan in the light of our real-world experience. Were we too ambitious, or were we too cautious? The readership of this review should be the stakeholders in our business plan. If necessary, we may need to support the report with a series of discussions to explain any variances and seek approval for any changes we wish to make.

Theoretical case study – reprise

Your brief is to develop and market a range of services to the public and service sectors based on expertise drawn from insurance and broader financial services. You will go on to create and then lead a team of high-performing consultants to sell and deliver the services. In your reflections section at the end of the last chapter, you described several options, selected one, and drafted a three-year business plan for its creation and delivery as a profitable service and a high-level task list covering the first 12 months.

Reflections

Please draw on your experience and current situation or use the theoretical case study.

- In 200 words, prepare a convincing narrative for a service you are launching. Edit this so that you can deliver it as "an elevator pitch" in 30 seconds, designed so that the hearer will respond by asking, "Can you tell me more about that?" Hint: Start with an earthquake and work up to a climax.
- Prepare task descriptions for two major launch tasks.
- Prepare a Gantt chart showing the timeline for your service launch.
- Describe the principal skills required in delivering your service's launch phase, and identify the staff numbers for each of the first four quarters.
- Explain briefly how you would determine the pricing for your service.
- Identify five performance indicators that you might use to determine your success in launching your service. Research and set suitable target levels for each one.

Notes

1 Not a prophetic statement because within two months, the war in a neighbouring state threatened to cross the border. Jon's hotel became the base for the international press core and visiting politicians. There were regular worried TV interviews from the hotel's front porch with distant shell fire in the background. In consultancy, timing can be everything. To complete the story, Serge was only in the basement for a few days and contributed to the due diligence report.

2 We had one client who was reluctant to pay for travel and accommodation costs, which they always referred to as "suitcase costs." If that is the case, estimate the costs and include them in the total fee. In another case, a client saw that they would get tax advantages in paying travel costs directly to the consultant, so we agreed a contract to permit that.

4 Talent

Who Will Deliver the Service for Us?

Aim of this chapter: To understand how to attract and retain the talented individuals we need to work with to meet our business and service delivery plan.

Learning outcome: To understand the necessary steps to acquire and maintain the talented resources to build our consultancy service's delivery vehicle. This includes the frontline "talent" working for clients and the back-office services, which provide the business infrastructure for the consultancy operations.

The importance of building an effective consultancy team cannot be over-emphasised. It is the equivalent of a manufacturer building its factory, supply chain, sales, and logistics functions. One wrong step at this point can completely derail our aspiration to develop a successful consultancy operation. Attracting, retaining, and managing the talent required to deliver our business is complex but can be broken into a series of processes and steps. As always, these may need to be varied to meet the requirements of different organisations and situations. Figure 4.1 sets out the main steps required to create and maintain talented, high-performing consultancy teams.

Step 1: Defining our talent needs

Before deciding how to proceed with our talent-building exercise, we need two visits to our continuing case study.

It's time for you to sit in the hot seat again.

In your role of creating a new consultancy service, your business justification has now been approved. It is early the following week, and you are meeting with Chris again. This time, he has brought along a human resource consultant, Kai.

Chris: "I have brought Kai here to help discuss the people aspects. Kai came to one of our early discovery sessions and has a background in what we are trying to achieve. So, I am handing this session over to Kai to talk about building a profile of the people we will need to fulfil your vision and deliver our service proposition."

Kai has experienced this situation many times with different clients and now switches into his full "explaining concepts to new clients" mode.

DOI: 10.4324/9781003490456-5

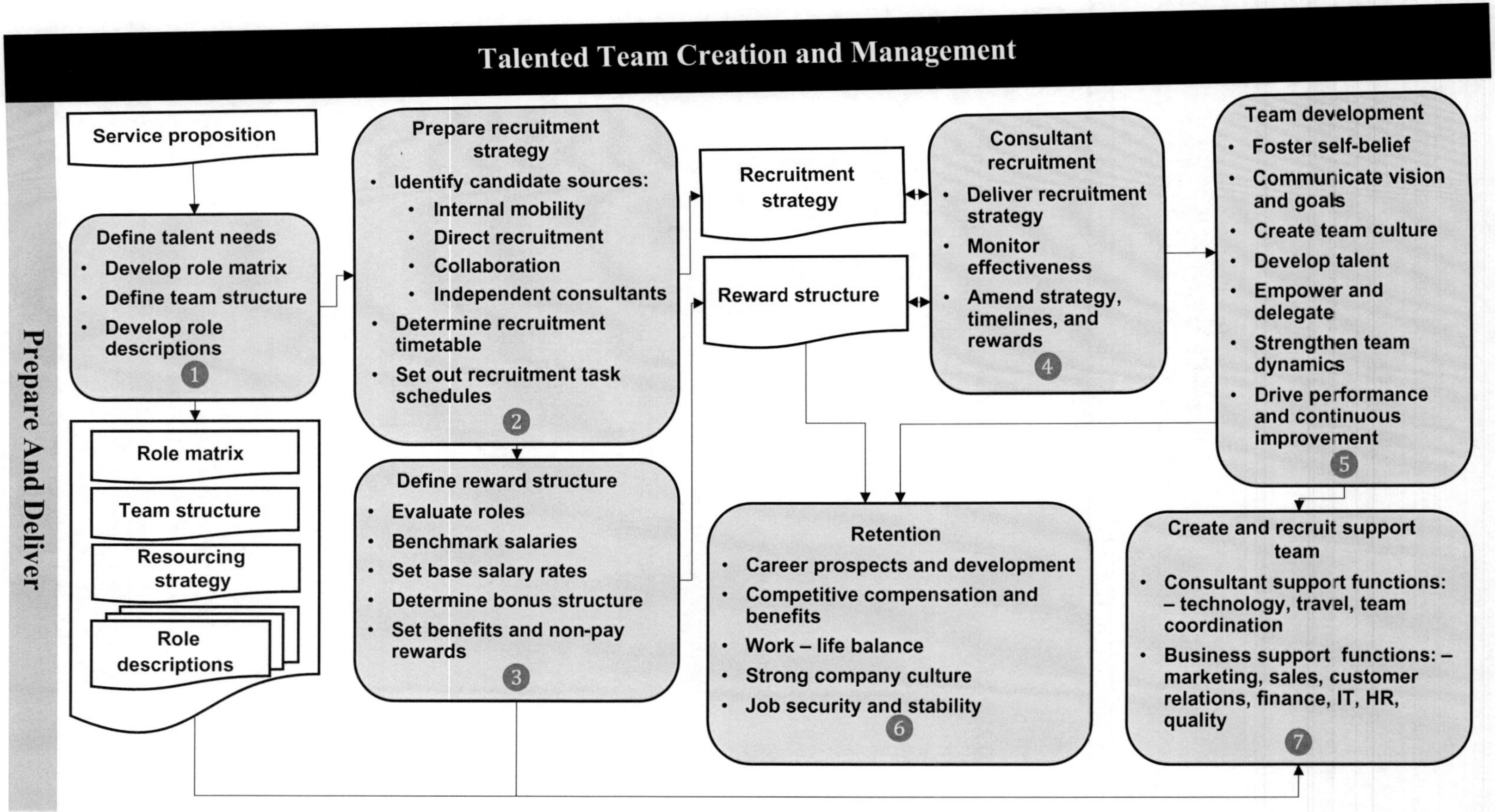

Figure 4.1 Talented Team Creation and Management.

Kai: "So far, you have been concentrating on how we might develop and sell a service. The simple truth is that what we sell is always people, their time and expertise – which I prefer to call their talent. But more than this, the people you need to recruit are both the talent you will sell and the means of selling it. Have in your mind the model of a small shopkeeper. Yes, they have to go out and get stock to sell – in our case, the consultants. However, they also have to recruit the shop assistants who will do the selling.

Now, to add the special consultancy twist. At different times, any of your team members could be a consultant delivering an assignment, a marketeer promoting the service, a sales rep closing the deal with a client or a thought leader developing an improved service. Consequently, we have a more pressing issue before considering how many staff we need, where they will come from, and how much we will need to pay them. We need to think in detail about what we will require from each member of our team and the skills and attributes they will need to have now and acquire in future. This thinking has to cover necessary attitudes and types of personality as well as the skills and qualifications needed for each role.

We need to establish our requirements at the outset so that we can shape the recruitment process to attract suitable candidates and ensure that we can address the only three questions we really must answer:

1. *Can they do the job?*
2. *Will they do the job?*
3. *Will they fit in?*

With those questions in mind, let's turn to developing a resourcing plan, which must address many complex and multifaceted issues. These include:

- *Skills and experience for each role:*
  - *What level of expertise will our consultants possess?*
  - *Do they require specific qualifications, and how should we evaluate qualifications against experience?*
  - *Is sufficient expertise available in the market, or will we have to train staff?*
  - *Will we have generalists or build teams with specific expertise?*
  - *Will our team have in-depth knowledge of our target client industries?*
- *Recruitment:*
  - *Will the team be fully employed by us, engaged on an assignment-by-assignment basis, or a mix of both?*
  - *How will we recruit, and in what time frame?*
  - *Will we transfer staff from other areas in the business, and if so, what subject and industry training might they require?*
  - *What are the market salary levels for the types of staff we wish to recruit, where will we need to pitch our offers, and how will this information affect our pricing model?*
  - *What should our induction processes include?*
- *Team structure:*
  - *What should our ideal team structure be?*
  - *How many teams will we aim to recruit?*
  - *Will we seek to build teams over time or create them immediately?*

- *Cultural fit:*
  - *How will we ensure our team can work effectively within our company's business and ethical culture?*
  - *How will we ensure our team can work effectively with diverse client cultures?*
  - *How will we ensure that our team can work collaboratively with each other?"*

Chris: "Thanks, Kai, that was excellent."

Turning to you, Chris continues: "I just want to add a word of warning about team balance in consultancy. We need flashy, bright stars, especially at the start. These are our pioneers who like breaking new ground and dislike rules and processes. Always charging on to new horizons, they never deliver the bulk of our work. For that, we need the settlers. The stayers who develop and follow methodologies and understand why we have a consistent approach to resolving client issues. You'll see what I mean if you think of a soccer team composed only of strikers, all of whom want to score the winning goal; it just doesn't work.

Today, we covered a huge amount about building a talented team. However, if you start the thinking on which you based the business case, much of the work has already been done. We also have company policies covering many of the answers. For now, I think you should mull over these questions and then get back together with Kai for some detailed work later in the week."

Kai consults his diary and says: "Thursday afternoon and Friday. In preparation, please would you review your service proposition and the implementation plan and consider how to categorise your different skill requirements for each role."

You: "Thanks, Kai, and Chris. Oh, one thing I have learned: I promise I will get a charge code for your time."

Before reading on, please jot down your thoughts on what you might do concerning the skills requirements for your plans for the new consultancy in the case study.

We are not finished with Kai yet.

It's now Thursday afternoon, and after fighting to book a suitably private meeting room, you are meeting with Kai.

You: "Hi Kai, Let me be frank. I have struggled to put together a framework that would help me answer your question about detailed skills requirements. I wanted to kick this off privately because, to be candid, I don't want the rest of the company in that open office to know quite how much I don't know. As a newcomer to consultancy, I am unsure how to pitch what we need for internal approval that will also be attractive to the wider recruitment market."

Kai: "That's OK; before we start, can we do some admin? Can I confirm that you need me for two days and that your budget allows for the standard internal recharge rate for my grade? It's just that previously, I have been caught out on internal jobs with this, and then my partner gets upset with me and your partner. Suddenly, the whole thing escalates and goes out of control. That aside, actually, [insert your name here], you have made a great start. Too many of my clients assume that they know everything and that even when they don't know something, they are still right about it. So, let's start from the top. I'll give you some context, and then we can discuss your needs. OK?"

You nod your agreement, and Kai continues.

"The context is that there is guidance for our industry that more or less holds across all employers. The UK-based Chartered Management Institute (CMI) and the Management Consultancies Association (MCA) issued a competency framework for Chartered consultancy status, a model for defining consultancy talent, irrespective of which country we operate in. Other consultancy organisations across the globe have set standards in terms of a body of knowledge required to achieve Certified Consultant status based on standards set out by the International Council for Management Consulting Institutes.

The UK CMI and MCA defined three levels of consultant, which they called:

1. *Foundation, having up to two years of consulting experience*
2. *Applied, having from three to five years of consulting experience,*
3. *Chartered as having more than five consulting experience.*

The more commonly encountered terms are junior/consultant, senior/managing consultant and director (or partner), although usage varies in different companies. Here, we use a three-level model, which maps to the three CMI/MCA levels. Our twist is that new recruits at level one are given the title junior consultant, and we expect to promote them to consultant after a year; at level two, senior consultants are expected to be promoted after two years. Promotions at level three from director to equity partner are trickier and depend on many factors. Are you clear so far?"

You say: "Well, that's clear so far. We need to determine what skills my plans will need at each level. I have created a skills matrix before, but that was as a line manager."

At this point, Kai decides that he needs to continue his explanation.

"I get a bit out of line with some of my colleagues here because I feel there is a step we need to go through before preparing a skills matrix. That is because when we prepare a skills matrix, it is a response to a need we have defined for staff to do something, which we formulate as a role description. Only when we have amalgamated these role descriptions into a role matrix can we ask, 'What skills will our people require?'

There are a couple of other things that I must stress as we go on. First, we focus on our complete team requirements, not just consultants. We must include our back office team. You will find that these people will make our new business area run smoothly. They are normally the only ones with the bigger picture of what's happening on the ground. When you think about it, that's not surprising. Our consultancy staff can be locked away on client sites for months or engaged in very focused attempts to meet demanding client purchasing deadlines. However, our back office staff regularly engage with all the team members. They also are at the centre of the web of formal and informal information about our business.

The second area I wanted to stress is that we don't recruit everybody we need – well, not as permanent staff. We can source support from delivery partners, retained and other independents, and through short-term recruitment using agencies."

We can use a role matrix to flesh out the picture of our team's structure described in our service proposal and resourcing strategy. This will then feed into a series of role descriptions. Both of these outputs will also need to take account of specific professional knowledge areas. Table 4.1

Table 4.1 Consultancy Role Matrix

Consultancy Role Matrix		
Junior Management Consultant	**Senior Management Consultant**	**Director/Partner**
Core professional skills	**Core professional skills**	**Core professional skills**
Deliver high-quality specialist professional knowledge and expertise in multiple client situations	Lead teams delivering high-quality specialist professional knowledge and expertise in multiple client situations Act as a solo consultant, providing clients with high-quality professional advice and support	Oversee the delivery of high-quality knowledge and expertise in multiple specialisms and in multiple client situations Act as a solo consultant, providing clients with high-quality professional advice and support
Ethics	**Ethics**	**Ethics**
Apply the consultancy's ethics code to all personal work and ensure that all work is undertaken within the code, escalating any exceptions as necessary	Apply the consultancy's ethics code to all personal work	Ensure that the consultancy's and the client's ethics codes are fully understood and applied to all work
	Ensure that all sales, marketing, and delivery work is undertaken within the code, escalating any exceptions as necessary	Resolution of complex ethical dilemmas
	Actively advocate the importance of the ethics code within the consultancy and clients	Continuing development of ethical code in line with developing national and international standards
Business understanding	**Business leadership and team management**	**Strategic commercial leadership**
Understand and keep abreast of industry trends, market dynamics, and organisational structures	Identify and lead opportunities for service development in existing and new markets	Set business goals and strategic direction, for example for profitability and chargeability, manage implementation strategies and monitor progress
Understand the basic commercial principles of consultancy services and contractual needs	Manage consultancy teams, including meeting chargeability and profitability targets	Ensure the alignment of engagements with the consultancy's business goals
	Leadership of key business areas	Oversight of the performance of multiple teams, often across different disciplines
	Quality and financial management of all but the most complex engagements	Quality and financial management of key, complex, or high-risk engagements

(*Continued*)

Table 4.1 (Continued)

Consultancy Role Matrix		
Junior Management Consultant	**Senior Management Consultant**	**Director/Partner**
Strategic analysis and problem-solving	**Advanced strategic thinking**	**Advanced strategic thinking**
Dissect complex business problems, conduct market and comparative analyses, and propose actionable solutions	Develop new approaches to client issues and methods for engagement delivery	Develop new strategic approaches for meeting issues across targeted industries and sectors
Use standard consultancy analysis tools appropriately during client engagements	Align consult projects with clients' evolving organisational goals	Challenge consultancy teams on approaches and methods used to support clients
Quantitative and qualitative analysis	**Thought leadership**	**Thought leadership**
Interpret financial data, perform statistical analysis, and synthesise information from various sources	Contribute to industry thought leadership, publish articles and white papers, speak at conferences, and stay ahead of industry trends	Industry thought leadership, publishing articles, speaking at, and chairing conferences
Client change management	**Client change management**	**Client change management**
Support organisational change initiatives and guide client staff through transitions	Lead client organisational change initiatives and guide clients through transitions	Work with C-suite executives and other board members to explore ways of supporting change and overcoming resistance
Counter resistance to change and escalate as necessary to ensure successful adoption	Manage resistance to change and ensure successful adoption	Develop new approaches to managing change
Business development	**Business development**	**Business development**
Contribute to the development of proposals to clients, including research activities	Quantify and evaluate new business opportunities, including risk evaluation	Identify new business opportunities, networking, and expand client portfolios
Contribute to client presentations during the sales process	Lead the client proposal process, including the commercial elements of the proposal and any arrangements for resource sharing	Approve proposals within commercial limits or manage the approval process for more complex or higher-value proposals

(*Continued*)

Table 4.1 (Continued)

Consultancy Role Matrix		
Junior Management Consultant	**Senior Management Consultant**	**Director/Partner**
Effective communication and relationship building	**Effective communication and relationship building**	**Executive-level communication and relationship building**
Use clear, concise, and accurate communication skills for presenting findings and recommendations to clients and team members	Networking and expanding client portfolios	Present to C-suite executives, influence decision-making, and provide strategic guidance
Build rapport with clients, colleagues, and stakeholders	Build and maintain strong client relationships, understanding their needs and delivering value	Establish and maintain industry-wide networks at the C-suite and board level
	Influence and negotiate with diverse stakeholders, including balancing competing interests	Build new and maintain existing client relationships
Mentor and coaching	**Mentor and coaching**	**Mentor and coaching**
Act as a workplace "buddy" to new recruits	Develop talent and foster a learning culture	Develop talent and foster a learning and development culture
	Guide junior consultants, share expertise, lead training events, and foster professional growth	Guide senior consultants, share expertise, sponsor training events, and foster professional growth
Engagement management	**Engagement management**	**Engagement management**
Follow project management processes, for example planning, scheduling, tracking, and reporting	Lead complex engagements, including planning, scheduling, progress tracking, and reporting to clients and senior management of the consultancy	Oversight of key engagement metrics includes on-time delivery, profitability, client satisfaction, issues, and risks
Identification and escalation of issues or risks	Management, and if necessary, escalation of engagement risks and issues	Evaluation of risk and issue management
	Resource allocation and resource sharing across engagements	Oversight of practice resourcing and the resolution of conflicting demands
	Review of quality of engagement outputs	Approval of major engagement outputs

is an example of a generic role matrix for a consultancy team. We would tailor this when specific professional expertise is required and will have to add details of the support staff roles.

Once again, our PNX Consultancy Services case study indicates what a resourcing strategy being submitted for approval could look like. As always, it is not the document format that is important; it is the thinking behind it.

PNX Consultancy Services

Application of Advanced AI in Healthcare

Resourcing Strategy

Skills and Experience

To deliver the envisioned AI in Healthcare Consultancy Services, specialists will be based in or close to PNX regional headquarters in New York and Paris and draw on existing local support services. Each staff member must demonstrate relevant qualifications and a suitable track record of success.

We will foster unified skill-based work groups coordinated across both offices, including:

- AI specialists developing and implementing AI solutions.
- Industry experts with a deep understanding of healthcare or healthcare insurance to ensure that our AI-based solutions are tailored to meet the sector's challenges.
- Data analysts responsible for analysing vast datasets (such as electronic health records and laboratory results) and providing insights that can be used to develop AI models.
- Change management specialists responsible for engaging with stakeholders before, during, and after the transition to AI, implementing robust early engagement and training programmes, and providing ongoing support and effectiveness reviews.
- Data governance and security experts to ensure the highest data privacy compliance standards (HIPAA, GDPR) throughout the AI lifecycle, from data acquisition and storage to model development and deployment.
- Ethics specialists who will ensure that our teams and services adhere to the highest ethical principles throughout AI development, deployment, and use, ensuring fairness, transparency, and minimising bias in patient risk assessments.
- Senior managers who will oversee the daily operation of the teams, sales, and engagement delivery. They will also lead our tactical planning.
- Business analysts to work with clients to identify their unique opportunities to benefit from AI-powered systems and assess their readiness to transform.
- Sales and marketing professionals to build a presence in key markets, open client discussions, negotiate contracts, and set commercial terms.
- Legal experts are needed to ensure that all activities comply with relevant laws and regulations and handle any legal issues that may arise.

Roles designated as senior will typically be filled by staff with at least five years of relevant post-qualification experience; junior roles will require at least three years of relevant post-qualification experience.

Team Structure

The sector lead partner will be based in New York but spend significant time in Paris, and a partner based locally will lead each regional office.

To foster skills and collaborative working, team members will operate as a single pool across both offices, with assignment allocations being agreed upon by the leadership team. The basic team structure for each office by the end of year one would be as follows:

1 Office lead partner reporting to the sector lead partner.
2 Senior managers/associate partners responsible for sales delivery and engagement management
4 AI specialists (2 senior, 2 junior).
4 Health or insurance industry experts (2 senior, 2 junior).
3 Data analysts.
2 Senior change management specialists.
2 Data governance and security experts (1 senior, 1 junior).
1 Ethics specialist (junior).
2 Business analysts (junior).
2 Sales and marketing professionals (1 senior, 1 junior).
1 Legal expert.
3 Business support office staff (1 senior, 2 junior).

It's also important to note that some individuals may fulfil multiple roles depending on their skills and experience. Paris-based staff will be expected to be able to work effectively in English and at least one other European language.

In the future, additional recruitment will be planned in accordance with the growth of the practice.

Recruitment

We plan to recruit as many core team members as possible from our existing workforce to build new teams that fit within PNX's established culture. This could also allow redeployment from teams focused on areas with declining market penetration. Transferees from within the firm must demonstrate a good fit with the skills matrix to be developed for each role. The office lead partners are expected to be filled by promotion or transfer from within the partnership.

As this is a new and dynamic area, it is considered essential to build the firm's critical mass of talent. In this instance, we should not rely on external contractors to deliver engagements. We may, however, from time to time engage industry or academic experts to offer advice on the development of best practices.

Our current outsourced recruitment provider will conduct external recruitment exercises to find the best available talent in the North American and European markets.

We estimate that staff transfers into teams from other business areas will take three months until staff are in place. External recruitment will take four to six months. Consequently, internal transferees will form the initial core of teams in both offices. This has a significant advantage in ensuring the new teams are created within our current operating culture and fully understand our operating modes and standards.

Cultural Diversity

We are a culturally diverse organisation, mirroring our diverse client base in Europe and North America. Working with our in-house diversity team, we will seek to recruit talent that reflects this.

Remuneration

For each grade and type of staff, we expect to pay around the reported average salary and bonuses for IT consultancy. This accords with our benchmarked salary policy and will enable us to remain price competitive in our chosen markets.

Induction

All staff will receive a one-week programme to introduce the team's work, our clients, and our methodologies for delivering in the healthcare AI arena.

We hope to brigade internal recruits into one of four induction programmes, two of which are being run in New York and two in Paris.

All new recruits to the firm will separately undergo a full company induction process within the first month, in accordance with company policy. After induction, these staff will be paired with an internal transferee into the team to support them over the first few months. Wherever possible, teams on client sites will initially be composed of transferees and new-to-company recruits.

Training and Development

To increase the flexible deployment of staff, we will seek to develop multiskilling by investing in additional training, work shadowing, and mentoring for all staff members. Designated staff members will also be tasked to create standardised assignment approaches, methodologies, and toolsets as the basis for further in-house training. Our objective is to ensure that individual knowledge, skills, and expertise are shared and documented to increase the company's intellectual capital and decrease the risk of relying on key individuals.

Team structure

Our resourcing strategy should have set out our consultancy's core functions, size, and timings. In any existing organisation, there may also be expectations for "normal" team structures that must be met or overcome. Commonly encountered consultancy team structures include the following:

- **Function-based**: This approach is helpful for consultancies with a clear division of services and expertise. Separate groups are organised based on specific functions or departments, for example, strategy team, marketing team, and finance services. While this can provide for clear roles and the efficient use of specialised skills, it can also lead to siloed thinking and limited cross-functional collaboration.

- **Engagement-based**: Consultancies with a high volume of short-term engagements may form temporary teams around specific client engagements. An engagement-based organisation provides flexibility and adaptability to changing client needs but can lead to resource allocation challenges and a lack of continuity.
- **Matrix**: This structure combines functional and engagement-based structures, with staff reporting to functional and engagement managers. It fits consultancies with complex engagements requiring diverse expertise, efficiently uses resources, and fosters cross-functional collaboration. Such a structure can create complexity and the potential for conflicts between functional and engagement managers.
- **Flat**: Often found in early-stage consultancies, flat structures have a minimal hierarchy, perhaps founders and consultants, and a strong emphasis on collaboration and autonomy. They also provide high levels of flexibility and rapid decision-making. However, there may also be a lack of clear leadership and the need to increase the number of levels as the consultancy grows to prevent managers from having an unsupportable number of direct reports.

The factors to consider when choosing a team structure include the following:

- **Engagement complexity**: How complex are the engagements our consultancy will undertake?
- **Client needs**: What level of specialisation and expertise will our clients require?
- **Culture**: What kind of work environment do we want to foster? This includes, for example, supervising client work and checking outputs for accuracy, completeness, and accordance with established policies and procedures.
- **Team size**: How many consultants, managers, supervisors, and support staff will we need? A small team of five to ten consultants and support staff will need a different structure to one of more than 30.
- **Budget**: What is our budget for team structure, including staff management, engagement supervision, and team support?

Consequently, the optimal structure for our team will evolve as we grow and should flex in response to customer needs. Therefore, we should keep our team structure under review and ensure that we maintain alignment with our current and proposed future situation.

Role descriptions

We should use them to set expectations for the post holder's tasks and to profile the personal attributes, skills, or experience required to perform the allocated tasks. The good news is that we have already assembled much of the information about what the post holder will do in our role matrix. We must now tailor the professional skills entries in the matrix to reflect our particular needs. In our example matrix, the professional skills needed by a senior consultant were defined as follows:

- Lead teams delivering high-quality specialist professional knowledge and expertise in multiple client situations.
- Act as a solo consultant, providing clients with high-quality professional advice and support.

When we define the role of a senior consultant business analyst, this wording could be extended and updated to read:

1. Work on or off client sites, leading business analyst teams in translating business needs into technical requirements that will achieve client business goals.
2. Work with sales specialists and others to create, pursue, and close business opportunities.
3. Work independently to create technical and operational solutions.
4. Advise clients on current best practice business analysis methodologies and suitable software tools.
5. Testing of systems and models against requirements.
6. Conducting assurance checks of implemented systems and models.
7. Quality review of the output of junior team members.
8. Coordinate third-party activities and engagement meetings.

The remainder of the role description identifies the personal qualities, skills, and experience required:

- **Personal qualities**: A review of job advertisements for senior consultants showed them asking for a variety of personal attributes, including:

  1. Can lead teams and engagements.
  2. Able to contribute to work in multiple sectors and types of engagement.
  3. Motivated to deliver client satisfaction.
  4. Ability to develop a wide range of relationships.
  5. Works well in a collaborative team.
  6. Thinks strategically and provides innovative solutions.
  7. Demonstrates high ethical standards and integrity.
  8. Can handle pressure and challenging situations.

- **Skills and experience**: We have already established minimum experience requirements in our role matrix for each staff level. Taking the generalised senior consultant role as an example, we might specify a minimum of three years of consultancy experience, to which we add more specific requirements. The review of those skills commonly requested in job advertisements for senior consultants showed them including:

  1. Outstanding verbal and written communication skills.
  2. Track record of problem analysis in client situations.
  3. Confident in managing and delivering client engagements.
  4. Versatile, with an ability to perform many different roles within an organisation to support delivery.
  5. Able to manage conflicting demands from multiple tasks and deadlines.
  6. Sales and delivery experience, including direct engagement with clients to understand their requirements and prepare bespoke solutions for them.
  7. Proven leadership in developing and implementing change initiatives and performance improvement programmes.
  8. Can demonstrate experience of working in multiple industry sectors.
  9. Has a network that shows an ability to build relationships with senior stakeholders.
  10. Has data analysis skills and understands data can be used to inform decision-making.
  11. Has experience in developing potential clients and opening business opportunities.

To this general list of skills and experience, we should add specific requirements for individual roles. For example, for our senior consultant business analyst, we could add the following:

1. Bachelor's or higher degree in business, finance, IT, or a related discipline or an Advanced International Diploma in Business Analysis.
2. Proficiency in using multiple methodologies and tools to analyse and visualise data effectively.

Step 2: Develop a recruitment strategy

Having established what skills our team will require, we need to identify how we will source and engage them. For this, we require a carefully developed recruitment strategy covering acquiring the talent pool needed to launch our new service. However, this is not enough because we also need our strategy to support building our talent pipeline for future growth and replacing any staff who leave us.

A word of caution. Recruiting the right team members for our service launch is onerous and time consuming. This will come at a time when we are at full stretch with other launch activities and decisions. Fortunately, recruitment is an area where we can call on others to support us, and we will need to use them to free up as much of our scarce time as possible.

Our strategy also needs to recognise that we do not need to employ all of our consultants directly and that we can resource our team in several ways. These include internal mobility, external recruitment, collaboration with other consultancies, and the use of independent consultants, including those sourced through temporary staff agencies. Each of these options has advantages and disadvantages. However, we can often adopt a mix-and-match approach. Each option will require a different set of tasks and implementation timelines.

Internal mobility

Internal transfers have major plus points, including our candidates' familiarity with the organisation, its culture, standards, systems, and operating processes. Also, by negotiating with their current team leaders, transferees may be available more quickly than other permanent recruits. Alternatively, they may be loaned for a while to help the initial phases of our service. However, if our service area is new to the company, few internal candidates may meet our ideal requirements profile.

Candidates could be asked to self-identify through internal publicity or may also be identified by assessing current employees to determine those with the necessary transferable skills or abilities for our new roles.

There is always a question of how to motivate the most talented internal candidates to apply and then accept a role offered to them. We will attract some candidates if we communicate our excitement about the new service and our enthusiasm for the interesting and diverse work it will provide. Others may only be motivated to move for improved incentives such as increased salary levels and benefits, promotion or better promotion prospects, and improved training levels. However, the incentives we can offer to encourage transfers may be limited by organisation policies and available funds.

Key tasks specific to internal recruitment are set out in Table 4.2.

Table 4.2 Internal Recruitment-Specific Tasks

Internal Recruitment-Specific Tasks	
Task	**Activities**
Internal communication	Develop a clear communication plan to inform employees about the new consultancy and the available positions
Identify potential candidates	Leverage internal talent databases and employee referrals to identify potential candidates within the organisation
Internal job posting	Advertise the positions internally, highlighting career growth opportunities and the chance to be part of a new team
Assess internal candidates	Evaluate internal candidates based on their skills, experience, and cultural fit

External recruitment

Recruiting external candidates is time consuming and is an area in which we should call on others for support. Many medium and larger consultancies have internal teams who constantly recruit and thoroughly understand the specific requirements of consultancy recruitment. Where such support is not available, we should always consider outsourcing. Other factors that may influence our decision to bring in outsourced help include the following:

- **Rapid growth or high-volume hiring**: Consultancy firms often experience rapid growth phases tied to specific engagements or client acquisitions. This can overburden an internal recruitment team and delay filling roles, hence our implementation plan.
- **Specialised or niche roles**: We often seek candidates with particular (and unusual) knowledge or experience. Recruitment firms specialising in consultancy frequently have a network of contacts in key areas and industries which may be interested in working with us, or if not, can refer the searcher agency to others who may be.
- **Cost efficiency**: If our recruitment needs are intermittent, we may find that maintaining an in-house team is more expensive than bringing in an agency on an as-needed basis.
- **Geographical expansion**: When we seek to expand into a new region, we will find that recruitment consultancies with a local presence can help identify and attract candidates more quickly than an in-house team new to the area.
- **Cultural nuances**: Using locally based recruitment firms can be advantageous when we seek to expand into different markets as they understand local cultures and business practices.
- **Discretion**: Often, we can use the publicity in a recruitment campaign to indicate to potential clients its interest in a particular area as part of its service marketing campaign. As such publicity may also alert our potential competitors, if we use an agency for our recruitment, we can mask our plans for a while. However, once candidates are being interviewed, this masking ceases to apply.

Outsourcing also has potential disadvantages:

- **Loss of control**: An outside agency inevitably reduces our direct control over the entire process. This means that candidates that we may feel to be suitable are filtered out.

- **Potential for misalignment**: If an agency does not share or fully understand our culture or values, it can put forward mismatched candidates, which inevitably lengthens our recruitment period.
- **Increased costs**: If we will be running regular recruitment campaigns, outsourcing can be more expensive than building an in-house recruitment team.
- **Data security**: There are additional risks when sharing sensitive candidate or company information with any third party.

Several key tasks must be implemented, whether we use an external agency or internal recruitment teams or undertake the recruitment process directly. These tasks include those set out in Table 4.3. The exact way these are approached and our level of engagement with recruitment specialists depends on our preferences, organisational culture, and internal processes.

Table 4.3 External Recruitment-Specific Tasks

External Recruitment-Specific Tasks	
Task	**Activities**
Define recruitment channels	Determine the most effective channels to reach potential candidates of each type and location. This includes job boards, social media, industry networks, professional associations, paid advertising, and engaging with employee referral programmes to tap into existing employees' networks Engaging with relevant educational institutions and alumni networks can help recruit new and recent graduates Consider whether this is to be a branded or confidential recruitment exercise
Develop branding	Create a strong employer brand to attract top talent Highlight the company culture, values, and career development opportunities Encourage employee advocacy to promote the company as a great place to work
Advertising	Develop compelling job advertisements and posts that accurately reflect the role and company Include employee case studies and testimonials in your publicity for the role Publicise the role using the platforms most relevant to your potential candidates, such as websites and social media content
Sourcing candidates	Actively seek out qualified candidates through various channels, including • Networking • Referrals • Job board searches • Headhunting

Completing the recruitment process

Ideally, we would assemble all potential candidates into a single pool and verify, compare, and select the candidates to whom we wish to make an offer. This can be done through running a managed assessment centre process, which allows us to directly compare candidates' performances on set tasks and in interviews. This approach can provide significant advantages in helping to build our team (see further reading). However, in most cases, this extends the recruitment process, and scheduling commitments and costs will require us to carry out the process in a less focused way, as in the tasks in Table 4.4.

Table 4.4 Recruitment Tasks (All Streams)

Recruitment Tasks (All Streams)	
Task	**Activities**
Screening and shortlisting	Review resumes/CVs Conduct initial phone screening interviews Shortlist qualified candidates for interview Consider using pre-employment assessments
Interviews	Consider using a formal assessment centre process in which candidates are required to complete standardised and comparable tasks individually or in teams Conduct structured interviews with shortlisted candidates Assess skills, experience, and cultural fit (Remember, Can they do the job? Will they do the job? Will they fit in?) Take notes!
Background checks	Conduct thorough background checks on selected candidates
Offer and negotiation	Extend offers to successful candidates Negotiate employment terms Complete contractual process

Delivery collaboration

In our service proposition, we should have outlined our high-level approach to team building, including how much of the service we intend to deliver and how much we will provide through collaboration with other parties. Collaboration can allow consultancies to share insights, best practices, and industry knowledge. Its strengths include more rapid access to diverse expertise and accelerated learning. However, weaknesses may arise if a lack of openness or competitive concerns hinder knowledge sharing.

Another issue to consider with collaboration arrangements in any form is our cash flow. It is always helpful to agree to align payments with receipts from clients as far as possible.

Another site visit.

So, let's take a trip to the prestigious offices of WWWX, a small consultancy in central London. Just bring an umbrella; the skies in London can soak you unexpectedly at any time of the year.

Like fast-moving rivers, there can be hidden business dangers in consultancies collaborating. This one was unexpected but could impact anyone engaging in a collaborative path.

WWWX is a boutique consultancy and is well regarded by its high-profile clients. Some years before, it had capitalised on this reputation by creating a consortium of global 'A' list consultancies and IT suppliers to gain access to national frameworks and other contracts. The idea was very successful. WWWX now runs a system in which consortium members agree which member is most likely to win any contract. Later, WWWX bills the work, takes a small percentage fee, and pays the rest to the consortium member. There is a small additional cost to WWWX comprising the salary of a full-time clerical assistant with some time from one director. Yet the collaboration contributes nearly a third of the company's profits and half its total income.

Enter Myles. The consultancy's founding partners brought Myles in as its chief executive to prepare it for sale. We meet him in a small reception area. He is a small, neatly dressed man and not very happy.

Myles almost shouts: "I have a real issue about this useless consortium. To make WWWX more attractive to investors, I have set a target of a ten percent profit margin this year. The indicator we are using for this is EBITDA.[1] *My problem is that this collaboration, with its stupidly small margin, is dragging down our overall percentage EBITDA by nearly three percent. We must close it down, but the founding partners are wedded to it. I wish that I had never taken this job. Look at the weather. I could have been out playing golf this afternoon."*

You ask naively: "What happens to the income of the founding partners if you cut profits by a third at a single stroke?"

"I don't care. Either they want a good sale price, or they don't."

What route would you take when using collaboration partners to maximise your chosen financial performance indicators?

In WWWX's case, they didn't close down the consortium. The answer was found differently. The accounting relationships between the parties were changed. The books now showed fee income from the client being allocated directly to the consortium member, who paid a percentage management fee back to WWWX. This massively reduced WWWX's turnover but increased its performance on Myle's beloved EBITDA.[2]

There is a wide range of different types of collaboration between consultancies delivering client engagements, and each has its strengths and weaknesses:

- **Prime/Subcontractor**: One consultancy (the prime contractor) takes the lead and manages the overall engagement. Other consultancies (subcontractors) provide specialised services or contribute to specific engagement components. Prime contractors can scale engagements up or down by engaging additional subcontractors. However, this can create communication challenges, as coordinating multiple subcontractors can be complex. There is also increased risk, as overreliance on subcontractors may pose risks if they fail to deliver to agreed timelines and quality.
- **Specialist support collaboration**: This is where we collaborate based on our specialised skills. For example, in the PNX case, they might handle the overall strategy and implementation management for an AI system in a health insurer but bring in specialist HR and training consultancy to work directly with users during the system rollout. This approach has the advantage that each consultancy brings its own areas of excellence to the engagement, and clients benefit from comprehensive solutions and a well-rounded approach. However, there are integration challenges, including coordinating diverse specialists with different management structures. Also, gaps in service or knowledge may occur if consultancies do not align seamlessly.
- **Joint contracting**: Multiple consultancies cooperate to form a joint team to bid for and execute an engagement with shared responsibilities and risks. This benefits from diverse perspectives, as each party has different viewpoints and from shared risks between the collaborators.

Problems can arise due to the need to obtain a consensus, which may slow decision-making. We may also need processes to resolve conflict if consensus cannot be reached.

- **Consortium collaboration**: As in our site visit, under consortium arrangements, multiple consultancies form a consortium to market services or tackle larger-scale engagements, and they pool resources, expertise, and networks. This provides the client with access to comprehensive capabilities as consortia members are able to cover all aspects of an engagement. Joint efforts also enhance the reputation of each consortium member and, by providing a more comprehensive service, increase their range of viable sales opportunities. Set against this are potential difficulties in balancing the interests of all members and the administrative overhead of managing consortium logistics.

Each different approach to collaboration will require a careful review of potential partners and a separate task plan to supplement our recruitment strategy. The amount of time necessary to establish different types of collaboration can vary widely. Each collaboration must be supported by carefully thought-through contractual agreements, which will have to be negotiated and agreed upon by the other parties. Consequently, it is never too early to engage expert legal opinion if collaboration is a potential option.

Independent consultants

Using independent consultants forms a hybrid approach between recruiting permanent employees and delivery collaboration. As with recruiting permanent staff, we need to clearly define the support, specific skills, and experience required from independent consultants. We also need to establish our preferred engagement model, either a period contract or an engagement-based one.

Using independent consultants can have many advantages, particularly during the early stages of a new service, including the following:

- **Flexibility**: We can rapidly scale our use of independent consultants to meet client demands. This allows us to respond quickly to market opportunities without the time lag usually involved in engaging full-time employees. Using them initially means that we may be able to launch our service more quickly.
- **Cost efficiency**: Independent consultants are engaged on an "as required" basis and usually paid only for chargeable time at a rate fixed to reflect fees charged to clients. Consequently, using them can sometimes be more cost-effective than hiring full-time employees.
- **Specialised expertise**: Independent consultants often possess deep knowledge of specific industries or functional areas. This means that we can acquire specialised knowledge without the need to hire full-time experts for every engagement. They can also support knowledge and skills transfer into our permanent team. On a longer-term basis, we could also use them as mentors and quality assessors to help develop team expertise further.
- **Access to industry networks**: In addition to their specialised expertise, independent consultants often have broad exposure to potential clients across their industry. We may also engage them to support our marketing effort. Their specialised knowledge will also help us demonstrate a successful track record for inclusion in sales proposals.
- **Risk mitigation (1)**: When we seek to expand our services, we can start building our team without the potential risk of incurring the long-term costs associated with permanent team members.
- **Risk mitigation (2)**: If, for any reason, an engagement is unsuccessful and is to be closed early, or if we find that the consultant is not performing as expected, we can terminate an independent consultant without significant cost penalties.

Using independent consultants can also present difficulties:

- **Quality**: Maintaining our quality standards requires effective management and oversight. Overreliance on independent consultants, especially in senior roles, can make this problematic.
- **Loyalty and commitment**: Independent consultants may be less loyal and committed to the company than full-time employees. Commitment may also be an issue towards the end of an engagement when, to take advantage of longer-term work opportunities or to avoid work gaps, they may seek to move off before their work is completed.
- **Intellectual property risks**: Clear contractual agreements and confidentiality requirements are essential to mitigate any risk to our intellectual property.
- **Client relationships**: We must create strong links and relationships with our client base to ensure the growth and sustainability of our consultancy. This can be more difficult if our day-to-day relationships are through on-site independent consultants. We must ensure that the consultancy, not our independent contractor, maintains consistent client engagement and relationship management. We should also put in place contractual obligations to ensure that the independent consultant cannot poach our clients from us.

There may be routes for identifying independent consultants that we can use, which are additional to those for recruiting permanent staff, including professional associations, which may hold lists of suitable candidates, and temporary staffing agencies. If we are using temporary staffing agencies, we need to research carefully and select those that are reputable and specialise in our required skill sets. This latter point is critical as we should seek to deal with only those agencies who understand the skill sets that we need and have a pool of existing talent upon which to draw.

Agency briefing

We will succeed better in sourcing the right candidates if we draw up a detailed briefing for temporary recruitment agencies. Fortunately, we can draw on our extensive work defining our services and consultant requirements in preparing this briefing. The information for the briefing should include information under a number of headings:

- **Detailed engagement overview**: Goals, objectives, timeline, milestones, scope of work, and deliverables.
- **Company and team background**: Company culture and values, team structure and roles, and existing team members.
- **Consultant profile requirements**: Specific skills and expertise required, experience and qualifications, industry knowledge, and soft skills and competencies (e.g. leadership, problem-solving).
- **Engagement challenges**: Potential obstacles, risk assessment and mitigation strategies, and contingency plans.
- **Expectations and preferences**: Communication style and frequency, reporting requirements, and any other preferences (e.g. personality, work style).
- **Reporting**: To whom will the consultant report, and how frequently?
- **Recruitment decision-making process**.

Our selection process should be rigorous enough to ensure that the consultant has appropriate skills. However, it should also reflect a lower risk level than permanent recruitment. Negotiation and contracting, on the other hand, will often require more individualised attention as we will not be using a company-standard employee contract but one tailored to each situation and consultant.

Before moving on, it is time to revisit our case study.

Back in PNX.

You have followed the steps to identify potential internal and external candidates and independent consultants.

Now, you are becoming concerned about the volume of interviews you will be holding. Also, while you have recruited staff before, they were primarily juniors and did not have the range of professional skills and experience for which you are now looking. So, you call Kai to arrange for another coaching session.

You: "Hi Kai, I have been reading up on the candidates the recruiters have put forward. I am beginning to believe that management consultants are a bizarre bunch. You wouldn't believe the number of career summaries I have read that claim a key personal attribute, 'attention to detail', and then are littered with rubbish grammar, spelling mistakes, punctuation errors, and other typos. Don't these people realise that when they put in a job application or CV, it is their personal marketing document. . . . Sorry, I was starting to go off on one. I was calling to say that I have many interviews coming up and to ask if you could spare half an hour for an update on interviewing skills and tips. I'll provide coffee and sugared doughnuts."

Kai laughs and says: "Sugar doughnuts are a great tool in interviews for unsettling a candidate. You can't eat one and maintain professional credibility while covered in sugar. So, yes to the coffee, and how about chocolate biscuits instead? I have meeting room 3 booked all afternoon today, but we should finish by 3:30."

At 3.30, you arrive with the coffee and chocolate biscuits, and Kai starts.

"I normally go through this with clients over two days with planned scenarios, video mock interviews, and feedback sessions. So, I have decided to focus on a few key headlines and tips. One additional thing that I will say is that the skills we need for a candidate interview are not significantly different from those when we are interviewing clients during an engagement. We seek and verify key information, give as much information as possible, and maintain flexibility to follow up on other areas of interest. Firstly, do you remember the three key questions we, not the candidate, must answer?"

You nod.

"OK, here are my ten things to do and one thing not to do in an interview:

1. *Do know what you want to ask about the candidate and their experience before the interview. Create a custom question crib sheet for each role and use it consistently as your core script, adding any specific questions for each candidate. We have to take the lead and never expect the interviewee to start talking and direct the conversation.*
2. *Do always observe the candidate. I make a point of personally collecting them and delivering them back to the reception area. This extends the time I can observe them and lets me see them in a situation different from the interview room. I am not a great fan of body watching; it is too imprecise to be justifiable if challenged, but when asking questions, you may notice extra hesitation, confidence, or discomfort not conveyed by their words. In the jargon, it's called leakage, and if you think you have detected something, you can explore the reasons for it further.*
3. *Do set the candidate at ease. They may be pretty nervous – we never know quite how emotionally invested they are in the outcome of our interview. Offering refreshments, even if it's only a glass of water, is a simple way of establishing rapport, as is asking them about their journey. This last tactic also provides an excellent bridge into the interview.*

4. *Do ask specific questions, but make sure they are open. Asking a closed question that allows the candidate to say yes or no does not help the conversation flow.*
5. *Do ask only one question at a time, giving the candidate time to think and answer. If there is a pause, wait and only expand the question or ask a follow-up one if the candidate asks you to.*
6. *Do prompt the candidate. If they seem to have finished answering but you want more information, you can prompt either with a simple 'And?' Alternatively, use questions such as 'What was the result of that?' or 'How did that make you feel?' 'That's great. Can you tell me a little more about . . .?'*
7. *Do allow for a pause when they seem to have finished answering before moving forward. About 10 seconds is usually right. Often, they may add further information to fill the silence, which can be revealing.*
8. *Do follow the interesting lines of thought that arise – you can return to the crib sheet later. If the candidate says something interesting or unexpected, follow the path and see where it leads.*
9. *Do take notes to ensure consistency; creating space for them on your crib sheet is a good idea. But don't let your note-taking prevent you from observing the candidate.*
10. *Do make any assessments immediately after the interview. This is because interviewing several candidates over days or sometimes weeks makes it challenging to recall precisely who said what. Some interviewers take photos of the candidates to help their memories.*
11. *Don't stress a candidate by highlighting that it says in their CV that they pay attention to detail and then pointing out the errors you discovered, but it can be interesting to see what happens."*

You: "Wow, Kai, I'll try and remember half that."

Kai: "It's OK. I prepared you a set of notes. Thanks for the coffee and the chocolate biscuits."

Recruitment timeline

The final element of our recruitment strategy is the timeline. We have already considered a number of the required recruitment tasks. In theory, all that remains is to prepare a simple timeline. However, variations always depend upon elements such as the degree of involvement required from an internal human resources department and whether press advertising, including specialist magazines, is required. Other things that we need to think about are the availability of standard contracts for employees and contracted staff and the typical notice periods for the type of candidate we want to recruit. Even the time of year can have an impact as some industries or sectors might have traditional hiring periods or peak times for job changes, for example, academic institutions and government jobs. It can also be challenging to arrange an interview programme or an assessment centre that coincides with a main holiday period.

Above all, our single most significant constraint is the time we can make available to review candidates and conduct interviews. During our launch and ramp-up stages, there will be many other demands on our time. Consequently, application screening (now often automatic) and initial interviews are usually best carried out by others. We are then left to conduct final hiring interviews, which may be increasingly delegated to team leaders as we build our permanent team.

Figure 4.2 shows a Gantt chart that identifies how the principal tasks might be arranged to deliver a strategy that utilises all potential recruitment sources discussed.

PNX AI in Healthcare
Consultant Recruitment Timeline

Task No:	Task	Month 1				2				3					4					5		
		1	2	3	4	5	6	7	8	9	10	11	12	13	14	15	16	17	18	19	20	22
1	**Define Talent Needs**																					
1.1	Develop role matrix	■																				
1.2	Define team structure	■																				
1.3	Create role descriptions		■	■																		
1.4	Prepare skills and experience profiles			■	■																	
1.5	Prepare recruitment strategy			■																		
2	**Internal Recruitment**																					
2.1	Internal communication		■																			
2.2	Identify potential candidates				■																	
2.3	Internal Job Posting				■																	
2.4	Assess candidates					■																
2.5	Screening and shortlisting						■															
2.6	Interviews							■	■													
2.7	Background checks								■													
2.8	Offer and negotiation									■												
2.9	Recruits start												■	■	■	■	■					
3	**External Recruitment**																					
3.1	Define recruitment channels				■																	
3.2	Develop branding				■																	
3.3	Advertising					■	■	■														
3.4	Sourcing candidates					■	■	■	■													
3.5	Screening and shortlisting							■	■	■												
3.6	Interviews									■	■	■										
3.7	Background checks											■	■									
3.8	Offer and negotiation													■	■							
3.9	Recruits start																	■	■	■	■	
4	**Collaboration**																					
4.1	Research potential partners				■	■																
4.2	Negotiate type of relationship						■	■	■													
4.3	Agree contract terms									■	■	■	■	■	■							
4.4	Contract starts															■						
5	**Independent Consultants**																					
5.1	Define recruitment channels				■																	
5.2	Develop branding				■																	
5.3	Advertising					■	■															
5.4	Sourcing candidates					■	■	■														
5.5	Screening and shortlisting					■																
5.6	Interviews						■	■														
5.7	Background checks						■	■														
5.8	Offer and negotiation						■	■	■													
5.9	Recruits start								■	■	■	■										

Figure 4.2 PNX AI in Healthcare Consultant Recruitment Timeline.

Step 3: Reward strategy

The design and implementation of a well-structured reward strategy are crucial for attracting, retaining, and motivating top talent. In parallel to determining our recruitment strategy, we need to develop a strategy for the reward of our team members, and it is far more complex than arbitrarily fixing pay ranges.

We need to draw on the role matrix, team structure, and role descriptions we have already prepared and use these to set out a transparent job grading system. We will use this in two ways: immediately to help demonstrate our competitiveness in the war for top talent and in the longer term to establish our programme for the development, personal growth, and promotion of our team members.

In considering our attractiveness to candidates, our overall reward package for each team member needs to find a balance between those offered by our competitors, the financial viability of our service, and the need to retain and develop talent. As with our service offer, where we need to view the service from the client's perspective, here we need to view the whole financial and non-financial reward package from the employee's perspective. This should lead us not to ask:

> *What is the minimum that I can pay to persuade this person to work for us?*

But to ask instead:

> *What is the maximum reward I can afford to pay this person to come and work with us?*

This alternative question means we focus on retention and attraction from the start of our recruitment and engagement process. However, we should test that our reward package at least equals that of the alternative roles our candidates could consider. To do this, we should research the current salary benchmarks for consultants at the level we wish to recruit in each industry and geography where we are competing for staff. Information on competitive salaries can be found through commissioned surveys, specialist-published reports, job board searches, and AI queries. As always, we should exercise caution when reports, surveys, and AI responses are based on published data, as details of reward packages are considered confidential information in most jurisdictions.

There are three areas that we need to consider: base salaries, bonuses, and deferred and non-financial rewards. When we have decided on an affordable level of reward that is attractive to staff, we also need to determine how this will be split between base salary, bonus payments, and other rewards. Table 4.5 shows the results of a simple AI question showing how reward splits vary between different grades in a sample of countries (remember the warnings about AI data).

Setting the base salary

This is the least problematic of the decisions we must make regarding rewards. Based on our salary research, we can set the base salary structure for each consultant grade. To retain some flexibility, we may choose to set an acceptable (and affordable) range rather than a fixed point. We might, for example, ensure that our salary ranges allow us to increase pay within each grade annually for three years within our current affordability limit.

Table 4.5 Reward Breakdown

Reward Breakdown				
Country	**Grade**	**Base Salary**	**Bonus**	**Other Benefits**
Australia	Junior consultant	62%	23%	15%
	Senior consultant	52%	28%	20%
	Salaried director	42%	33%	25%
	Partner	27%	55%	18%
France	Junior consultant	62%	20%	18%
	Senior consultant	52%	25%	23%
	Salaried director	42%	30%	28%
	Partner	22%	60%	18%
Germany	Junior consultant	70%	15%	15%
	Senior consultant	60%	20%	20%
	Salaried director	50%	25%	25%
	Partner	30%	50%	20%
India	Junior consultant	50%	15%	35%
	Senior consultant	45%	20%	35%
	Salaried director	40%	25%	35%
	Partner	25%	40%	35%
UK	Junior consultant	60%	25%	15%
	Senior consultant	50%	30%	20%
	Salaried director	40%	35%	25%
	Partner	25%	55%	20%
USA	Junior consultant	65%	20%	15%
	Senior consultant	55%	25%	20%
	Salaried director	45%	30%	25%
	Partner	30%	50%	20%

Developing an incentive-based bonus scheme

This can be much more problematic and complex, but before we consider crafting a bonus scheme, we should make a couple of illuminating site visits.

First, we are joining a boutique consultancy firm's end-of-year party.

It is the day that everyone looks forward to, the last working day before the holidays. I hope that you have remembered to dress up in your favourite party clothes because everyone else is.

The morning always starts with Geri, the Chief Executive, distributing a couple of bottles of wine to every staff member. Then there is champagne and cake, followed by a staff briefing on how the company has performed wonderfully. Then, about 11:30 am, it's off to an excellent restaurant for lunch and a fantastic party, which lasts for the rest of the day and most of the night. Except this year, as we are about to find out, it will all fall flat. Most people will go home after a quiet and sullen lunch.

Let's sip the champagne, eat the cake, and listen to Geri to discover what's happening.

"Thank you all for coming together. I will get straight to it. Although we have been busy, and as you know, we have won more work than last year, we have failed to meet our growth targets. We failed to meet our stretch target, meaning there will be no level two bonuses this year, and we also failed to meet our normal growth target, so we will not be paying the level one bonuses either."

There is stunned silence as everyone in the room, consultants, support staff, and others, has been working flat out all year.

What Geri is not saying is that the company is less profitable than last year – in fact, it is much more profitable. Nor is Geri saying that the staff in the various divisions have not worked hard, which they have. Nor is Geri saying that the company has not grown, which it has. In fact, compared to the previous year, it has more cash available to pay bonuses. Yet it had pinned staff bonus payments solely on achieving aspirational company growth targets, over which most staff had little or no influence.

Now you understand why it is not going to be a good party.

Second, 11 months later, we are visiting another boutique consultancy.

As it happens, they have offices only a stone's throw away from where Geri made his speech. This consultancy also likes to have a good end-of-year party.

We will eavesdrop on a call between CJ, one of the directors, who is having difficulties arranging this year's party, and Em, a senior consultant.

"Em, I am disappointed that you are one of the ones who has declined to come to the party. We have a great day arranged. I have an amazing motivational speaker arranged for the morning – an Olympic gold medallist, no less – and some fun team-building exercises in the afternoon. I feel that this is important as most consultants work alone on client sites and get little chance to interact with each other. As a relative newcomer, this is a great opportunity for you to get to know everyone a bit better. There is the formal dinner in the evening, with an opportunity for those like you who have to come from quite a distance to stay over."

"I am sorry, CJ, but I am needed on the client site, and I don't want to take time out – with travel time, it would mean two full days. But you also have to understand that the new bonus scheme pays a bonus of ten per cent of fees charged above the monthly minimum fee earnings level. I have achieved this this month, so I would lose two days' bonus for attending the party, and so would many of my colleagues."

CJ's new individual bonus scheme is having unintended consequences.

Please take a few moments to write down your thoughts on the main features of a bonus scheme for management consultants.

Bonus structures and supporting performance metrics are created to foster high performance, drive business success, and reward excellence. Our two site visits highlight issues that we should test for when assessing the effectiveness of bonus schemes, including the following:

- **Performance**: Is the proposed bonus directly linked to individual or team performance? We wish to ensure that bonuses are based on merit and that there is no scope for arbitrary payments. Geri's scheme was unrelated to personal or team performance and relied on meeting a completely arbitrary set of company targets. We could establish individual-level performance metrics to support bonus payments covering engagement delivery, business and personal development, and contribution to team management. At a team and company level, metrics could be based on revenue growth, profitability, client retention, health and safety, and client and employee satisfaction.
- **Alignment with all relevant company goals**: Bonus criteria should help support the employee's focus on those activities that contribute most to the company's overall strategic objectives. While CJ's scheme was generous and rewarded fee-earning work, it effectively penalised activities the company wanted to promote, such as training, team meetings, sales, and marketing. In contrast, the scheme that Geri had designed centred on one aspirational goal, growth, and it simply ignored every other significant goal for the company.
- **Transparency and fairness**: The criteria for earning a bonus should be clear, understandable, and applied consistently to all employees. There should be no room for ambiguity or favouritism. CJ's arithmetic calculation of a 10% bonus on all fees earned above a monthly minimum was a good example of transparency.
- **Attainable but challenging**: Bonus targets should be ambitious but achievable, motivating employees to strive for excellence without being so far out of reach as to demoralise them. One of the dangers here is that where targets are met in one year, they are increased the following year without supporting changes in the business, for example, if CJ raised the monthly minimum fee requirement without a corresponding increase in fee rates.
- **Communicated effectively**: Employees should understand the bonus scheme, including the criteria, potential rewards, and how their performance will be evaluated. Regular communication helps build trust and engagement. By making a single annual performance announcement, Geri was not communicating effectively, and as we saw also chose probably the worst time to give bad news. In a practical scheme where staff behaviour changes can influence achieving targets and hence bonus payments, that is, not like Geri's, it is essential to share regular performance updates as these will help motivate staff.

Completing the rewards package – non-financial rewards and other benefits

Finalising the third element of the reward package, non-financial rewards, other benefits, and conditions can, again, be complex. This task is made more so as different jurisdictions have different legal requirements concerning aspects of the packages that we can offer, including minimum paid leave, maximum working hours, pension contributions, public holidays, and parental leave. For example, the UK currently requires a minimum of 28 days paid leave (including public holidays), and France stipulates a maximum 35-hour working week. Legal requirements in the USA and Australia may vary by state and city. However, no requirement prevents us from becoming more attractive as an employer by offering more than the legal minimum requirements.

Our research will have shown the nature of our competitors' packages, which is the measure we should use. Local taxation rules must be considered when designing a package as these may limit our scope or change the attractiveness of different benefits, making additional professional advice invaluable.

We should also consider how we provide various short-term and long-term incentives designed to encourage immediate results and sustainable performance. We can draw from a number of basic concepts in developing our own benefits mix:

- **Comprehensive benefits**: Taking local legal requirements as a baseline, we can add on further benefits such as enhanced health insurance and retirement plans, service-related additional leave, and professional development opportunities. Some consultancies offer flexible benefits choices, possibly based on salary sacrifice schemes, which allow individual employees to choose benefits such as additional leave, gym membership, and season ticket loans. One London-based consultancy provided staff with a free lunch and another fresh fruit every day.
- **Long-term incentives**: A profit-sharing scheme aligns staff and company interests. Similar incentives to reward long-term contributions include equity-based compensation, such as stock options or share ownership plans. As with bonus schemes, these should be transparent and fair.
- **Non-monetary rewards**: A robust recognition programme to acknowledge and appreciate employee contributions is a strong example of a non-monetary reward. We can also include wellness initiatives, mental health support, and work–life balance initiatives under this category.

Step 4: Recruitment programme delivery

Having worked hard to establish clear strategies to guide our recruitment and a timeline for its delivery, we cannot assume that everything will happen as planned. The Prussian general von Moltke the Elder is famously reported as writing that "No battle plan survives first contact with the enemy." Consequently, we need to:

- **Monitor delivery**: The timing of this monitoring process is critical, and the shorter the timeline for delivering any task, the more frequent such reviews should be. For example, in a three-week engagement with a recruitment agency, we may want updates from the agency twice a week, but during a week of first-round interviews, we may wish to receive feedback daily.
- **Evaluate**: As ever, our planning was based on assumptions around how well each task would perform. If the output from any task fails to meet these expectations, we need to ask why and take action, either adjusting our plans or modifying the task. For example, suppose PNX posts an opportunity for a senior consultant/analyst on a job board which fails to generate sufficient interest from suitable candidates. In that case, the posting may have to be modified to make the role more attractive, or other recruitment channels may have to be looked at.
- **Update**: When adjusting individual tasks or altering a range of tasks to help meet our objectives, we must reconsider timelines and resources. For example, in the case of PNX's failing job posting, it may be necessary to increase the application period or engage an agency to undertake a candidate search. However, this will impact timelines, which may have knock-on effects elsewhere in its recruitment and service launch plans.

- **Strategic review**: If our plans to offer an attractive opportunity to potential candidates are not meeting our expectations, we may need to backtrack and consider where adjustments need to be made. This may also mean taking a further step back and reviewing our overall service design and delivery plans.

Step 5: Team development

Much of a management consultant's work is carried out directly with clients and often in isolation from the consultancy and other team members. This means that perhaps more than almost any other industry, our continuing success depends on having highly qualified and self-motivated staff committed to marketing, selling, and delivering the highest standards of client service. To establish a high-performing consultancy team, whether comprised internal transfers, recruits, or a mixture of both, we need to work with them to create a culture that supports achieving our objectives, motivates them, and fosters internal bonds between them. The areas that we should address all interconnect into a comprehensive culture of open communication, performance monitoring and support, including the following:

- **Self-belief**: When employees believe in the company's mission and their abilities to organise and deliver the required actions, they are more likely to be engaged, motivated, and resilient. This positive mindset is called collective efficacy, and it has been shown that there is a positive relationship between it and team performance (Alexandria K. Elms, 2023).
- **Communicate vision and goals**: We have already established our vision and goals for the consultancy service. We should articulate a compelling team mission and vision that communicates the team's purpose, values, and aspirations and aligns them with our organisational objectives. We can cascade our overall SMART goals (remember specific, measurable, achievable, relevant, and time-bound) into ones tailored to the role of each team member. This provides us and the team members with a way to monitor progress fairly and openly. This should be supported in two ways. First, with a team communication programme, face-to-face or online meetings are best, depending on how the team is located. Second, where possible, in one-to-one discussions with each team member individually so that we are confident that they understand their role and responsibilities, our expectations of them, and their contribution to the team's goals.
- **Create team culture**: High-performing teams are positive about their contribution to overall goals and have a collaborative and inclusive culture. Teams with a higher level of collective efficacy will tend to have higher levels of collaboration in their work. For example, a team member lacking an area of knowledge may feel more able to engage with others to cover the gap if they feel safe in exposing their ignorance and are sure of support.

  In building a positive, supportive team culture, we will need to create a psychologically safe environment where we work with the team to build trust, respect, and open communication channels to encourage diverse perspectives and ideas. We then need to foster a culture of cooperation, shared goals, and mutual support among team members. This is often challenging, especially with consultants who frequently work in isolation from each other. Whilst "away days" and team-building exercises help create our desired culture, they are often expensive to run and have high costs in terms of loss of fee earning. Good results, however, can be obtained through proactive teaming of consultants to work with various colleagues on different engagements and sales or marketing opportunities.

Recognising and rewarding achievements fairly are an important aspect of maintaining a high-performing team. We should always acknowledge and celebrate both individual and team successes, which can boost morale and motivation. However, we must exercise caution and sensitivity because such schemes may be perceived negatively by individuals or groups who regularly feel they have not been recognised or celebrated. This can occur when support staff feel excluded from schemes recognising consultants' sales and engagement delivery successes. In these cases, we need to seek other recognition opportunities.

A final aspect of team culture is diversity and inclusion. Multiple research papers, including two by McKinsey (in 2015 and 2018), have shown that teams that are diverse and inclusive tend to deliver significantly improved outcomes, such as enhanced innovation and creativity or improved productivity and performance.

- **Develop talent**: Although we have recruited the most talented and motivated team members available, a programme of continuous development is essential for maintaining a high-performing team and for staff retention. It also builds our talent pipeline, enabling us to fill future senior opportunities from within. Achieving this requires us to foster a continuous learning culture through feedback, coaching, training, work experience, and experimentation. Consequently, we should regularly conduct comprehensive skill assessments which identify skill gaps and create individual learning and development plans to help staff to reach their full potential. We need to provide ongoing learning opportunities to fulfil team members' learning and development plans. These opportunities may include internal, online, and external training courses, workshops, and conferences, as well as assigning them to work on sales or client engagements alongside more experienced or qualified staff. Implementing a mentorship programme which pairs senior and junior team members will also facilitate knowledge transfer and skill development. As an adjunct, we could also set up a peer-based buddy programme, where every recruit to the company is "buddied" with a peer on the same level who is already working within the team.
- **Empowering and delegating**: The long-term success of our consultancy is determined by our ability of consultants to work autonomously and to take responsibility for their work. This requires us to create space for this to happen by empowering our staff to manage their work and delegating tasks to them. In smaller companies, delegation also helps reduce the critical load on directors and senior staff. Encouraging autonomy and initiative, especially for more junior staff, requires that we provide support to them when given tasks or when raising issues that they feel may be outside their level of confidence or competence.
- **Strengthening team dynamics**: Strong team dynamics are essential for effective collaboration and problem-solving and contribute to a cohesive and productive team environment. We need to consider how we can build strong relationships by fostering social connections and camaraderie among team members, including through work-led and separate team-building activities and informal gatherings. Linking with our team culture, we should work to create a safe environment with open and honest communication. Our objective should be to build trust and understanding by encouraging open dialogue, active listening, and open communication where team members respect each other's viewpoints. One aspect of this is being able to manage conflict effectively, including developing a shared understanding that conflicts often arise from misunderstandings and approaching conflicts from a non-emotional position.
- **Drive performance and continuous improvement**: A culture of continuous innovation and improvement is essential for long-term success. This requires working to support a culture of innovation that encourages experimentation, risk-taking, and creative problem-solving to drive our continuous improvement. To achieve this, regular performance evaluation and

feedback are critical, and we should start by defining key performance indicators (KPIs) and performance improvement goals for individuals and the team. We should also conduct objective performance reviews to evaluate performance to identify the team's strengths and areas for development. These reviews also feed into the team member's learning and development programmes.

Step 6: Retention

The preceding sections show the effort that is required to recruit talented staff. This is always delivered at the expense of other essential business activities. However, this is only one of the reasons we need to focus on maximising staff retention and minimising its opposite, high turnover rates. These reasons include the following:

- **Knowledge and expertise loss**: Our consultants develop in-depth knowledge of our clients and methodologies. Consequently, any staff member leaving may result in a loss of our organisational knowledge, adversely affecting the quality of the work we deliver. This may represent a significant risk if such staff resignations reach a high level.
- **Client relationships**: Building strong client relationships takes time and trust. Another danger from losing experienced consultants is the disruption of our relationships, coupled with our former consultant carrying them forward to a role for their new company. It's essentially a double blow.
- **Engagement continuity**: Consultants often work on long-term engagements or multiple engagements for the same client. Even low staff turnover levels on critical engagements can result in delays, increased costs, and decreased client satisfaction as new team members ramp up their knowledge of the engagement and the client.
- **Talent development**: High turnover rates undermine our talent development programme. This makes it challenging to develop our future leaders and may lead our competitors benefiting from our investment in talent development.
- **Company reputation**: Our reputation as an employer of choice may be damaged if it becomes known that we have a high turnover rate, making it harder to attract top talent in the future.

We need to keep under continuous review multiple factors to ensure that they continue to meet our needs and maintain high levels of staff retention, including career prospects and development, competitive compensation and benefits, work–life balance, a strong company culture, and job security and stability.

Career prospects and development

In order to prevent staff from moving to competitor companies, we need to ensure that we have a clear and attainable career path. We need our staff to recognise that there are better opportunities for growth, skill enhancement, and advancement through our regular training, mentorship, and coaching programmes rather than moving elsewhere. Additionally, exposing employees to challenging engagements that expand their skill set and broaden their industry knowledge is essential to keep them engaged and motivated. Consequently, a continuous learning and development culture is vital to retaining top talent. The following is an example of how PNX Consultancy set out its promotion pathway as part of its policy of attracting and retaining top staff.

PNX Consultancy Services

**AI in Healthcare
Consultancy Career
Pathway**

Overview

Maintaining a transparent, open, and fair career path is integral to our aspiration to be recognised as one of the top employers in the management consultancy industry.

PNX's career structure is designed to provide clear progression paths for employees based on increasing levels of responsibility, expertise, and contribution to the firm. This career structure provides a clear path for employee development, recognises and rewards high performance, and provides a strong talent pipeline for our future growth. It is supported by a comprehensive learning and skills development programme and a performance-based appraisal system.

All roles identified in the team structure will be allocated to one of four core levels: junior consultant, consultant, senior consultant, and director/partner. Promotions between these levels are based on a comprehensive assessment of an individual's performance against specific professional expertise, sales, team leadership, knowledge leadership, and business management criteria. The promotions process will operate twice annually, with new promotions effective on 1 January and 1 July each year. During each promotion round, the management team will review and consider all consultancy staff for promotion. Exceptionally, promotions may be considered to meet the business's needs at other times.

Promotion Criteria:

Junior Consultant (0–2 years' experience)

- **Primary focus**
  Develop core consulting skills, build industry knowledge, and contribute to engagement delivery.
- **Criteria for promotion to consultant**
  Record of client and manager feedback showing:
  - Proficiency in one or more core consulting methodologies and toolsets.
  - Record of successful completion of assigned engagement tasks with minimal supervision requirements.
  - Increasingly effective communication and interpersonal skills.
  - Positive contributions to team working and culture.
  - Active participation in consulting and professional skills development.

Consultant (2–5 years' experience)

- **Primary focus**
  Develop specialised expertise, take ownership of engagement deliverables, and contribute to business development.

- **Criteria for promotion to senior consultant**
  Record of client and manager feedback showing:
  - In-depth knowledge of specific industry sectors or functional areas.
  - Proven ability to lead engagement workstreams and deliver high-quality outputs.
  - Shown practical client relationship management skills.
  - Undertaken a range of sales and business development activities.
  - Demonstrated ability to mentor and coach junior staff.
  - Contribution to knowledge management initiatives.

Senior Consultant (5–7 years' experience)

- **Primary focus**
  Develop engagement and team leadership skills, expand industry knowledge, and contribute to strategic business development.
- **Criteria for promotion to director**
  Record of client, manager, and director feedback showing:
  - Proven ability to lead and manage complex engagements.
  - Strong business acumen and strategic thinking.
  - Led successful business development activities, including new client acquisitions.
  - Ability to develop and implement new client service offers.
  - Demonstrated consultancy team leadership.
  - Has successfully mentored junior staff.

Director/Partner (7+ years' experience)

- **Primary focus**
  Drive business growth, develop and manage client relationships, and lead and develop teams.
- **Criteria for promotion to partner/director**
  Record of client and director feedback showing:
  - Proven track record of successful business development and client management.
  - Strong leadership and team-building skills.
  - Demonstrated that they have excellent industry knowledge and can provide thought leadership.
  - Financial acumen and business management expertise.

Note: Promotion usually is first to a salaried role. Promotion to equity partner is aligned with the firm's strategic goals and is typically based on performance over multiple periods.

Compensation and benefits – remaining competitive

We established a reward strategy as part of our recruitment process. However, over time, we need to ensure that we maintain robust compensation packages that align with market standards and employee contributions. On an individual basis, we should regularly ensure that base salaries and other elements of the employee's package remain competitive and reflect the employee's value to the organisation. This requires reviewing packages offered by our competitors regularly.

Work–life balance

A healthy work–life balance is increasingly important to employees in today's demanding professional landscape. Consultancy is often demanding, requiring being away from home, travel, and working long hours to meet deadlines. A genuine commitment to employee well-being can, therefore, improve job satisfaction. Providing access to wellness programmes, stress management resources, and mental health support creates a supportive work environment that reduces "burnout" with its associated sick leave and underperformance. We could also offer flexible working arrangements, such as remote work options, employee-chosen hours, and compressed workweeks. Generous holiday and sick leave policies show that we value our team members' time and encourage them to prioritise their health. For example, one consultancy enforced a mandatory month's leave for its equity partners each year.

Strong company culture

We have already established that fostering a culture of employee engagement, loyalty, and inclusivity is essential. However, this culture must be maintained over time and needs processes to support it. We could conduct periodic employee surveys to understand any drift away from our high-performing culture we need to monitor staff views. This should include issues such as openness of communication, collaboration, satisfaction and engagement, and feelings of support and belonging. These must be conducted at least annually, with additional "pulse checks" as needed. For a more continuous process, we could develop staff focus groups to investigate and explore areas of concern, such as challenges in collaboration, barriers to open communication, and support systems effectiveness, and also provide a channel for employee suggestions for improvement.

Two further areas to consider are assessing cultural indicators through direct observation, which can uncover hidden areas for improvement. These observations could include frequency and quality of cross-departmental interactions, levels of participation in team and other meetings, willingness to share information and ideas, and amount of support offered to colleagues. Second, we could establish key performance indicators (KPIs). Various KPIs related to culture and employee experience can be collected and analysed, including employee turnover rates, client feedback on engagements, and recorded staff time (as an indicator of collaboration).

Step 7: Create and recruit a support team

So far, this chapter has focused on creating the consultancy team, but we must also consider our administration and support team. These unsung heroes and heroines form the backbone of a successful consultancy. Consequently, all the steps outlined for creating our consultancy team apply equally to our support team. However, buying some support services in smaller consultancies is more cost-effective.

The benefits of a well-functioning support team include freeing up consultant time to focus on their core competencies rather than administration, which leads to increased productivity and higher-quality deliverables.[3] We can also see reduced costs from centralising administrative functions. As the team, unlike the consultants, is continually present, they can smooth administrative processes, which will support a positive client experience, which in turn increases client satisfaction and loyalty. Errors and legal issues are also less likely to arise, as the team should ensure our compliance with our own procedures and external regulations. Increasingly effective data management is crucial for any consultancy, and the support team can ensure that our data is accurate, secure, and readily accessible.

We can divide support teams' duties into two essential areas, support for consultancy teams and support for the business.

Support for consultancy teams

A great support team assists consultants by ensuring they are not diverted from fee-earning work and helping them arrive at the right place and time with the right IT equipment. The types of support commonly found include the following:

- **Technology**: The team ensures that the company and its consultants have the necessary tools to operate efficiently. This role includes managing central and personal IT hardware and software and providing a technical support hotline. They should also stay updated on industry trends and new technologies that could enhance productivity and client service.
- **Travel**: The support team books flights, accommodation, and ground transportation, which should save the consultant time and reduce stress. This work should not be underestimated and can be complex, especially when dealing with individual requirements, client preferences, and obtaining discounted prices.
- **Coordination**: The team is a central hub that coordinates schedules, meetings, and appointments. They often manage diaries, handle correspondence, and distribute information.

Support for the business

The central administration team needs to support the consultancy's broader business operations, and in this, it mirrors many other businesses. However, the principal functions that we require to support our unique type of business may have different emphases:

- **Marketing**: Our marketing team supports us by owning all marketing materials and activities. This includes all our promotional activities and may involve specialists maintaining websites, designing graphic materials, producing video content, and creating thought leadership pieces from notes scribbled by senior consultants in haste!
- **Sales**: The team supports an engagement sales team, including maintaining standard documentation to support proposals, conducting research, and managing client information and sales systems. They may also coordinate the work of authors of different parts of a sales proposal, prepare and monitor submission deadlines, and prepare and submit final documentation.
- **Customer relations**: Many of our support team members interact directly with clients, receiving inquiries, giving information, and resolving queries. They also typically manage our customer relationship management system (CRM) and may gather client engagement feedback.
- **Finance**: The administrative team is responsible for financial management, including invoicing, payments, and payroll. Working with practice leadership, they monitor the financial

health of the business, including cash flow forecasting and management, budgetary control, and the essential work of ensuring that fee invoices are promptly raised and pursued and that debtors are paid (possibly not so promptly).

- **IT management**: In addition to providing technical support to consultants, the team oversees IT infrastructure, data security, and system maintenance. They implement and manage IT systems to support business operations and ensure data integrity.
- **Human resources**: Effective human resources functions are critical to success in a business that relies on people rather than products. The team also ensures compliance with labour laws.
- **Quality management**: Maintaining high-quality service delivery is essential for a consultancy's reputation. The team supports the firm's quality management systems, which its accreditations may mandate, tracks engagement performance, and ensures compliance with industry standards.

Support team recruitment

All of the advice and guidance on how to source consultants applies equally to our support team. Above all, we always need to answer our three basic questions:

Can they do the job?
Will they do the job?
Can they fit in?

Taking time to find the right people who work well together in a support role and equally well with our consultants and clients is not essential to our success, but it will make the journey much easier.

Reflections

Once again, please draw on your personal experience and current situation or use the theoretical case study.

- Prepare a tailored consultancy matrix and team structure for your proposed team.
- Pick two roles and create detailed role descriptions for them.
- Draft an outline recruitment strategy for your team and prepare a recruitment timeline using a Gantt chart.
- Draw up a brief for an external agency to support recruiting a senior consultant and a consultant for your team.
- How would you design a reward structure for all your team members, including the support team, that ties total rewards to performance?
- As part of your onboarding process for the new team, what steps will you take to create an effective team culture?
- Identify how you will deliver the required support functions for your planned consultancy service.

Further reading

The CMI has also set out details of training courses for consultants at three levels, which correspond to UK vocational training levels four, five, and seven:

- Level 4, foundation, junior management consultant, the entry-level role in the consultancy profession
- Level 5, professional consultants seeking to develop key consultancy skills further
- Level 7, professional consultants wishing to lead consultancy activities in a senior capacity.

The Chartered Management Consultant Accreditation (CHMC) Competency Framework
Certified Management Consultant (CMC) ICMCI Summary Common Body of Knowledge
Assessment Centres and Global Talent Management by George C. Thornton Iii, Nigel Povah
The Five Dysfunctions of a Team by Patrick Lencioni
Building High-Performance Teams: A Practical Guide to Developing World-Class Teams by Richard Hackman
Crucial Conversations: Tools for Talking When Stakes Are High by Kerry Patterson, Joseph Grenny, Ron McMillan, and Al Switzler

Notes

1 An acronym that refers to Earnings Before Interest, Taxes, Depreciation, Amortisation, and any other costs that you think you can get away with excluding.
2 Accountancy can be as weird as sub-atomic physics. Don't get me started on the financial reasons why you might choose to build partition walls on carpets or spend time taking handlebars off bicycles.
3 I can still hear the cry of pain from a very senior consultant who had made a slip in trying to get a consultant's time moved from being recorded as Work in Progress to a point where it could be billed. No, I don't understand why it should have been so problematic, but we were working for the consultancy arm of an accountancy partnership!

Bibliography

Alexandria K. Elms, H. G.-M. (2023). Confidence Is Key: Collective Efficacy, Team Processes and Team Effectiveness. *Small Group Research*, 191–218.

5 Marketing and Promotion

What Do We Have to Do to Engage with Our Market?

Aim of this chapter: To introduce marketing and promotion as an intelligence-led process and to emphasise the importance of developing a market profile and trusted relationships as a precursor to successful consultancy sales.

Learning outcome: To confidently prepare and successfully implement service marketing strategies that create a recognised and trusted service profile among potential clients and enable business growth.

In a quote attributed to Ralph Waldo Emerson in his journal of February 1855, he said that he trusted a good deal to what he called "common fame" for generating interest in our products or services:

> *If a man has good corn, or wood, or boards, or pigs, to sell, or can make better chairs or knives, crucibles, or church organs, than anybody else, you will find a broad hard-beaten road to his house, though it be in the woods . . . . the first witness tells it to a second, and men go by fives and tens and fifties to his door.*
>
> (Emerson 1912)

If Emerson's view that we could rely on this "common fame" to bring orders to us was ever accurate, today's globalised information systems and high competition levels in management consultancy have long since made it difficult to achieve.

Marketing and sales skills are new to many established professionals transitioning into consultancy. Yet being able to market, sell, and deliver innovative services is essential to our success as consultants.

So, let's start with a quick site visit.

You are making a phone call . . . .

"Hi. Is that Zeph?"

You hear an affirmative grunt.

"This is [insert your name here]. We haven't met yet, but I have been brought in to create and lead a new high-value service. Chris has given me your name as someone in the

DOI: 10.4324/9781003490456-6

business I should talk to about marketing and sales. Let me be open and honest. I have experience running a team concerned with online marketing campaigns for insurance. I am in uncharted waters when I come to the bigger picture of marketing. Sales even more so."

Zeph chuckles and replies: "Why is it that Chris always suggests me as the right person to help people? Ah, well, I suppose it's because I do. I ran our marketing team, a grandiose term for just three of us, and I assisted in developing our marketing strategy. Now, that is devolved to practice leaders for action. Let me give you my marketing 101. I can come to you at three this afternoon. I generally work for good coffee and decent biscuits."

You agree – and slip out of the office to buy the best biscuits you can find.

Fast forward to the afternoon. You have met Zeph, established a friendly rapport, and watched the chocolate biscuits magically disappear from the plate.

Zeph: "I know from Chris that you are already progressing in building your ideas into a service. There are things that I will cover that you have already started or completed. But you may want to review where you are, so my perspective may be helpful.

Before we begin, one thing to remember is always to be your client. I mean, look at everything from their point of view and honestly test everything against a straightforward question:

'What would our clients think of this?'

So, here is my Consultancy Service Marketing 101. Make notes there will be an exam later.

- ***Clients want to buy solutions**: So that is what we sell. We do not sell services; we only develop our services as a way to solve client's problems.*
- ***Don't seek clients for our service**: Design solutions that naturally attract them by resolving their problems. They need guidance along the way, so give them signposts like "When we do that, you will experience this."*
- ***Innovation transcends novelty**: In addition to inventing new products or services, we often reimagine solutions to longstanding challenges using fresh approaches, creativity, adaptability, and a willingness to break from convention.*
- ***Advertising requires payment**: However, innovation often yields free publicity. By investing our effort in creating and promoting innovative solutions, we significantly reduce the need for costly advertising campaigns.*
- ***Satisfaction is key**: A satisfied client is the best salesperson ever, but a dissatisfied one will tell ten times more people how awful we are than a satisfied one will tell that we are extraordinary.*
- ***Brand is a promise, but service is fulfilment**: Having both in harmony results in increased trust, loyalty, and long-term success.*
- ***Keep it short and straightforward**: This is the age of information overload. Simplicity and brevity are ultimate luxuries, but remember, building client trust relies on consistent, repeat interactions.*
- ***Targeting is vital**: A service for everybody is a service for nobody, and we don't have the time to deal with nobody.*
- ***Prize relationships over services**: We are a people business. Most clients will interact with a company whose people build trust and foster strong connections. When we nurture these relationships, we convert leads into loyal clients.*

- ***Emotional resonance is essential:*** *It may be a more substantial selling point than functional benefits. It's not the service we sell that people relate to; it's the story we tell.*
- ***Visibility is everything:*** *We are either a shining beacon or in total darkness."*

You: "Thanks, Zeph. There are so many layers within that. But first, it's comforting that we have done the research and put clients at the front and centre of designing our service. Can I catch up with you when we start planning how we handle sales?"

Zeph: "Certainly, but don't leave it too long. We need to get your new team to handle leads effectively and guide prospects from being lukewarm interest into converted clients."

The main objective of our marketing approach is to move potential clients from ignorance of our company and our services through stages of knowledge to trust, to contracting with us to deliver a solution to their problems or issues, and finally to becoming a repeat client. We may now have to use every means to create our own "common fame" and stand out in a competitive market. Figure 5.1 highlights the broad steps to take when marketing a new service. Whilst many of the steps are interconnected and follow sequentially, we may also need to commence some tasks before others are fully completed.

Step 1: Analyse client motivation

"Our clients buy from us," said a senior partner of a global consultancy, "based only on five factors: fear, uncertainty, doubt, greed, and envy." They may have had a point, and no doubt these five factors motivate some clients. However, there is a wider range of reasons for engaging management consultants, which change in importance depending on the client's situation. However, we should start by considering the challenging attitudes that clients can exhibit:

- **Time poverty**: Our clients are almost invariably busy, with multiple demands on each hour of their day. It is a challenge to gain their attention so that they can receive and evaluate our message.
- **Cash poverty**. Clients also have multiple claims on available financial resources. They need to recognise that we can provide value to them above the costs they will incur by buying from us.
- **Scepticism**: Most experienced consultants will have heard variations of the old joke. "A consultant is a person who, when you ask them the time, borrows your watch, tells you the time, puts your watch in their pocket and walks off." However, this joke expresses a view prevalent within some potential clients that engaging consultants will leave you worse off.
- **Fearfulness**: Our clients may be fearful of exposing vulnerabilities and worry about the unknown outcomes of implementing new strategies.
- **Complacency**: Some organisations fail to recognise when they are facing problems that consultancy could help them resolve.
- **Lack of trust**: Clients prefer consultants they've seen or heard about. Building visibility, authority, respect, and trust is crucial if we are unknown to them.
- **Uncertainty**: Some clients hesitate because they are concerned about whether any workable, cost-effective solutions to their issues exist.

In addition to understanding these negative attitudes, to reach clients with our marketing messages, we must also understand why they are concerned about a perceived problem and may consider buying our consultancy services. We should research our clients' drivers that may lead

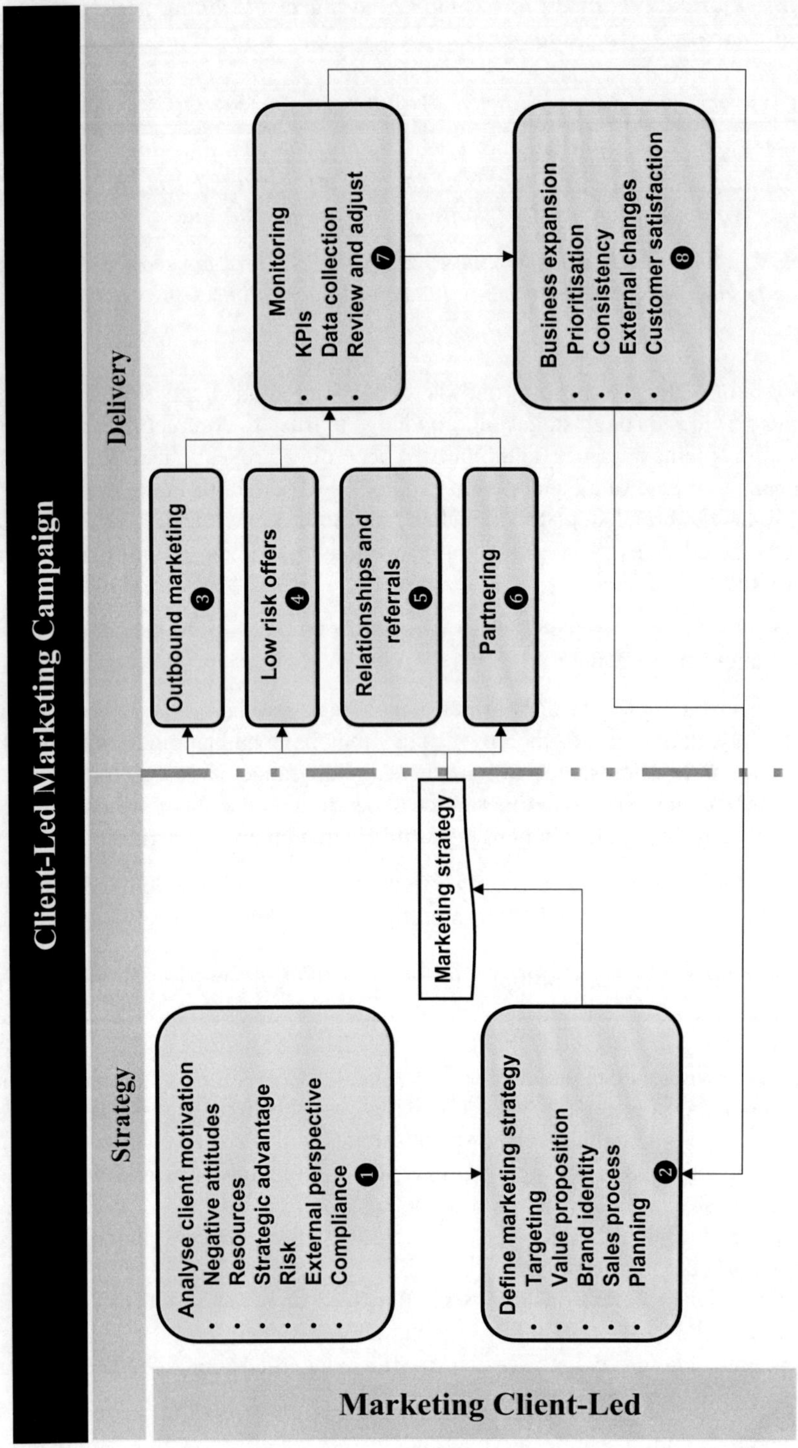

Figure 5.1 Client-Led Marketing Campaign.

them to engage with us. However, most of their concerns usually fall into one of the following categories:

- **Perceived resource and capability gaps**: These gaps can result from a lack of specialised expertise for specific projects or initiatives. For instance, a company might require data scientists for a complex analytics project or digital marketing specialists for a rebranding campaign. Even when a company has capable resources in-house, they may already be fully committed to other work. Equally, where challenges are multifaceted, interconnected, or require in-depth technical knowledge, the client may lack the necessary expertise, structured approaches, and relevant experience in similar work in other organisations. Many consultants also have developed proprietary frameworks and methods for specific types of engagements, which can reduce the time required for planning, analysis, and implementation that are not available to client staff.
- **Need to drive strategic goals and growth**: Client managers used to focusing on daily operations may lack the knowledge and experience to achieve strategic goals and drive growth. An unbiased view of strengths, weaknesses, opportunities, and threats often leads to more informed decision-making and improved strategic planning. This is supported by specialist management consultants who have experience in, for example, leveraging industry benchmarks and best practices to improve performance and competitiveness or providing strategic guidance and operational support during significant changes, such as mergers, acquisitions, and digital transformations. Similarly, many managers lack the external perspective of consultants who can assist clients by bringing innovative approaches to resolving problems or generating new ideas and solutions that require fresh perspectives and specialised knowledge.
- **Competitive advantage (1)**: Another area where clients often call on consultants for assistance is in developing and implementing strategies that will enable them to outperform their competitors. This assistance may include providing market analysis and competitive intelligence or identifying how the latest technologies could enhance their performance. A prime example of this is where clients operate in industries and markets where change, including technology-driven change, is rapid, and the speed of their response to such changes is often critical to their success. Using consultants with proven methodologies can accelerate timelines and enable clients to seize new opportunities.
- **Competitive advantage (2)**: Bringing in consultants who are experts in cost management approaches such as Lean helps organisations achieve cost savings through process optimisation and technology implementation.
- **Risk management**: A specialist external perspective is extremely valuable to clients faced with assessing and mitigating risks impacting operations, reputation, regulatory compliance, or financial performance. These may include areas such as IT exposure and supply chain resilience and recruitment, employee development, succession planning, and organisational culture.

When interacting with clients, we should understand that many have multiple interlocking issues across different categories. An example might be a company wishing to enter a new geographic market. They need local expertise to ensure that the country's regulations are understood, and operational processes are modified for local needs. They are also under time pressure to meet seasonal market deadlines for launching their product.

Step 2: Defining a marketing strategy

Our marketing strategy will be based mainly on information already collected. However, it is an opportunity to review and update previously gathered information and decisions, and it will have a different audience, many of whom will not have seen our previous documentation. Core to are the answers to the following questions:

Where will we target our efforts?
Who will we interact with?
Why might our clients buy from us?
How will we interact with prospects and clients at different levels of interest?
What tasks must we complete to move clients first to awareness and ultimately to a closed sale?
When do we need to complete these tasks?

and, of course,

How Much do we need to spend?

The answers to these questions can be neatly tied into a structure for our marketing strategy as follows:

Targeting

Our time and marketing resources are always limited, so prioritising their use is essential. We should start by revisiting our understanding of our potential client base to identify the areas to target with the best possible return on effort and spending. Our actions should include the following:

- **Understanding our solution from the client's perspective**: The first step in identifying potential target clients is clearly defining their specific problems that our service is designed to solve and the client benefits it will bring. Remember, "It is not about US. It is about YOU." So, determine the benefits for each target type, including business owners, managers of a particular department, or end users.
- **Identifying high-potential clients**: Prioritising our marketing effort requires identifying the industries or sectors most likely to benefit from the solutions that we intend to target and segmenting them accordingly. We should consider the size of businesses or other organisations that best fit our service. Factors such as revenue, employee count, and industry maturity will help us determine the ideal target market. We should research locations or regions with a higher concentration of potential clients (and competition). For example, we could decide to prioritise owners of multiple retail outlets in region X who are over 55 and may wish to retire.
- **Evaluating market potential**: Once we deconstruct the total market into smaller segments, we can assess the overall opportunity by determining the potential of each segment. We can also identify our potential competitors, their pricing, and their market share by segment. This should give us sufficient information granularity to help determine our marketing priorities.
- **Defining the ideal client contact profile**: Clients are not monoliths but are composed of individuals in many roles. When we understand our ideal individual types of contact profiles within each segment, we can decide on the most effective marketing channels and messages to reach them.
- **Understanding client needs and challenges**: If we align our service with specific client needs, we will be perceived as authors of a valuable solution. If we also understand how potential clients currently address these challenges, we can identify gaps in the market where

our service will provide a unique solution. Researching the decision-making processes within potential clients also helps determine individuals involved in purchasing decisions at different expenditure levels.

Let's revisit our example in Chapter 2 of an accountancy firm targeting potential clients. You will recall that managing consultant Jay later used this work to jump-start his solo consultancy after his team was unexpectedly "downsized."

This example reveals the following:

1. *The identified client problem was a lack of demonstrable control over the use of information technology for administrative and finance services.*
2. *The proposed solution was based on independent computer audits of at-risk systems, which clients could use to improve system and process security.*
3. *The market to be addressed was initially restricted to local bodies within the UK National Health Service.*
4. *The key decision-maker in each body was the Finance Director.*
5. *There were about 250 individuals to contact. They were strongly networked through regional and national bodies and could be expected to discuss any significant approaches from a major accountancy firm.*
6. *The accounting firm identified 25 partners, each of whom was to write to an average of ten target clients using a standardised letter – which they may wish to rewrite and then follow this up with a programme of personal contacts.*

As a solo consultant, Jay signed all the letters in fountain pen (stuffed the envelopes, stamped them, and took them to the Post Office) and made the follow-up calls.

Value proposition

Our objective in developing our key or unique value proposition is to communicate a value-driven message. It should describe the value we offer to potential clients in a compelling manner and let them see us as the trusted partner in their business success. Again, we should put ourselves in our clients' shoes.

Remember that whilst we are busy creating and launching consultancy services, our clients only buy solutions to their perceived problems. Consequently, our value proposition should address the following:

- **Problem definition**: We must clearly define our potential clients' problems using their language, demonstrating our understanding of their business, and showing that we are a credible service provider with whom they could work. We do this by briefly setting out our understanding of our clients' pain points, challenges, or opportunities.
- **Targeted solutions** to address these challenges and showcase our ability to provide practical and effective recommendations.
- **Unique value proposition** differentiates us from competitors by emphasising the client benefits from our unique strengths, for example, expertise in a particular industry, proprietary methodologies, or proven track record of success.

- **Measurable outcomes** that quantify the benefits our clients can expect to achieve, such as increased revenue, reduced costs, or improved efficiency. Where we do not have comparable past assignments, we draw on our market testing with volunteer clients.
- **Success stories,** either case studies or client testimonials, demonstrate our ability to deliver results, thereby further building trust. (Note that in our initial marketing, we can focus on the history of the team members who will deliver solutions for the client.)
- **Experienced team,** setting out the qualifications and experience of our team, emphasises their industry knowledge and track record, and reassures clients that they are working with experts. (Note: Preparing tailored profiles and short success stories is helpful; multipage career profiles are not.)
- **Collaborative approach,** emphasising that we work in collaboration with client staff and managers helps to spotlight our aim to deliver success through strong partnerships and tailoring our inputs to solve their problems.
- **Strong ethical foundation,** emphasising our commitment to ethical business practices and our adherence to industry standards, further builds trust and confidence in our ability to deliver client solutions.

The test of a great value proposition is for the client to complete the sentence truthfully:

I would buy from PNX Consultancy because . . .

Brand identity

We need to clearly define how we want to be perceived by our potential clients and recruits and consider the following:

- **Core brand values**: We should clearly and concisely state our fundamental beliefs underpinning our actions and decision-making. In our case study, PNX Consultancy's core brand values are innovation, expertise, trust, and a results orientation.
- **Brand promise**: This is a brief statement communicating the benefits clients will obtain from working with us. It should be memorable, engaging, and reflect our key value proposition. PNX Consultancy's brand promise is "Improving patient and business outcomes through empowering healthcare organisations to harness the power of AI."
- **Brand positioning**: This defines how we want to be perceived in the market and should highlight our strengths to differentiate our brand from competitors. The PNX Consultancy brand, by emphasising its expertise and experience in solution delivery, is seeking to position the company as a trusted partner for healthcare organisations seeking to leverage AI.
- **Brand personality**: This is a reflection of the human-like characteristics that a brand embodies. It's how a brand is perceived by consumers, going beyond its products or services, for example, is it seen as friendly, professional, or innovative? For example, a tech company might want to be perceived as modern, innovative, and cutting edge. A financial consultancy brand could be seen as discreet, formal, and dependable. The brand personality we project should be consistent with our target audience and messaging. PNX Consultancy's brand personality aims to show that it is intelligent, reliable, collaborative, and innovative, aligning with its focus on providing cutting-edge AI solutions.
- **Brand voice**: A strong brand voice helps create a consistent and memorable customer experience and should reflect our brand's personality and values in the language of our target audience. A consultancy's brand voice should be professional, informative, and engaging. For example, McKinsey & Company has developed an authoritative brand voice style. In consequence, their reports and articles are based on in-depth analysis and may use complex

language. Our case study consultancy, PNX, has a brand voice designed to be informative, professional, and forward thinking. This aligns with their focus on innovative AI solutions for the healthcare industry.

- **Strapline**: A short, catchy phrase that encapsulates the essence of a brand or product and is often used as a tagline or slogan. Our strapline should be memorable, easy to understand, and reflect our unique value proposition. PNX Consultancy's strapline, "AI for Healthcare, Delivered," concisely conveys its expertise in successfully delivering healthcare AI solutions.
- **Brand visual identity**: This should include our logo, colours, typography, and imagery. Our visual identity should be memorable, consistent, and aligned with the brand's personality and values. For example, Bain & Company's logo has a bold, geometric shape, using red and white colours to convey energy, innovation, and leadership. Our brand visual identity includes ensuring that print colours (Pantone numbers) are reflected in online screens (described by RGB or CMYK codes). We also need to ensure that all materials produced are of the highest quality and error-free. Any format, grammar, or spelling slip-ups will cause potential clients to question the quality of our work. (Note care must be taken in certain countries and societies to ensure that logos fall within cultural and legislative norms.) It always pays to institute a rigorous independent check and sign-off on any prepared material.[1]
- **Thought leadership**: An area that is a cornerstone for management consultancies and is a prime way of positioning our brand as an industry authority that sits outside a competitive sales process. Sharing innovative insights and expert opinions consistently demonstrates our deep understanding of industry trends and challenges and helps us build trust and credibility with potential clients. It should also differentiate us from our competitors and help attract top talent to our consulting teams. We should, therefore, invest time and resources in thought leadership activities, which could include preparing white papers, hosting webinars and round tables, and speaking at or chairing conference discussions. These allow us to shape the future of our field and influence industry standards and practices. Ultimately, thought leadership helps drive business growth by creating a strong, recognisable brand that clients and partners respect and seek out for their most critical challenges.

Comprehensive sales process

A robust sales process includes defining sales stages, developing sales collateral, and training. Our sales process is designed to progress a potential client through the various stages of a purchase decision, often called the sales funnel. This sales funnel is a visual image representing a client's journey, which starts at the top with many prospects gradually reducing in number through different stages, finishing with contracted clients at the bottom. Instead of a funnel with potential clients implicitly drawn by gravity from top to bottom, regard achieving sales as a prospect moving gradually up a stepped pyramid level by level. Figure 5.2 sets out the different steps in the sales pyramid. We must actively guide and support our prospects upward as they climb each step, starting with initial awareness at the bottom and ending with loyal customers at the top. By working closely with each client to support their ascent, we will create a more effective buying experience and increase sales. This continuing engagement with them ensures that we align our marketing efforts with their needs and build trust and loyalty throughout the process. To maximise conversions of leads that we have identified, our sales processes should:

- **Be built on adequate preparation**: Including defining sales stages (pyramid steps), developing solution-centred sales collateral, training our sales team in effective sales techniques, and supporting them with effective systems.

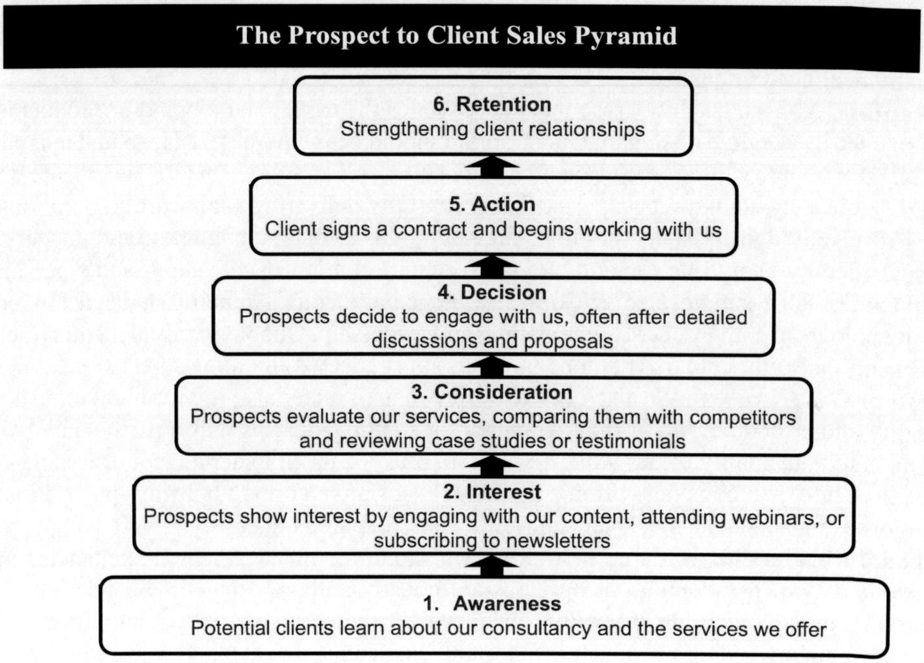

Figure 5.2 The Prospect to Client Sales Pyramid.

- **Identify client personas**: Their pain points, needs, and motivations to ensure that we continue targeting the right audience with the right message.
- **Track prospects**: We need to monitor their journey and each contact with them to ensure consistency in our relationships and messages. Inconsistency will undermine the trusted relationships that we are seeking to build. A client relationship management (CRM) system can track sales activities and client interactions. Ideally, the CRM will integrate with our calendar system and prepare reports on sales activities and the value of potential sales over time weighted by the prospect's position on our sales pyramid.
- **Provide educational content**: Engaging and informing potential clients at the bottom of our sales pyramid with content that meets their needs and supports them as they move to higher pyramid steps. This content could start with general blog posts, videos, or social media posts but become more specific to the prospect as our understanding of their needs evolves.
- **Deliver in-depth resources**: As prospects reach the middle of our sales pyramid, we understand more about the evaluation criteria they may use to select a consultancy to work with. This might involve white papers, case studies, webinars, client site visits, opportunities to meet the team members, or demonstrations showcasing our service's benefits and addressing potential concerns.
- **Tailor our messaging**: When prospects reach the top levels of the pyramid, tailored messages should address their final concerns and encourage sales closure. This tailoring often involves bespoke offers, clear calls to action, and follow-up communications to reinforce understanding of the value of our solutions. Where we are in a competitive tendering process, our entire sales effort may be focused on this end of the sales process.

Effective planning

We now have a long list of tasks identified in our strategy, and the final stage is to determine the resources each task needs and get it underway. If only life were that simple, as ever, as soon as we have a plan, we will find that the people we require to help us are committed elsewhere, on vacation or taking time out sick; printing our collateral will take longer than we have before the conference and exhibition we plan to visit – and because we missed the deadline the only stand available is too small and in a part of the hall where we can expect little footfall. But all of these can be managed if we start with a robust idea of what we are trying to achieve and when. Table 5.1 shows the timing, resources, and staffing required to deliver the marketing strategy for our consultancy service. Remember, when setting out a timeline, the first rule of planning is that it always takes longer than you think.

Table 5.1 is a general timeline, and we should adjust it based on the unique needs of each service being launched. While these phases are presented sequentially, some tasks can be done concurrently. For example, gathering client testimonials may occur throughout the process. Resource allocations are an estimate and may vary depending on our budget and team structure.

Table 5.1 PNX Consultancy Services Launch Marketing Tasks

PNX Consultancy Services Launch Marketing Tasks					
Weeks	**Phase**	**Activities**	**Resources**	**Staffing**	**Leadership**
1 to 4	Client analysis Targeting	Internal workshops Market research Competitor analysis Buyer persona development	Market research reports Industry publications Analysis tools	Marketing manager Market research analyst	Marketing
5 to 8	Key value proposition Brand identity	Service refinement Value proposition development Brand identity definition	Competitive analysis reports Brand development tools	Marketing manager Copywriter Graphic designer Senior manager for sign-off	Marketing
9 to 12	Content Marketing Sales Enablement	Content creation Email marketing Social media Web site development Sales collateral development Sales process definition Sales team training	Content management system Email marketing platform Social media management tools	Marketing manager Content writer Social media manager Web developer Graphic designer Print company Sales team Senior manager for sign-off	Marketing Sales
13+	Sales and lead generation	Telemarketing campaign Lead nurturing Sales closures	CRM system Sales training materials	Sales manager Telemarketing team Sales team	Sales

Effective communication and collaboration between marketing and sales teams are crucial for success. Table 5.1 shows how engagement and leadership move between the teams as the strategy progresses. However, it is a good practice to ensure that the sales team leadership is engaged throughout the strategy's development and delivery and that the marketing team remains in contact during sales delivery as part of the monitoring and review process.

PNX Consultancy has developed the following market strategy for its AI in health services using this general framework.

PNX Consultancy Services

Healthcare AI Services in the USA and Europe

Go-To-Market Strategy

Executive Summary

PNX Consultancy aims to become the first choice for AI-led management and IT consultancy services for clients in healthcare services and related industries.

This strategy outlines a targeted approach to engaging key decision-makers within health insurance companies, government bodies, and healthcare providers in the United States and Europe.

Target Audience Segments and Messages

- **Health Insurance Companies (USA and Europe)**: Focus on AI-driven solutions for claims processing automation, fraud detection, and personalised medicine integration. Target CIOs, CMOs, and Heads of Claims Processing.
- **Government Bodies (National, State, Local – USA and Europe)**: Emphasise AI's role in population health management, disease prediction, and resource allocation optimisation. Engage with Public Health Department Directors, Healthcare Policy Unit Leaders, and Chief Technology Officers.
- **Healthcare Providers and Maintenance Organisations (USA and Europe)**: Use messaging to convey the beneficial impact that AI can have on clinical decision support, patient care optimisation, and preventative care programmes. Target CMIOs, COOs, and Heads of IT.
- **Establishing Thought Leadership:**
    - Health insurance companies: Participate in industry webinars and collaborate with analysts to establish PNX as a thought leader in AI-powered claims processing and fraud detection.
    - Government bodies: Develop white papers and research reports focused on government healthcare priorities (e.g. chronic disease management, rural healthcare) leveraging AI.
    - Healthcare providers and maintenance organisations: Partner with healthcare IT companies to establish PNX as a trusted advisor on AI integration for clinical workflows and patient care optimisation.

Key Value Proposition

PNX Consultancy provides our clients with assured access to the industry-leading, independent experts they need to enable them to transform their business delivery results and patient outcomes through rapidly and effectively harnessing AI solutions.

- **Key benefits for clients working with PNX-led AI solutions:**
  - Enhanced efficiency and cost-effectiveness: Our AI expertise will enable them to select and implement best-of-breed AI solutions to streamline processes, reduce error rates, and optimise the use of resources.
  - Improved patient care: Our consultants put patient outcomes at the heart of our work. This includes using AI to personalise care packages, improve the accuracy of patient diagnoses, and enhance patients' experiences, outcomes, and satisfaction with the service they have received.
  - Reduced health delivery costs: Our experience with AI in health and other industries allows us to design client solutions that optimise resource allocation and minimise operational expenses.
  - Improved strategic decisions: We support clients through the learning process of adopting data-driven decisions, enabling them to maximise the value they obtain from the data that AI enables them to collect.
  - Increased compliance and security: We share our experience from across the health sector with clients faced with the need to meet the challenges of evolving regulations and the increasing need to implement the highest data security standards and monitor compliance.
  - Tailored AI solutions: Every client has a unique set of interacting needs and goals. Our AI consultants work with client managers and staff to uncover and prioritise these to ensure the "best fit" AI solution.
  - Competitive advantage: Our AI consultants work with client staff and managers to deliver competitive advantage through supporting innovation in effective service delivery and improved patient results.

Brand Identity

- **Core Brand Values:**
  - Innovation: PNX Consultancy works across healthcare to exploit AI-enabled systems and processes to drive innovative solutions to our client's complex challenges.
  - Expertise: We demonstrate deep domain expertise covering the triple aspects of healthcare, information technology exploitation, and AI.
  - Trust: Core to PNX Consultancy's DNA is building lasting, trusted client relationships based on transparency and integrity.
  - Secure: PNX has robust data security protocols and is committed to HIPAA (USA) and GDPR (Europe) compliance.
  - Results-oriented: Delivering tangible, measurable results confirmed by our clients that improve patient outcomes and drive efficiency.

- **Brand Promise:**
  - "Improving patient and business outcomes through empowering healthcare organisations to harness the power of AI."
- **Brand Positioning:**
  - Trusted partner: PNX Consultancy is the first choice for healthcare organisations seeking to leverage AI to transform their operations and improve patient outcomes. We tailor solutions to address client-specific needs and challenges within healthcare.
  - Proven track record: Client engagements will be more successful because of our team's experience delivering successful AI projects across the healthcare sector.
  - Deep domain knowledge: Our team members become acknowledged thought leaders, sharing their in-depth knowledge and understanding of healthcare challenges and AI applications.
  - Commitment to excellence: PNX consultants are renowned for providing clients with the highest quality of service and exceeding the client's expectations.
- **Brand Personality:**
  - Intelligent: PNX Consultancy is knowledgeable and forward thinking.
  - Reliable: We are dependable and consistent in our approach.
  - Collaborative: PNX consultants work in close collaboration with our clients to achieve their objectives.
  - Innovative: PNX consultants always seek evidence-driven, better ways to do things.
- **Strapline:**
  "AI for Healthcare, Delivered."
- **Brand Visual Identity:**
  The core concept is blending modern technology with healthcare to reflect the innovation that AI brings to healthcare.
  - Overall aesthetic: Our brand's visual identity evokes trust, innovation, and progress. The deep and lighter blue, teal, or turquoise shades create a visually appealing brand. A dedicated logo for the service is proposed, which should be distinctive and easily recognisable. All typography and imagery will complement this aesthetic while remaining consistent with the overall PNX brand guidelines.
  - Colour palette:
    1. Primary. Deep navy blue: This is used to symbolise trust, reliability, and expertise. Recommended colour: Pantone 19–3923 TCX Navy Blazer.
    2. Secondary. A lighter shade of blue: This is used to represent innovation and progress. Recommended colour: Pantone 16–4132 TCX Skydiver.
    3. Accent. A vibrant teal or turquoise: This is used to convey the energy. Recommended colour: Pantone 15–4722 TCX Turquoise.
  - Typography:
    1. Primary: A sans-serif font, Helvetica or Roboto, should be used for readability and modern aesthetic.

2. Secondary: A serif font, such as Times New Roman or Garamond, adds sophistication to headlines and titles.

- Logo:
  1. Main element: A stylised "PNX" that incorporates elements of medical imagery and a circuit board to symbolise the intersection of technology and human health.
  2. Secondary element: A tagline or phrase like "AI for Healthcare" or "Empowering Health" is placed beneath the main element.
- Imagery:
  Focus on technology and healthcare: Use images of medical professionals, patients, modern medical equipment, and AI-driven visualisations.
- Colour scheme: Follow the PNX brand colour palette to maintain consistency.

Tailored Marketing Channels

- **Multilingual website (English and French)**: This website showcases PNX's expertise with resources like case studies and white papers specific to each target segment, which can be downloaded in exchange for contact information.
- **Targeted social media marketing**: Share industry insights, thought leadership content, and success stories using high-quality written content and short information videos. Channels to be used for targeted campaigns include LinkedIn.
- **Targeted email marketing**: Develop email campaigns highlighting the potential for using AI and client success stories.
- **Industry Events and Conferences**: Actively participate in relevant healthcare IT conferences in the USA and Europe. Consider sponsorships for high-visibility opportunities.
- **Direct outreach**: For high-value prospects, consider personalised outreach (emails, phone calls) tailored to specific needs and challenges.

Sales Process

The existing company processes will be adhered to and strengthened as follows:

- **Initial Contact:**
  - Sales specialist: Reach out to potential clients through emails, calls, and networking events. Identify and review advertised tender opportunities. Qualify client leads based on their needs, budget, service fit, and readiness to adopt AI solutions.
  - Delivery team: Attend industry networking events and participate in initial meetings to determine client needs and provide technical insights.
  - Interaction: Sales specialists provide narratives and support the delivery team in communicating our value proposition and evaluating client potential.
- **Needs Assessment and Proposal Development:**
  - Sales specialists: Conduct in-depth needs assessments to understand our client's specific challenges and goals.

  - Nominated engagement manager and delivery team: Gathering technical requirements to support a tailored proposal outlining the AI solutions and their benefits to the client.
  - Proposal managers: Oversee the proposal development process to ensure it aligns with the client's needs and the company's capabilities. Take responsibility for the quality of the final proposal.
  - Service team leaders: Review and approve fees, profitability, risk, and proposed approach, referring to senior management in accordance with standard company policies.
  - Interaction: The engagement manager and the delivery team work closely with sales specialists to ensure the proposal addresses all client concerns and highlights the unique value of the AI solutions.

- **Presentation and Negotiation:**
  - Sales specialists: Lead the proposal presentation to the client and contract negotiations, including pricing, timelines, and deliverables.
  - Nominated engagement manager and delivery team: Offer technical support during the presentation and answer the client's detailed questions.
  - Senior management: Set the parameters for contract negotiations and may step in if required to provide additional assurance and finalise terms. May also lead major client presentations.
  - Interaction: Sales specialists coach the delivery team on effective presentation techniques and negotiation strategies.
- **Contract Finalisation and Onboarding:**
  - Sales specialists: Finalise the contract terms and ensure that all legal and compliance requirements are met. Engage the legal team as necessary.
  - Nominated engagement manager: Develop plans to transition the client smoothly from sales to service delivery.
  - Delivery team. Prepare for the project kick-off by familiarising themselves with the client's systems and requirements.
  - Senior management: Review, approve, and sign the final contract in accordance with company policies.
  - Interaction: Sales specialists give the engagement manager and delivery team a final briefing to ensure a seamless transition.

Measurement and Adaptation:

The effectiveness of the strategy is demonstrated by tracking key metrics, including

- Website traffic.
- Engagement with content and marketing materials.
- Press and other media coverage.
- Leads generated by target segment.
- Conversion rates at each stage of the sales pyramid.

Data-driven insights will guide strategic adjustments to maximise PNX's reach and client acquisition success.

Timeline

Weeks 1–4

1. Commence client analysis and target identification.
2. Confidential outreach to existing clients.
3. Define campaign success metrics.
4. Agree on the campaign budget.
5. Set out a detailed content strategy and calendar and engage content writers and producers.
6. Book attendance at relevant AI, IT, and healthcare conferences.

Weeks 5–8

1. Craft unique value proposition.
2. Prepare narratives, including case studies, success stories, elevator pitches, and consultant profiles.
3. Design brand identity following agreed guidelines.

Weeks 9–12

1. Complete marketing content, including blog posts, articles, white papers, videos, call scripts, social media posts, and email sequences.
2. Issue press releases focusing on the service, client success stories, and added value.
3. Launch a multilingual website (English and French).
4. Commence targeted social media marketing.
5. Commence targeted email marketing.
6. Actively participate in relevant AI, IT, and healthcare conferences.
7. Commence direct personalised outreach for high-value prospects.
8. Train the consultancy sales team on the new services and solutions being offered, including familiarising them with marketing content and handling objections.
9. Commence primary outbound sales campaign (email, follow-up calls, letters).

Week 13

1. Ongoing sales activity and lead generation.
2. Monitoring and review process.

Step 3: Outbound marketing

Adopting a structured approach to outbound marketing means that we can build on our previous work, honing and refining it by personalising our messages and contacts. Consultancy marketing is unlike consumer marketing, which targets vast audiences with short sales cycles and emotional appeals. Instead, outbound marketing for high-value consultancy services focuses on a select group of businesses and decision-makers, has longer sales cycles, and needs intellectual content. We aim to build lasting partnerships with a select group of clients, while consumer marketing focuses on maximising short-term sales.

Consider the example of Jay, our newly independent consultant, who we first met in Chapter 2 and revisited earlier in this chapter.

When subsequently asked about his experience of creating a boutique consultancy, Jay said, "I created a thriving niche consultancy offer with just a single carefully crafted letter. Yet, out of 250 letters sent, only one led initially to a long-term contract. This became a cornerstone of my business for several years through referrals to similar bodies and from repeat sales to the initial client.

The point about not always getting immediate results was firmly driven home to me after taking an exhibition stand at a major industry conference. We were put in a back corner and had no significant conversations over the three days. Yet nearly a year later, we won a large contract, and when asked what tipped the balance in our favour, the client said that they had seen our stand and realised that we were bigger than they had thought."

Any of our outbound marketing activities are often only the first step in a journey that leads to sales. Unlike consumer marketing, these activities are not about immediate conversions but about moving prospects towards becoming paying clients.

It typically takes multiple interactions, or "touchpoints," to persuade any client to engage with a management consultancy. Such touchpoints include emails, phone calls, in-person meetings, or other forms of communication such as websites, social media posts, traditional collateral such as "leave behind" brochures or press advertisements, and even word of mouth. The number and type of necessary touchpoints vary according to factors such as the complexity of the client's challenges, the industry, and the identified client profile. A conservative estimate would range from six to ten touchpoints; less than that is fortunate, more than that, and we may have to investigate the effectiveness of our communications.

While the quantity of touchpoints is significant, their quality is crucial. By ensuring the quality of our interactions, we can increase our chances of converting prospects into clients. Consequently, we must craft each touchpoint carefully to provide value and build trust with the potential client. Each one should offer insights, address concerns, and demonstrate our expertise from the client's perspective.

We also need to maintain brand quality at each touchpoint to reinforce our brand in the prospect's mind. Be warned: collateral that is poorly produced, badly laid out, or appallingly spelt will rapidly, even fatally, undermine our prospects' confidence in our ability to deliver high-quality consultancy.

Before commencing an outbound marketing campaign, we must review, update, and extend the data we prepared earlier. In particular, we need to reuse and update the ideal client profile and prospect data gathered previously. From now on, a customer relationship management system (CRM), preferably one that integrates with our calendar system, is a valuable tool. Usually, this requires some investment, either as a monthly subscription or as an outright purchase, although some more limited software may be free.

If you choose not to use a CRM package, it's all down to manually record your activities on index cards for each prospect. Either approach requires discipline and effort, but from now on, everything is about personalisation, consistency, and relationship building. Relying on memory, diary notes, and calendars is not an option for effective marketing and sales.

The tasks that we need to complete for a successful outbound marketing campaign include the following:

- Understanding our target audience.
- Harnessing Artificial Intelligence (AI).
- Making our value proposition compelling.

Understanding our target audience

- **Identify the ideal client profile**: Clearly define the characteristics of our ideal client, including industry, company size, decision-makers, and pain points. For example, we might target mid-sized tech companies facing scaling challenges. Remember, rather than large numbers, we want to build a focused picture of high-quality prospects.
- **Segment our target audience**: We can segment our audience of colder contacts into smaller, more manageable segments based on factors like industry, location, and company size. Segmenting by industry (e.g. healthcare, finance) allows us to tailor our messaging and select more likely contact opportunities.
- **Conduct thorough research**: We should research our warmer contacts and gather in-depth information about their needs, preferences, and behaviours through market research, surveys, and industry analysis. This research will assist us in understanding where and how we need to personalise our messages and adjust our contact strategy. For example, using tools like LinkedIn Sales Navigator can help identify key decision-makers and their interests. Researching online data about our contact's organisation is helpful in identifying corporate strategies and progress and perhaps allows us to infer potential pain points.

Harnessing Artificial Intelligence (AI)

As an alternative to commissioning research, buying, or renting qualified lists of prospects, we can use AI to help identify potential client prospects. By analysing datasets from various sources, we may select targets by company size, financial performance, recent growth, leadership changes, market and economic growth, and other published information.

However, AI is not a panacea, and although it can automate data collection and analysis, saving time and resources for marketing teams, it also has the limitations including:

- Reliance on available data means that if the data is flawed or outdated, the insights will be too. This means that we have to check the data produced.
- Correlation of data does not imply causation of events.

- AI may struggle to understand subtle nuances of human behaviour that a seasoned marketeer would quickly grasp.
- AI may be less beneficial when we are already engaged with a defined market and have built a contact network and database.
- Some people may have ethical concerns about AI's ability to analyse social media interactions and might feel that it is too intrusive.

Making our value proposition compelling

Storytelling is a way of sharing information about our value proposition that resonates with our target audience. Using narrative storytelling as a communication technique enhances fact retention for several reasons:

- **Emotional engagement**: People are more likely to pay attention to our message and remember information when they are emotionally connected to it. We can use stories to connect with the listener or reader in a way which is impossible with a litany of dry facts and figures. For example, "The chief finance officer of ABC company was faced with major issues over their year-end. It seemed that their accounting systems and processes were always changed, ready for the new year. When his staff were busiest, they had to take time out to learn new systems and processes. It was hard for everyone. But we came in and did XYZ, which really eased the pressure."
- **Contextual understanding**: Stories provide context, helping listeners understand how facts relate to each other and the broader picture, making information more meaningful and easier to recall.
- **Memory anchors**: As in our short example, stories tie facts together into a coherent whole. Recalling the story makes our prospects more likely to remember the associated facts.
- **Mental imagery**: Stories stimulate mental imagery, which can enhance memory and visualising a scene helps solidify information in the mind.
- **Relevance and personal connection**: Stories can make facts more relevant to the listener or reader by connecting them to their personal experiences or aspirations, creating a strong sense of ownership and engagement.

Appropriately used, narrative is the most powerful tool for building clients' understanding of why we will be their ideal partner. A cohesive narrative helps reinforce trust and credibility and underline our advantages over competitors. The benefit of creating consistent narratives is that it allows us to root narratives into every aspect of our marketing and sales, including our staff training.

Our narrative needs to make us stand out. We should highlight our unique or high-value selling points and modify these for each target prospect. These should clearly articulate the benefits and value we offer that differentiate us from our competitors. For example, if our consultancy has a proven track record in reducing operational costs by 20%, we should highlight this in our messaging. It should also allow us to tailor our message to resonate with the detailed needs and challenges of each segment and individual we wish to engage with. For instance, PNX's campaign targeting healthcare companies might focus on improving patient care efficiency, but this needs to be worded in the light of information on each prospect. Using data and case studies demonstrates the tangible results our consultancy can deliver for each particular client. For example, showcasing a case study where our consultancy helped a client decrease costs by 30% through process optimisation is useful when a target client is reported to have declining profits. We would need an alternative slant if the target is growing fast and needs process optimisation to increase throughput. We should select the most appropriate illustrations for our narrative from a library of different case studies and testimonials so that we can tailor our narrative stories to resonate with each target client.

Crafting effective outbound marketing tactics

- **Personalised outreach**: A personalised email campaign that addresses the recipient's specific pain points can increase engagement rates by up to 29%. Consequently, wherever possible, we should use data to select contacts and personalise our outreach efforts to their needs, including targeting emails that address their issues or making phone calls with tailored scripts.
- **Content marketing**: Creating high-quality content like blog posts, short videos, white papers, and case studies ensures our audience feels informed and knowledgeable about our services and helps reinforce our position as thought leaders in our sector.
- **Social media marketing**: We should engage and connect our audience to our brand and services through social media messages to our target audience, share valuable content, and support lasting relationships.
- **Public relations**: We should seek media coverage to increase brand visibility and credibility. For instance, getting featured in industry publications or speaking at conferences can position our consultancy as an authority. Engaging public relations specialists can help increase impact in this area.
- **Networking events**: Selectively attending industry conferences and networking events allows us to connect with target potential clients and build relationships. For example, participating in events like the "TechCrunch Disrupt" provides opportunities to meet tech industry leaders while speaking at chamber of commerce events allows us to meet local small businesses.
- **Email marketing**: Developing targeted email campaigns with compelling subject lines, personalised content, and a clear call to action can capture our target's attention. For instance, an email campaign with a subject line like "Discover How to Reduce Operational Costs by 20%" can be very effective. However, be clear that you follow local legislation and good practice. The last thing we need is for any adverse reactions from any part of our outbound marketing.
- **Paid digital advertising**: We can use paid advertising platforms like Google Ads and LinkedIn Ads, which can be very effective at reaching a selected target business audience. We could choose targets based on many factors, such as their job titles, industries, areas, or company size. This will ensure that our message reaches the "right" people. Additionally, it allows us to monitor the effectiveness of each advertisement.

Addressing different types of prospects

Our marketing is attempting to convert prospects into profitable clients, and we need to understand that prospects need to be addressed in various ways based on our previous relationships with them. Conversion rates for known clients are typically higher due to our existing relationships and trust, possibly. For example, conversion rates for existing clients can be as high as 30–50%.

Conversion rates can be almost as promising for companies with whom we have previously engaged, built a strong relationship, and shown that we understand their needs. Re-engaging with such warm leads may give conversion rates of 20–30%.

Conversion rates for cold prospects are generally lower; for example, personalised cold email campaigns can achieve between 1% and 5% conversion rates. However, effective outreach and personalisation can improve our chances of success. Consequently, we need to adopt different strategies for each prospect category.

Nurturing existing relationships through regular communication, personalised offerings, and exceptional service is critical to maintaining our existing client base. Having spent time acquiring a client, the last thing we need is to lose them through neglect. For example, quarterly newsletters containing industry insights, client success stories and updates on our services, and occasional short calls can keep us firmly in the client's view as their partners in success. We can use similar means to maintain relationships with previously encountered companies. Re-engaging with contacts who have previously expressed interest in our services helps to keep our potential client base alive to our services. We should always personalise our follow-up messages with these contacts to show that we understand and can address their unique needs and goals. For instance, a follow-up email or letter referencing a concern expressed in a previous conversation can reignite interest and support building a relationship.

Cold prospects are where we start our engagement process and identify potential clients through research and outreach. Essentially, we are aiming to bring a previously unknown contact onto the base level of our sales pyramid. As always, we should use a targeted approach, focusing on possible pain points and showing how our services can address them. We should use our compelling value proposition and narratives that resonate with our understanding of the needs and challenges in their industry or sector. For example, a cold email campaign highlighting how our consultancy solved a common industry problem for a well-known company can generate an expression of interest. It should usually be promptly followed up with an outreach call.

Step 4: Low-risk offers

We must recognise that engaging management consultants is a significant investment for many businesses in terms of management and staff time as well as cost. If we allow them to test our services without a substantial upfront commitment, they can reduce their level of perceived risk. If we deliver quick wins through a low-risk engagement, we can demonstrate our value, making it easier for clients to justify a longer-term commitment. Our low-risk offers could include minor engagements, such as free initial consultations, discounted trial periods, and money-back guarantees.

Low-risk offers should attract more potential clients, increasing our pool of leads. This is particularly useful for new consultancies building their client base and established firms entering new markets or creating new services. We should also ask the client to provide feedback and, if possible, testimonials to help us refine new services and support our marketing to other clients. Table 5.2 discusses several key types of low-risk offers.

Step 5: Client relationships and referrals

Our most essential sales assets are not our sales team, our investment in outbound marketing campaigns, or the content we have so carefully created. It is satisfied clients. As organisations and individual contacts, our clients often become our best advocates, sharing their positive experiences with others. This word-of-mouth marketing is invaluable and free and leads to new business opportunities. We need to foster this, for example, by creating opportunities for satisfied clients to tell their stories to other clients at industry events or in articles, videos, and news coverage in suitable publications.

Referrals multiply our marketing efforts. For example, a leading USA consulting firm is now renowned for its expertise in the healthcare industry. The firm earned its clients' trust and respect

Table 5.2 Low-Risk Consultancy Offers

Low-Risk Consultancy Offers			
Type	**Advantages**	**Disadvantages**	**Example**
Benchmark review An analysis comparing the client's performance against industry standards	**Competitive edge** Provides insights into a company's relative position in the market **Action-oriented** Identifies clear areas for improvement and strategic advantage **Credibility booster** Demonstrates the consultancy's expertise and analytical capabilities	**Data-intensive** Requires significant data collection and analysis **Misinterpretation risk** Clients may need guidance to understand the data and its implications	Process improvement consultancy A offers comprehensive benchmarking services to help clients assess their performance against industry leaders, identifying opportunities for cost reduction, revenue growth, and strategic differentiation
High-level process audit A short strategy session, often 30 minutes long, to discuss the client's challenges and potential solutions may be on-site or remote	**Efficiency finder** Pinpoints inefficiencies in operations, leading to increased productivity **Quick wins** Often reveals immediate opportunities for improvement, generating tangible results **Trust Builder** Demonstrates the consultancy's ability to deliver value quickly and efficiently	**Surface level** It may not address underlying systemic issues that require deeper analysis **Follow-up needed** Often necessitates more in-depth audits to identify root causes and implement sustainable solutions	Global consulting group B provides high-level process audits to help clients identify bottlenecks and streamline their operations, leading to increased productivity, cost savings, and improved customer satisfaction
Free initial consultation A short strategy session to discuss the client's challenges and potential solutions, often 30 minutes. It may be on-site or remote	**Low commitment** Straightforward for potential clients to accept, reducing the barrier to entry **Relationship building** Establishes initial trust and rapport, laying the foundation for future collaborations **Lead generation** Attracts a wide range of prospects, expanding the consultancy's potential client base	**Time consuming** It can be resource intensive without guaranteed results **Low conversion rate** Not all consultations lead to paid engagements, requiring careful qualification and follow-up	International strategy consultancy C often offers potential clients free initial consultations, during which it assesses the client's needs and identifies opportunities for tailored solutions

(*Continued*)

Table 5.2 (Continued)

Low-Risk Consultancy Offers			
Type	**Advantages**	**Disadvantages**	**Example**
Pilot project A small-scale project to demonstrate capabilities, such as optimising a single department's workflow	**Proof of concept** Demonstrates the consultancy's capabilities in action, reducing risk for the client **Trust Builder** Allows clients to evaluate the consultancy's services on a smaller scale before committing to a larger project	**Resource intensive** Requires careful planning, execution, and monitoring **Limited scope** It may not fully showcase the consultancy's expertise or the solution's full potential	Tech consultancy D offers pilot projects for digital transformation initiatives, allowing clients to experience the benefits of new technologies before committing to a full-scale implementation
Workshops and webinars Content designed to provide value to potential clients	**Educational value** Provides valuable insights and showcases the consultancy's expertise **Lead generation** Attracts a broad audience and generates potential leads	**Resource intensive** Requires preparation, promotion, and facilitation **No immediate revenue** It may not lead to immediate sales but can build brand awareness and thought leadership	Finance and services organisation E regularly hosts free webinars on various business topics, attracting potential clients, and demonstrating its thought leadership in the industry
Money-back guarantee A simple refund offer if the client is unsatisfied with the service provided	**Risk reduction** Assures clients of satisfaction or a refund, building confidence, and trust. **Trust builder** Demonstrates the consultancy's confidence in its services and ability to deliver results	**Financial risk** Potential for refunds if clients are not satisfied, impacting profitability **Perceived desperation** It may be seen as a sign of uncertainty or lack of confidence in the services	Coaching guru F's coaching programmes often come with a money-back guarantee, offering clients a risk-free trial and demonstrating his commitment to delivering results
Discounting A fixed discount offer for the first project with a client or the first projects of a new service	**Attracts clients** Lower initial costs can entice clients to try the consultancy's services It may give a price advantage over competitors **Value showcase** Provides an opportunity to prove the consultancy's worth and build long-term relationships	**Revenue impact** Lower initial revenue from discounted projects **Perceived low value** Clients may expect lower prices in the future, potentially impacting future pricing strategies	Multidisciplinary consultancy G offers discounted rates for initial projects to new clients in emerging markets, building long-term relationships, and establishing a foothold in new geographic regions

A prominent USA strategic adviser known for innovative and bold approaches developed the ultimate approach to low-risk offers. He decided to implement a high-risk strategy to attract serious clients. His offer was a simple yet daring example of risk reversal: He would agree to meet with a client for an hour if the client placed a cheque for $10,000 on the table at the start of the meeting. The deal was that if the client felt they had not received adequate value from the discussion by the end of the session, they could pick up the cheque and walk away with no questions asked.
This strategy worked on many levels:

1. ***Low-risk offer**: If a client was unsatisfied, the only cost was their time.*
2. ***Demonstrated confidence**: It showcased the adviser's belief in his expertise and the value he could provide, which built confidence in potential clients.*
3. ***Filtered serious clients**: Only those genuinely serious about their business and willing to invest in high-quality advice would agree to such terms.*
4. ***Created a sense of urgency**: Clients were more focused and engaged during the meeting because they had only an hour to get their money's worth.*

This approach was a testament to the adviser's confidence in his ability to deliver substantial value in a short amount of time and was remarkably effective. Clients were often impressed by the adviser's insights and felt that the value they received was well worth the $10,000. Only rarely did the client pick up the cheque and leave.

The lesson is that calculated risks and demonstrating confidence in our abilities can lead to successful outcomes, even in high-stakes situations. It also underscores the importance of believing in our added value and being willing to stand by it.

through exceptional work with one client, a major USA hospital network. This work led to a referral to other prominent healthcare providers, resulting in significant new engagements, which further enhanced the firm's reputation. Another significant consulting firm is well known for building enduring client relationships. This is based on first understanding each client's unique challenges and then designing individualised solutions for them. After a successful engagement for a retail chain which followed this model, the company generated referrals to retailers in other areas facing similar challenges. The result was a significantly expanded client base and revenue growth. These examples illustrate the power of client relationships and referrals in driving new sales. However, they were not chance events; effort and planning are required to create a client satisfaction culture that leads to increased opportunities and long-term business success. We need to implement a carefully designed customer relationship strategy to successfully transform our clients into our advocates. A vital element of such a strategy is recognising that everyone within our company is a component of our relationship with our customers. Consequently, we need to ensure the broadest involvement of our consultants and support staff in a range of customer relationship activities, including the following:

- **Proactive client management**: Too often, consultancies leave the client relationship management to the engagement manager. This confuses completing the current contract and maintaining a relationship to win new contracts. Appointing a relationship manager for the client overcomes this confusion. It enables us to develop our relationships with the broader client management team rather than just the sponsor of the current work.

- **Active listening**: We pay close attention to clients' needs and concerns, which shows genuine interest in their challenges and goals. Our staff and team members, including contractors, may obtain information in formal meetings or informal "water cooler" moments, phone calls, or emails. We must ensure that the data they receive are fed to the client relationship manager to support our ongoing relationship.
- **Transparent communication**: Our consultants and support staff communicate with client staff and managers at all levels. Being open, honest, and upfront about expectations, timelines, deliverables, and current engagements builds trust and a long-term relationship. However, we also need to create formal communication channels within our contract terms and conditions to agree on how to resolve issues that may have a contractual impact. There can be tension between informal and formal communication channels. For example, in a close working collaboration between our staff and the client staff, a consultant individually agreeing to be helpful and take on a task outside the scope of work could incur irrecoverable costs and delay contracted deliverables. However, a formal communication of such a change request would have ensured that impacts could be fully assessed and a contract variation obtained.
- **Proactive problem-solving**: Anticipating potential risks and offering solutions before they become active issues for the client, even where they are outside the scope of our current work, demonstrates our commitment and reliability and may lead to engagement extensions.
- **Continuous improvement**: Seeking feedback from our clients and using it to refine our services and delivery methods shows them that their opinions are valued and helps improve service quality for themselves and other clients.
- **Personalised service**: Tailoring our approach to clients' unique needs and preferences enhances their satisfaction and loyalty.
- **Tracking contacts in addition to clients**: Our points of contact within client organisations are individuals. As they progress in their careers, this year's project facilitator might become next year's business sponsor and eventually a board director; they also often move on to new companies. We can expand our network and increase our opportunities by tracking these career moves and maintaining engagement with the original contact in their new role, who is now a warm contact in a new potential client, and with their successor in our client. There are two ways to do this: the original way of asking, "Where have they gone?" when we are told they have moved on, or the more effective way of posting "Congratulations on your new role" when a contact uses social media to announce a move. Don't forget to research their new email address and update your CRM system.
- **Seeking referrals**: If we consistently deliver exceptional value, we can respectfully request referrals from existing contacts when appropriate. This approach generates "warm" new leads, strengthens existing client relationships, and fosters long-term business growth. Do not, however, expect referrals between clients who are arch-competitors.

Time for a short virtual site visit

Do you remember our independent consultant, Jack, from Chapter 1?

Jack has been successfully independent for a few years now. Before then, he had worked for a couple of large consultancies, the first of which was in the healthcare team. He hasn't done much marketing except network with his old managers, who now all run small specialist consultancies. He is about to discover the power of client relationships – even when you haven't been attending to them.

This time, we are going to listen to a call.

It was a dark and stormy night (no, it really was). Jack was driving to his hotel to be available for a client meeting early the following day. An accident had closed the motorway, and now he was crossing a desolate moor in the storm. His hands-free phone chirps, so he pulls into a parking area. He doesn't recognise the number but takes the call anyway.

"Good evening, this is Jack. Can I help you?"

"Jack, tracking you down has taken me a little while. My name is Marianne. Do you remember me?"

In his head, Jack sees an old-fashioned card index of contacts. He mentally ripples through the cards. There is only one Marianne, but that was from at least seven years ago when Jack was still working for a large consultancy.

"Blank Hospital?" he asks.

"That's right. Well, not anymore."

Jack had worked for Blank Hospital's Chief Financial Officer, modelling the impact of nursing service changes. Marianne had been a finance team leader and his principal contact. He knew she and the Chief Financial Officer had moved on because two years later, he won another assignment for Blank Hospital, leading the procurement of a patient administration system.

"You know that the Chief Executive left to form a new body responsible for a network of specialist hospitals. He took Freda, the Chief Financial Officer, with him, and Freda recruited me. The point is, Jack, that we have a capital spending plan, and Freda and the Chief Executive asked me to find you to help us model its implications."

"Of course, I'd love to help. Do we need a call with Freda?"

Perhaps, Jack should move his mental card index into a Customer Relationship Management database and proactively manage his contacts. At least they could find him more quickly, and perhaps he could move on from subcontracting to doing more profitable work directly for clients.

Step 6: Partnering with complementary businesses

In Chapter 4, we considered different collaboration models with other organisations in delivering engagements. We can also collaborate more widely with organisations that provide services or products that complement our services. This collaboration can create mutually beneficial relationships that increase both companies' revenue, market share, and client satisfaction. One of the primary advantages of partnering with complementary businesses is the ability to cross-sell and upsell our services. Combining our strengths with our partners can provide our clients with more comprehensive and practical solutions. For instance, a consulting firm focusing on strategic planning could partner with a technology consultancy to offer end-to-end solutions that address strategic and operational needs and technology implementation support.

Partnering with complementary businesses in other geographic areas can help us expand our reach and enter new markets. Working with our partner's customer base and distribution channels lets us reach new clients and increase our visibility. An example could be a consulting firm based in the UK specialising in transportation policy, which could partner with one based in the United States with a significant interest in automated fare systems design and implementation. Each firm could serve clients in both markets and draw on the expertise of the other to provide end-to-end services. Partnering is not easy, and when considering a partnership, we need to evaluate our possible partners carefully to ensure their degree of fit with our business, including their reputation, financial stability, and alignment with our values and culture.

Examples of potential partnering based on complementary services could include the following scenarios:

- Consulting firm A partners with software integration company B to offer comprehensive digital transformation solutions. They are able to combine firm A's strategic consulting and implementation support with company B's software customisation and training. This partnership allows them to provide comprehensive solutions to their clients, increasing both firms' value proposition and market share.
- Consulting firm C partners with a public relations agency, D. They successfully collaborate and are able to provide their clients with an integrated service that combines strategic marketing advice from firm C with the delivery of effective public relations campaigns by agency D. This partnership offers a better solution for their clients. It allows both companies to increase their number of warm contacts and generate more high-quality sales leads.
- Consulting firm E specialises in human resources issues and partners with training and development firm F. Their joint offer to clients is centred on leadership development programmes that combine strategic consulting and succession planning from firm E with practical training from firm F. This provides clients with an integrated solution which is more attractive than separate services, allowing both firms to increase sales.

However, partnering can have challenges, and from the outset, to reduce the potential for conflicts, we must understand each other's goals, objectives, and values. We also need to consider how far and if we need to integrate our organisational cultures and operations. For example, one potential problem area is overlapping service. Tension that undermines our partnership can arise when each partner feels they should compete for the same opportunity. Another essential task is conducting a due diligence review that covers our potential partner's reputation, services, and financial stability. If we have any doubts at this stage, we should aim to "fail safe" and halt the process to protect our reputation.

Often time is pressing, especially where the partnership is required to take advantage of a particular opportunity. However, we need to take time to design, negotiate, and agree on a clear and explicit partnership agreement. This must outline the scope of the partnership, our respective roles and responsibilities, our profit-sharing arrangements, and, most importantly, dispute resolution processes. It is also essential to promptly address any issues or concerns that arise between the partners. Consequently, our agreement should also establish effective communication channels that will ensure all partners communicate with each other openly and honestly.

Another aspect of a successful collaboration is regular performance monitoring. To ensure equitable outcomes, we need to agree on how and when to evaluate the benefits and challenges of parentship. As our experience operating the partnership evolves, we will need to adapt our joint work and make adjustments to our partnership contractual arrangements.

Step 7: Monitoring and adjustment

Monitoring and adjusting our actions during the implementation stage are critical to ensuring that we are optimising our efforts, maximising our return on investment, and achieving successful outcomes. This is achieved through the following.

Key performance indicators

To monitor our marketing strategy effectively, we need to establish clear KPIs that align with our overall business objectives for each of the tasks and activities in the strategy. These KPIs can vary depending on our service's specific goals, but some common examples include the following:

- **Website traffic**: Tracking the number of visitors to our website and their behaviour can help us evaluate how effective our online marketing is and make adjustments to the website as necessary to improve client experience. We should also track downloads of different marketing materials, for example, white papers, from the website.
- **Lead generation**: Monitoring the number of leads generated through each of our marketing activities provides essential insight into their effectiveness.
- **Conversion rates**: Tracking the conversion rates at every step of our sales pyramid, from interest and leads to contracted clients, can help us measure the efficiency of our sales process.
- **Return on investment (ROI)**: Calculating the ROI for our marketing activities will help us determine if our efforts have generated a positive return. We can also break this down to consider the costs and effectiveness of different elements of our strategy. We need to consider the period over which any return is calculated, as we are essentially engaged in long-term relationship building rather than short-term sales.

Data collection and analysis

To gather the necessary data to monitor our KPIs, we can use a variety of tools and techniques, such as follows:

- **Website analytics**: Tools such as Google Analytics will provide detailed insights into website traffic, user behaviour, and conversion rates.
- **Customer relationship management (CRM) software**: CRM packages, while useful at an operational level, should also provide us with comprehensive reporting functions that facilitate our analysis of leads, opportunities, and customer interactions. In some cases, additional reporting software may be required if we wish to integrate data from different systems for reporting.
- **Social media analytics**: In the same way that a raft of tools are available for analysing website traffic, other tools are available for collecting and analysing social media performance. These tools can provide insights into our social media engagement and reach.
- **Surveys and feedback forms**: We should use these regularly to collect prospect feedback data and identify areas for improvement in our marketing approach and materials.

Once we have collected the necessary data from all sources, we need to integrate and analyse it to identify trends, patterns, and areas for improvement. Data visualisation and statistical analysis tools are extremely helpful and can automate much of the analysis and presentation process. Some tools allow for creating dashboards that provide one-page overviews of key data and trends, which can significantly assist in decision-making.

Regular review and adjustment

Hopefully, once we have gathered our data and reported using our performance dashboard, we need to review our KPIs and consider if we need to adjust our strategies to maximise our impact. How frequently we hold such reviews depends on the length of the marketing campaign, but a weekly check-up is a good starting point. In each review, we should consider the following:

- **Is our target audience still the right fit?** Despite our careful planning, we may find that our target audience isn't positively engaging with our messaging, and we need to adjust our targeting strategy. Retargeting could mean that we identify other parts of our market, perhaps by widening a geographic area or refocusing on those parts of our target audience, showing a higher response rate. Also, we should always ask the following question:

  Are we reaching the right people within organisations?

  Depending on the answer, we should consider adjusting our ideal customer profile to include different organisational roles, such as switching from the operations director to the chief executive.

- **Is our message resonating?** If it isn't, we must rethink how we communicate the value of engaging with us. This may mean revisiting our value proposition and considering whether we need to tailor our messaging more precisely to the prospect's pain points we identified in our research. We should also consider using language that the prospect finds more persuasive. Remember, "It's not about **US**. It's about **YOU**." So, ask the following supplementary questions:

  Have we put the client front and centre in our messaging?
  Have we emphasised the benefits the client should expect sufficiently?
  Have we written our messages in a way that reflects our ideal customer's use of language?

- **Are our resources targeted to the best effect?** If certain activities or channels are not giving us the results that we expected or are performing less well than others, we should consider allocating our time and effort elsewhere. For example, if a paid advertising campaign is underperforming, we might reallocate our resources to other activities, such as attending conferences or outreach to warm prospects and current clients. We should always ask ourselves the following questions:

  Are the results from each marketing activity justifying our investment in time and resources?
  Are other activities yielding better results?

  When considering our answers, we should remember that some channels may be slower to yield results than others.

- **Are our marketing experiments yielding results?** Over time, we should explore new channels, test different messaging approaches, and experiment with content formats. Our twin objectives from such experimentation are to increase our success rate at each level of the sales pyramid and manage our costs. We should treat each of our revised marketing tactics as a pilot and carefully analyse its results and costs before fully adopting it.

Other factors to consider

As we implement our strategy, several other key factors will make adjusting our approach necessary. First, change. We must keep ourselves fully informed about the emerging trends and developments in the industries and sectors we are targeting. By keeping ourselves well informed, we will be able to respond quickly to change. This means that our service offer will remain relevant to our clients and competitive in the market place. Similarly, maintaining a close watch on our competitors' marketing efforts is also essential. By understanding their strategies, we can gain valuable insights into their thinking and identify ways to maintain our differentiation in the marketplace.

Our short-term decisions or tactical adjustments to our marketing strategy must be evaluated to ensure they do not conflict with our firm's overall policies and goals. We saw this in action with Jay's original proposal for marketing an IT security service, where the senior partner emphasised the firm's policy of allocating each prospect to a single partner for all services being promoted.

Step 8: Marketing, sales, and business expansion

Business growth will undoubtedly stretch our marketing and sales resources. Adjusting our marketing strategy and tactics as we seek to move new prospects up our sales pyramid while nurturing our existing clients' targets may be necessary.

Prioritisation

Even within a larger consultancy, allocating our time is one of the primary challenges we face as our business grows. With a growing number of client engagements and staff demanding our time, it is difficult to dedicate sufficient resources to marketing and business development. We may be stretched thin personally, juggling client meetings, engagement deliverables, staff management, and marketing initiatives. To address this challenge, we must prioritise and delegate effectively. By identifying the critical marketing activities and reassigning them to team members with the appropriate skills, we can free up our time for other essential tasks. For example, we might delegate social media management to a junior team member and focus our activities on client meetings and building partnerships.

Consistency

Maintaining a consistent brand message and identity as our business expands can be difficult. Growing means that we will hire additional team members who lack a detailed appreciation of our brand and perhaps deliver new services, which may dilute our brand. We can avoid this by maintaining a strong brand strategy and ensuring all our marketing efforts align with our core values and messaging. This will involve documenting our brand style requirements, developing a consistent tone of voice in all communications and regularly updating our website, training, and marketing materials. It is essential to ensure that we allocate sufficient time to onboarding new marketing team members or outsourced providers to ensure that they align with our culture and values.

External pressures

Growth means we may face increased competition from other consultancies as they respond to our marketplace challenges and changes in our chosen industry sectors. During a period of growth, it is even more imperative that we continuously monitor industry trends and adapt our marketing strategy accordingly. This might involve investing in new marketing technologies, exploring new channels, or refining our messaging. To do otherwise may result in our growth stalling. As we scale our business, we must always focus on our clients and maintain high levels of their satisfaction. Our existing clients will remain our greatest advocates, and their referrals will be a valuable source of new business. To grow sustainably, we must continue to meet their needs and exceed their expectations to reinforce those strong relationships that will deliver repeat business and expand our client base.

Reflections

As before, please draw on your personal experience and your current situation or use the theoretical case study.

- Prepare an analysis of why different categories of clients might be motivated to buy the consultancy service you propose. Please pay particular attention to the pain points that might cause them to close a deal with you.
- Draft a profile of your ideal client, including their type of organisation and role.
- How would you explain the main points of your key value proposition:
  - To a client in a brief conversation. This is your 90-second explanation (often called an elevator pitch – but who talks in elevators?)
  - To your internal decision-makers who need to understand your proposals in more depth before approving your proposition.
- How would you brief an external agency on your desire to develop an integrated set of promotional materials, including website content?
- What outbound marketing activities do you propose, and what timeline would you follow to deliver them?
- Can you identify potential complementary businesses to help expand your marketing reach, and how would you introduce the concept of partnering with them?
- What key performance indicators would you use to monitor the effectiveness of your marketing efforts?

Further reading

Marketing Management: A Strategic Perspective (2016) by Philip Kotler, Kevin Keller, and Michael Brady
Building a Story Brand: Clarify Your Message So Customers Will Listen (2017) Donald Miller
Selling Services The ABC of Professional Selling (2024) Clifton Warren

Note

1 Pulping expensive printed material because of unseen errors is a costly business. Naming no names, but on one notable occasion, after approving the proofs for four high-quality, full colour, and costly brochures, I went on holiday. The responsible director and the group marketing director added a short sentence to my carefully vetted and rechecked text. When I returned after two weeks, the 500 copies of each brochure had been beautifully printed. However, when I spotted the glaring spelling mistake they had introduced, I had to order the 2,000 brochures to be pulped. In order to meet a conference and exhibition deadline, all four brochures then had to be reprinted at very expensive express print rates, and my marketing budget took a substantial hit.

Bibliography

Emerson, R. W. (1912). *Journals of Ralph Waldo Emerson 1820–1872*, Vol. 8. Boston and New York: Houghton Mifflin Company.

6 Sales

How Will We Turn Our Market into Our Clients?

Aim of this chapter: To explain why mastery of the sales process is the major contributor to the success of a consultancy operation and to explain the necessary steps in identifying valid prospects and converting them into profitable clients.

Learning outcomes: To understand what motivates individual clients to buy our services and to be able to define and operate the processes which deliver an effective mechanism for each of the consultancy's services. To understand different sales approaches and how they may suit different client circumstances.

We are at a stage where we have designed our service and told the whole of our potential market about it by delivering our highly effective marketing strategy. Clients are about to flock to us, eager to pay premium rates. So, in Ralph Waldo Emerson's term, we wait for them to create that "*broad hard-beaten road*" to our door.

A few prospects may journey to our door, but usually, we have to seek out opportunities and work to convert our prospects into our clients, that is, to close the deal. This work is needed regularly to provide a sound pipeline of work and keep our teams profitably occupied. Maintaining this pipeline requires creating a repeatable sales process that consistently delivers profitable engagements. Figure 6.1 sets out the general steps in such a sales process.

Step 1: Prospecting for clients

During our outbound marketing activities (see Chapter 5), our focus is not on selling services but on building trusted relationships. We have recognised the imperative of spending time and resources creating our trusted relationships with clients, which will deliver more future opportunities. However, we must also acknowledge that it is imperative to close new business deals and recognise that our cliff edge is approaching every day.

Consider the following question from a senior consultancy partner to one of his managing consultants:

Each morning, how do you decide which direction you will point your car?

The partner's real question was not about compass points but about prioritising sales prospecting work to generate quality opportunities in the shorter term. Outreach marketing and previous research should have developed a process already generating warm leads for the managing consultant to follow up on and relationships to nurture.

DOI: 10.4324/9781003490456-7

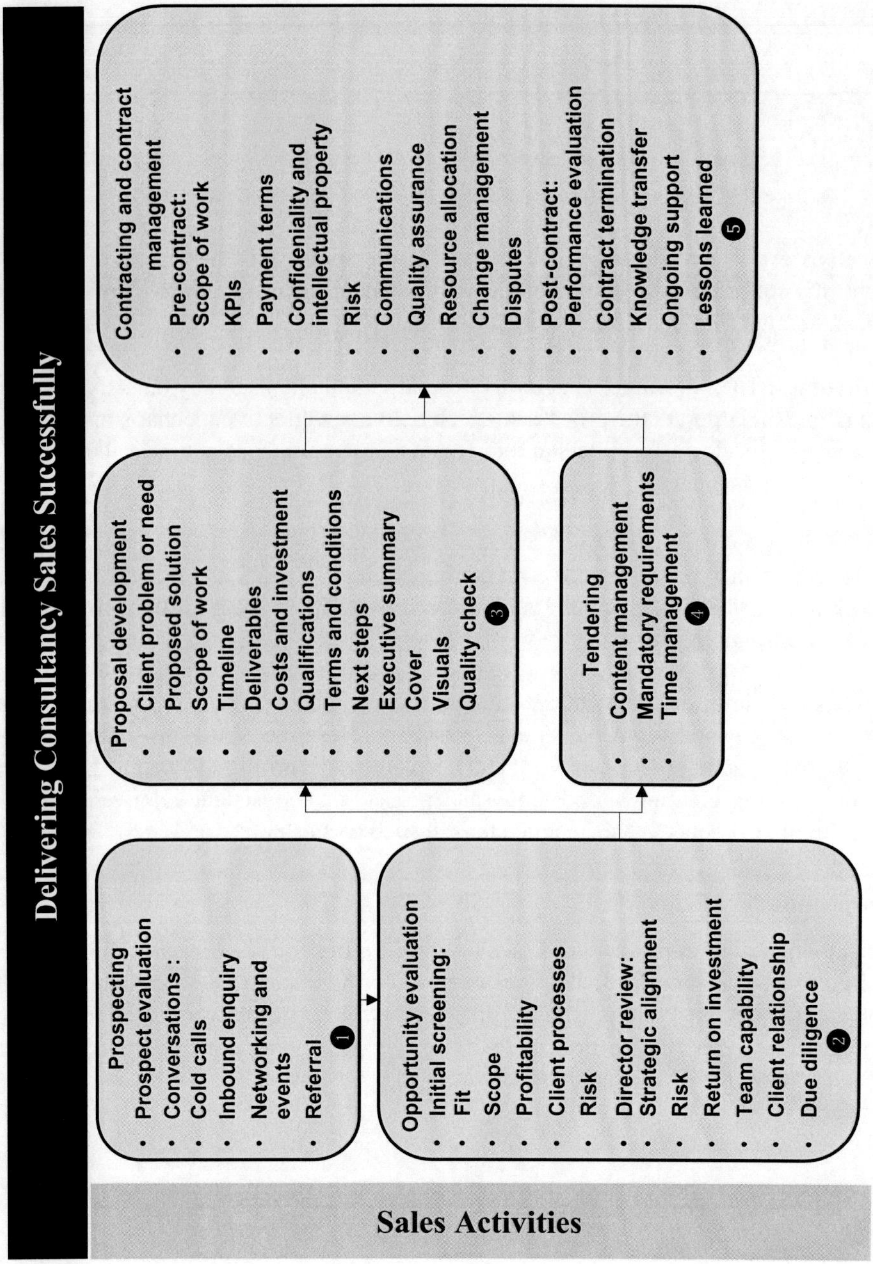

Figure 6.1 Delivering Consultancy Sales Successfully.

Sales prospecting is challenging for many transitioning to independent consultancy or consultancy leadership roles because it requires a skill foreign to most people:

Talking to strangers.

To make it harder for those new to prospecting, this "talking to strangers" skill is better described as

Talking to strangers about what we are good at, why we can best meet their needs, and why everyone else is inferior. Observing and actively listening to their responses and modifying our message to reflect their needs and priorities.

Let's take a short site visit to look at prospecting in action.

We are going to snoop on a call being placed by a marketeer from an IT consultancy called ITX. El is following up on an industry conference, contacting targeted attendees who weren't logged as having been met by the company's team.

El is very, very good at getting positive results. First, though, El has to get through a gatekeeper.

"Hi there, I'm El from ITX. I'm following up on Ms. Exxe's attendance at our IT security session at the conference and my follow-up letter to her. I know she's busy, and I'd like to see if she might have a few minutes to discuss a potential solution that could benefit her team. . . . Perhaps just a quick word now, and if necessary, she can schedule a call at a better time."

After a hurried conversation on mute at the other end.

"Good morning, El, I am Ms. Exxe. Your session was beneficial, but I am not sure that I saw your letter. Can you tell me what this is about?"

"My letter said that we were particularly sorry to have missed having a conversation with you at the conference, as I understand from a press release that your company is currently implementing AI-based solutions across the business. I am glad you found the session on AI and data security helpful. After last week's conference session, we had insightful one-on-one discussions with other industry leaders, and I believe our solutions could benefit your company and your current AI implementation. Based on our discussions, we'd be happy to share an updated briefing on the AI challenges that the industry is facing and explore where our AI security assessment services could help you ensure a smooth transition. Would you be available for a 15-minute call with one of our industry experts in the next few days?"

"El, it was an interesting session; the Q and A at the end were thought-provoking. Yes, I think a chat might be helpful. When did you have it in mind?"

What do you think were the objectives of the call, and did El achieve them?

Please take a moment to deconstruct this example and list ITX's steps to enable this call.

You should see that ITX has developed a tactical prospecting plan and has:

1. *Sponsored a targeted session at a conference building visibility.*
2. *Held one-on-one discussions with some, but not all, attendees.*
3. *Sent a follow-up letter to everyone, including a personalised version to those like Ms Exxe that they failed to contact at the conference.*
4. *Reached out by phone as a follow-up to the letter to create an opportunity for a discussion.*
5. *Set up a plan for resourcing a series of short information meetings as the next step.*

El was highly experienced at "Talking to strangers" and worked on a carefully designed process with built-in loops to handle potential objections and bring the conversation to a successful conclusion. Like all skills, "talking to strangers" requires practice to engage the prospect, allow them to set out their issues and desires, and then weave this into our narrative about how using our service will help them to succeed.

It's time to take on your role in the consultancy company again.

Having mainly worked internally, you have not had any experience of "Talking to strangers about what we are good at, why we can best meet their needs, and why everyone else is inferior," so you call on Zeph for some advice.

Zeph has asked if you could meet in a local café.

Zeph arrives accompanied by Bobbie, who has recently completed the consultancy's sales coaching programme.

You: "Zeph, thanks for offering to help again. I don't mind admitting that I am really queasy about walking up to strangers and starting conversations. But why are we here?"

Zeph: "I thought we might try something different today. By the way, my price is that you pay for the coffee and the doughnuts. Actually, scrub the doughnuts, as getting covered in sugar or icing can undermine our professional credibility. Bobbie is here to help me, and the two of you are going to do a role-play. I thought being here would add realism as well as decent coffee because the setting for the role play is a café at an exhibition centre."

Zeph: "Bobbie, you are playing the prospect, the operations director of a small tech startup. Please sit there at the next table. First, icebreakers and introductions. Remember how Great Britain's late Queen Elizabeth was known for her famous icebreakers? 'What do you do?' and 'Have you travelled far?' You could also say something that draws attention to something you have noticed about the person that's interesting or unique, but that can have difficulties. For now, it is best to keep it simple and stick to the Queen Elizabeth technique."

You: "That's a great way to start a conversation, but how does that work?"

Zeph addresses Bobbie: "Excuse me, would you mind if I joined you? I noticed we're both attending the [exhibition name]. It seems to have pulled in people from all over. Have you travelled far today?"

Bobbie: "Not at all; please join me. Yes, I came over from Manchester. We're a small tech startup trying to make a splash in the light engineering market."

Zeph: "OK, now you must do something I imagine that Queen Elizabeth never had to: introduce yourself. You need to add where you are from and what we do."

You: "I'm [Insert your name here] from PNX. We work with leading-edge companies to help improve their performance over a wide range of areas."

Zeph: "That was spot on, and I liked sneaking in client benefits. Now, move on to your elevator pitch. It's about the value you bring to the client. And remember, people recall best what you say first and what you say last. So, ensure these parts of your conversation contain key messages."

You: "Our consultants have a track record of helping clients to optimise their operations and achieve enviable growth rates. They get customised support to help them get a long-term competitive edge. We do this by harnessing the expertise and insights we have gained by working for the world's leading-edge finance companies."

Bobbie: "That sounds interesting, but I'm unsure if we need any new services right now. Our current advisers seem to be doing a good job."

Zeph: "Great objection. Now, how would you handle that?"

You: "Many of our clients initially felt the same way, but they found that our data-driven approach helped them reduce costs by an average of 15% and increase revenue by 20% within six months. Could we discuss how we might be able to achieve similar results for you?"

Zeph: "Excellent. Numbers – a good way to address the objection. Now, practice asking for a meeting and addressing objections. Remember to reiterate your key message at the end."

You: "Since we're both here at [exhibition name], dedicated to improving performance, this is something that you are interested in. Would you be available to meet next week to discuss your specific goals and how we can help you achieve them? Our data-driven approach has helped many businesses reduce costs and increase revenue, so I'm confident we can do the same for you."

Bobbie: "I'm quite busy next week. Maybe some other time."

Zeph: "Another good objection. How would you respond?"

You: "I understand. How about we schedule a quick 15-minute call instead to see if there's a fit between us? It can be as brief as a coffee break. Remember, our goal is to help you achieve your business objectives."

Zeph: "Excellent. Now, add one more question. When the contact has agreed, ask if they can think of anyone else who might benefit from our services. This is a great way to expand your network."

You: "That's a great idea. Perhaps I could ask, 'Do you know of any other businesses in your industry that might be facing issues similar to yours?' I'd love to share how we've helped other companies achieve major cost reductions and revenue growth."

Bobbie: "Actually, I do know a couple of people who might be interested. They're also attending this exhibition and might be looking for similar services."

Zeph: "Excellent. Make sure to get their contact details."

You: "Could you please share their contact details with me? Also, may I have your contact information? Do you have a card?"

Bobbie: "Sure, I can give you their details. Here's my card."

Zeph: "Perfect. The more people you talk to, the more opportunities you'll have."

You: "Thank you for the guidance, and thank you, Bobbie. I feel more confident about prospecting now."

Zeph: "That's great to hear. Keep practising, and you'll be a pro in no time!"

Zeph has woven many elements into this one conversation. Before moving on, it is worth analysing it and noting your findings.

We need to develop reusable elements to incorporate into our conversations with sales prospects. As before, we are building on our previous work for the information but using it for a new purpose: moving our prospects towards a sale or filtering them out entirely.

Remember that any conversation is a two-way exchange of information. Throughout it, we must actively listen, analyse what our prospect is saying, acknowledge it, and use it to steer the conversation's flow and content to keep a prospect engaged and receptive to us.

There are at least six key building blocks of conversations with prospects that we need to master and be able to use in the correct circumstances:

- **Pain points**: Understanding the prospect's specific challenges, problems, and pain points is a precondition to building a successful relationship. We need to use active listening techniques and ask open and probing questions to uncover the root causes of their issues. Consider the following example of a sequence which runs: Ask an open question, actively listen to the answer, and ask a second probing question:
    - *Q, Are there any areas causing you concern at the moment?*
    - *A, There's been a significant drop in productivity last quarter, and we're unsure why.*
    - *Q, Is this across the board, or have you noticed productivity changes in specific teams or departments?*
- **Goals**: We often need to probe further to understand the client's true objectives, and these may not be immediately apparent and are frequently vague. If, however, we can flesh out a picture of what the client is trying to achieve, we can move on to the next step in the conversation. Unfortunately, while we may have established a set of SMART goals, that may not be the case with our client. Still, we can try probing as in the following example:
    - *Q, What are your immediate strategic goals for performance improvement?*
    - *A, Our goal is to streamline operations, reducing costs by 15% by next year.*
- **Value proposition**: To communicate the benefits of our services effectively, we must first have a firm and fluent grasp of our value proposition and be able to adapt our presentation to align with the client's specific pain points and goals. Our goal is always to demonstrate that our services will resolve their issues.
    - *Example: We specialise in helping you reduce operational costs and improve productivity by optimising business processes.*
- **Expertise**: Building credibility with prospects requires demonstrating our knowledge and experience in their industry or domain. We can use credentials, certifications, and stories of past successes and share insights from industry trends and best practices.
    - *Example 1: Our team includes certified Six Sigma Black Belts with over 20 years of experience who have successfully helped numerous similar companies in your industry achieve their operational goals.*
    - *Example 2: We have been very fortunate to have engaged Professor Chen, the leading academic expert globally in this area, to guide our practice and mentor our consultancy team.*
- **Case studies**: Sharing success stories from clients provides concrete evidence of our capabilities. Case studies should include details about the client's initial situation, challenges, solutions implemented, and results achieved. Numbers are always a strong feature of any case study.
    - *Example: We recently helped a major insurance company reduce their £11m telephone costs by 30%, increased quality, and reduced time for moves and changes from one week to one day.*

- **Next steps**: Outlining the process for moving forward, such as a follow-up meeting or a more in-depth assessment, maintains momentum and ensures that both parties are aligned on the process.
  - *Example 1: Let's schedule a follow-up meeting next week to discuss a tailored engagement plan to help you on this.*
  - *Example 2: After an initial consultation, we could prepare an overview of how your current processes match up against industry standards. That's a pretty small piece of work. After that, we can discuss creating a customised engagement, hitting those areas with the most scope for improvement. I will send you a proposal for the overview by Monday. (Note: This is an example of the assumed close technique, although not for a sale in this case.)*

When we have a clear grasp on and fluency in using each of these elements, we can start building them into common conversation scenarios, as in the following examples:

Cold call

Often, it is a telephone call, but it could also be used for an impromptu meeting.

- **Pain point**: It is essential to identify our prospects' pain points as early as possible during a cold call to keep them engaged.
  - *Example: Many companies in your industry struggle with challenges with [specific issue]. Is this something you're experiencing as well?*
- **Value proposition**: Our value proposition statement should be concise and highlight key benefits that address the prospect's pain points.
  - *Example: Many companies in your sector have benefitted from working with our highly experienced team to resolve [specific prospect pain point, or points]. Theirs is an enviable track record of success in developing tailored solutions for clients that help have delivered [specific benefit or benefits].*
- **Next steps**: To demonstrate your commitment and keep the conversation moving, propose a specific time for the follow-up.
  - *Example: Would you be available for a follow-up call next Tuesday to explore this further?*

Inbound enquiry

This will usually be an unscheduled telephone call and requires us to be ready to pick up and apply our conversation framework immediately.

- **Pain point**: When handling an inbound inquiry, the client has already shown interest, so focus on clarifying the specific issue or problem the client is facing. Ask detailed questions to clarify their pain points.
  - *Example 1: What specific issues are you encountering with your current supply chain processes?*
  - *Example 2: Are there particular areas where you see delays or increased costs?*
  - *Example 3: Can you tell me more about the specific challenges you're experiencing with your IT operations?*
- **Expertise**: We should always highlight our expertise by discussing similar projects we have handled and sharing relevant case studies, provided that we can do so without breaching

client confidentiality. The unbreakable rule should be that we should only ever name previous clients who have agreed to be identified.

- *Example 1: We have extensive experience in supply chain optimisation and have delivered successful engagements for several Fortune 500 companies.*
- *Example 2: Our team has successfully implemented supply chain optimisation strategies for leading companies, resulting in significant cost reductions and improved efficiency. I know that [name of industry figure] is happy for us to tell you that [company] is one of our satisfied clients.*

- **Case studies**: Provide specific examples demonstrating success in addressing similar challenges.
  - *Example 1: We recently worked with a global electronics company streamlining their supply chain. We reduced average lead times by 20% and cut international transport costs by 15%.*
  - *Example 2: On my last assignment, we helped a major insurer slash their telecommunications costs by over one-third and reduce their response rate to requests for moves and changes from four days to one.*
- **Next steps**: Suggest a discovery call to understand the client's needs further and tailor your proposed actions accordingly.
  - *Example 1: I'd like to arrange a discovery call to learn more about your specific challenges and discuss how our solutions can help you achieve your goals.*
  - *Example 2: Let's schedule a discovery call to discuss your needs in more detail and see where our team could help.*

Networking event

This is often a prearranged, specific opportunity to meet potential clients. Still, it may also be applied in less structured situations, like visiting an exhibition, as in our last site visit.

- **Pain points**: Conversations at networking events are often more casual. Focus on discussing industry trends and everyday challenges.
  - *Example 1: I've noticed that many companies face difficulties with digital transformation. How is your company handling this transition?*
  - *Example 2: Many companies in our industry are struggling with digital transformation. Is this something you're dealing with as well?*
- **Value proposition**: We should provide a general overview of how our services address common industry challenges. This can help drive the discussion forward. Adapting our message to show how this meets the prospect's perception of the issues affecting their company is essential
  - *Example 1: Our consultancy offers comprehensive digital transformation services, from strategy development to implementation, helping companies navigate this complex process successfully.*
  - *Example 2: From your comment, I understand your company is about to start an AI-led digital transformation. One of the areas that we specialise in is guiding companies in your position through the transformation to ensure that you have a smooth and effective transition.*
- **Next steps**: Exchange contact information and follow up with a personalised email that references your conversation and suggests a more formal meeting.
  - *Example 1: It was great meeting you at the networking event. I'd love to discuss how our digital transformation services can benefit your company. Are you available for a call next week?*
  - *Example 2: Here's my card. I will call you next week, and we can discuss further how we could help your company deliver a smooth and successful digital transformation.*

Referral

Referrals lend us the reputation of the referrer and, so, have some built-in trust that we need to respect. However, they decay over time, so we must be prepared to follow them up quickly and effectively.

- **Pain points**: Use the referral's insights about the prospect to tailor the conversation to their needs.
  - *Example 1: I was talking to [Referrer's Name], and they suggested you are looking to improve levels of customer satisfaction. Can you tell me more about what you want to achieve?*
  - *Example 2: [Referrer's Name] suggested that I give you a call. Is it right that you wish to improve your customer satisfaction scores?*
- **Value proposition**: Customise our value proposition to address the client's known challenges.
  - *Example 1: Our customer systems improvement team has an enviable track record of supporting organisations to find the right CRM systems that meet their needs without breaking the bank.*
  - *Example 2: Our dedicated customer experience improvement team measures your operational performance and identifies multiple areas of easy marginal improvement which build into higher customer satisfaction scores.*
- **Case studies**: Provide relevant case studies demonstrating our success in addressing similar challenges.
  - *Example 1: We worked with a telecommunications company to revamp their customer service processes, resulting in their improvement of customer satisfaction scores of 30% over six months.*
  - *Example 2: We recently helped a client in the same industry increase customer satisfaction scores.*

> *One consultancy partner had a novel and highly confident approach when prospecting. They would close the first part of an initial conversation with a prospect as follows:*
>
> *"Our team is undoubtedly the most experienced and successful in the industry in delivering client benefits. However, I understand that you may want to explore other options. Feel free to reach out to our competitors, and you may even be able to pay them a little less. I am okay with that, but I am confident that, as others have, you will find their services lacking in comparison. However, I assure you that we will still come and help rescue you from the mess that will inevitably follow.*
>
> *But let me set out the main benefits that we would seek to deliver for you."*

Step 2: Opportunity evaluation

Not all opportunities are created equal, and we must assess each one and prioritise the effort we are prepared to invest in it. We may decide not to pursue some opportunities for any one of a variety of reasons.

Before looking at a simple process and the factors that we might want to consider in deciding whether to invest time and resources in pursuing opportunities, there are two key and very useful guidelines:

- Work hard to work with people you like (and like you).
- If making the sale is too hard, then delivering the engagement probably will be as well. Usually, it's best to walk away.

It's time to drop in on our independent consultant, Jack, again, this time much earlier in his career. He had just started as a junior consultant in a regional office of the UK consulting arm of one of the world's most significant accounting partnerships. Opportunity-seeking antennae were in full operation when, during a family dinner to celebrate the new job, Jack's sister said,

"At a meeting yesterday, our MD, who founded the company, dropped a bombshell: retirement and the sale of their majority shareholding to the XYZ conglomerate. The MD will support the transition, and then it's off to the sun somewhere. Now, we will have to integrate all their systems with ours, which will be a huge task."

While saying to her, "Will you be all right, Sis?" Jack wondered, "Systems integration, is this an opportunity to use our track record to secure a major job?"

The next day in the office, Jack researched and found that XYZ had been an audit client for years. So, Jack emailed the audit partner responsible, suggesting that they have a chat about the opportunity.

Now, let's join Jack as the phone rings.

"Is that Jack?" a pleasant female voice.

"Yes. Can I help you?"

"Please wait; I am putting you through Sir Benjamin Doolittle."

Jack hears the name, and suddenly, the room spins. Out of 10,000 people, he thinks, why is the firm's senior UK partner, number two in the global firm, calling me a junior consultant? Jack is beginning to sweat, more than a little – fearing this will not be good. Mentally, Jack is clearing his desk.

"Jack, I was calling to thank you for the intelligence on XYZ's acquisition. Good work. You don't know that I used to be the manager of their audit contract, and I have been engaged with them for a very long time. I wanted to tell you that for years, we have had a policy that, whilst we do their audits, we will not accept any other work from them, not tax work, and certainly not management consultancy."

Jack: "Thank you, Sir Benjamin. Am I permitted to ask why?"

Sir B: "No, Jack, you are not. But you are new to us, and I will tell you that we assess the business risk for every opportunity. We are content to do audit work for this client, where clearly defined standards and protocols make it low risk. All other work, for them, however, is judged to be too high a risk, so we don't offer, and if asked, we politely refuse."

At this, the line goes dead.

There are two primary points at which we must assess opportunities. When a proposal is required, we need to establish if the time and effort required to develop it are justifiable. After the proposal is prepared, we need to judge if there are sound commercial reasons to support submitting it to the client.

Initial screening of requests

Table 6.1 shows a worked example of a weighted assessment of an opportunity by the PNX Consultancy. The proposal reviewer has assessed how the opportunity scores against each criterion, which has been allocated a standard weight across all opportunities. The resulting

Table 6.1 PNX Consultancy Services Opportunity Assessment Score Sheet

PNX Consultancy Services Opportunity Assessment Score Sheet			
Opportunity Name/Client	**Health Insurance AI Claim Processing XXX Insurance**		
	Weight (1–5) 1 = Low	**Score (0–10) 0 = Poor**	**Weighted Score**
Total score (out of 700)			**533**
Score below 350	~~*Rejected*~~		
Scores 351–500	~~*Director Approval required*~~		
Scores 500 plus	**Manager Approval**		
Total score (out of 700)			**533**
1. Client fit			**68**
Industry and sector	3	9	27
Company size and maturity	3	7	21
Geographic location	2	10	20
2. Engagement scope and complexity			**106**
Nature of the problem	5	8	40
Scope of work	5	6	30
Level of engagement	4	9	36
3. Potential revenue and profitability			**79**
Engagement fee	4	7	28
Engagement duration	3	7	21
Resource allocation	3	10	30
4. Client's decision-making process			**50**
Key stakeholders	2	4	8
Approval process	3	4	12
Timeframe	3	10	30
5. Risk assessment			**230**
Client: Management stability	3	10	30
Client: Payment history	3	6	18
Foreign currency exposure	3	0	0
Payment profiles	4	9	36
Reputational risk	2	10	20
Regulatory compliance	5	10	50
Competitive landscape	3	5	15
Technological risks	3	7	21
Data privacy and security	4	10	40

weighted scores are totalled and compared against the firm's approval rules. PNX's quality control process also subjects the scoring to an independent review by an uninvolved manager.

Director or partner review of high-level proposals

We should develop an outline proposal if an opportunity is approved to progress. This is not the whole document for submission to the client with supporting evidence and text. It should summarise the main business and financial elements around which the final proposal will be built and any exposure risks. We should include an overview of the engagement, including objectives, scope, methodology, timeline, and financial estimates. In many firms, this is passed to a director or partner for review, but depending on its criticality, it is also referred to other specialists, for example, to a legal team. Table 6.2 shows a format for PNX's weighted assessment of the proposal, following the same approach as the opportunity assessment.

Table 6.2 PNX Consultancy Services Proposal Assessment Score Sheet

PNX Consultancy Services Proposal Assessment Score Sheet			
Proposal Name/Client	**Health Insurance AI Claim Processing XXX Insurance**		
Total Fee Income	**Margin %**		
$150,500	**25%**		
	Weight (1–5) 1 = Low	**Score (0–10) 0 = Poor**	**Weighted Score**
Score below 700	***~~Rejected~~***		
Score 700–850, or fees above £250,000	**Senior Director Approval Required**		
Score 851+, and fees less than 250,000	***~~Director Approval Required~~***		
Total Score (Out of 1000)			**811**
1. Strategic alignment			**93**
Core competencies	4	9	36
Market positioning	4	9	36
Differentiation	3	7	21
2. Risk assessment			**329**
Engagement complexity	4	3	12
Client commitment	4	8	32
Resource availability	4	6	24
Management stability	4	9	36
Payment history	4	9	36
Foreign currency exposure	3	10	30
Payment profiles	3	7	21
Reputational risk	4	7	28
Regulatory compliance	5	10	50
Competitive landscape	3	5	15
Technological risks	3	5	15
Data privacy and security	3	10	30

(Continued)

Table 6.2 (Continued)

PNX Consultancy Services Proposal Assessment Score Sheet			
Proposal Name/Client	**Health Insurance AI Claim Processing XXX Insurance**		
3. Return on investment (ROI)			**81**
Financial benefits	5	10	50
Non-financial benefits	2	5	10
Cost–benefit analysis	3	7	21
4. Team capability			**85**
Expertise	2	10	20
Availability	5	10	50
Workload	3	5	15
5. Client relationship			**88**
Cultural fit	4	10	40
Communication style	3	8	24
Trust and rapport	3	8	24
6. Due diligence			**135**
Financial information	3	10	30
Legal and regulatory compliance	3	10	30
Client reference checks	3	10	30
Industry analysis	3	5	15
Engagement feasibility study	3	10	30

Step 3: Proposal development

If the engagement is a good fit, we can develop a more detailed proposal for submission to the client. We aim to win the work and to set the client's expectations about how the work will be delivered. Remember that we place the client at the centre of all our work. This applies equally to proposals. Our objective is to persuade the prospective client to engage us, and by ensuring that we focus on them and their needs, we will write a more persuasive proposal.

At a high level, our winning proposal must fulfil a number of needs. It must demonstrate our credibility and track record to help the client build their trust and confidence in us. We will strengthen this trust if we consider any risks which we identified during our due diligence process and set out how we would mitigate them. Also, as the proposal will often be the basis of our contract, we should always outline our proposed scope of work and detail the required financial and commercial arrangements.

The following points list the sorts of details that a client would expect to be covered in a winning proposal, with examples of good practice:

- **Client's problem or need**: We should open by using storytelling techniques to illustrate our understanding of the client's challenges in a relatable way. We should back up our claims with data and evidence and use case studies or stories to describe similar situations.

- *Example: This is a proposal for a retail client facing declining sales and increased competition. Our analysis identifies the root causes of the decline, including a lack of omnichannel integration and outdated store formats, and includes case studies from clients who had experienced similar problems.*

- **Proposed solution**: We should illustrate our proposed solution using relevant visuals, such as diagrams and charts. Sometimes, we can include details of the main headings in a final report. Any visuals we use should be high quality and reflect our brand value. Using AI-generated images may introduce errors, and we should check them carefully. When describing the methodologies and tools we will use, we should be specific but not so descriptive as to give away our intellectual property.[1] We should differentiate ourselves from competitors by highlighting the unique value proposition of our solution.

  - *Example: A technology company is seeking proposals for a go-to-market strategy for its expansion into new markets. The consultancy sets out the different tasks that the consultants will undertake and provides examples of the output from its graphical approach to analysis and reporting.*

- **Scope of work**: The importance of presenting the scope of our work in a clear and concise format, such as a bullet-point list or short paragraphs and even tables, cannot be over-emphasised. Being crystal clear at this stage sets client expectations and removes many potential causes for disappointment or dispute during and after the engagement. This precision includes being specific about the limits to our research and deliverables and any assumptions that we need to make about client and resource availability. We could also consider including a contingency plan for unexpected challenges.

  - *Example: A proposal from a global consultancy for a significant financial systems review for a large multinational corporation. The scope of work outlines the procedures that will be followed, including testing controls, reviewing databases and outputs, and assessing risk. It also includes a statement that the client will provide on-site accommodation, access to company systems and data, and suitable meeting rooms for the team during the engagement and that staff and managers will be available for interview as required during the engagement.*

- **Timeline**: We can use a visual representation to make the timeline more straightforward to understand. Gantt charts, for example, are widely used. When preparing a timeline, we should again consider including a contingency buffer for unexpected delays and stating any assumptions on which it is based that are external to our control, such as the availability of client staff for interviews.

  - *Example: A large systems and consultancy provider is submitting a proposal for a digital transformation engagement. The timeline includes key milestones such as engagement initiation, timing of intermediate deliverables, requirements gathering, solution design, development, testing, user acceptance, and deployment.*

- **Deliverables**: We must align our deliverables with the client's goals and objectives. We should specify the outputs the client can expect and quantify the expected benefits of each deliverable. The dates for each deliverable should also be included in our timeline.

  - *Example: An expert customer experience (CX) consultancy is submitting a proposal for developing a CX improvement programme for a significant online and catalogue retailer. They identify that they will prepare several deliverables during the assignment, including a customer journey map, an analysis of the current website's use by customers, a redesigned website with user experience testing, and a training programme for customer-facing staff.*

- **Costs and investment**: It is critical to be transparent about the costs involved and, if necessary, explain how they are calculated. We may need to give detailed consideration to the charging model to be used (e.g. fixed price, benefit sharing, day rates), which will be included in our contract. It is worthwhile to check out the client's requirements for handling consultants' travel expenses; some clients want to see them itemised, others don't, yet others want them detailed and aligned with their policies and even to reimburse consultants directly.
    - *Example: A proposal from a specialist strategy adviser for a strategic planning engagement. The cost breakdown includes consulting fees, travel and accommodation expenses, and third-party costs. The consultancy also justifies the cost by calculating the potential return on investment.*
- **Team and company qualifications**: Testimonials and case studies showcase our team's expertise. We should also highlight any relevant certifications or awards of the company and the team members. It is worth considering including a brief profile of each team member (however, we always need to reserve the right, with client agreement, to substitute team members when necessary).
    - *Example: In a proposal for a supply chain optimisation engagement, the team qualifications section highlights the consultants' experience in logistics, supply chain management, information technology, and data analytics.*
- **Terms and conditions**: Clear and concise language avoids misunderstandings. We should ensure that the terms and conditions are fair to both parties and consider using a standard form of contract (the NEC family of contracts is well tested).
    - *Example: A proposal outlining standard terms and conditions, such as confidentiality agreements, intellectual property rights, and dispute resolution procedures.*
- **Next steps**: Provide clear instructions on how the client can proceed and how we will respond to any questions or concerns the client may have.
    - *Example: A proposal encouraging the client to arrange a follow-up meeting with a nominated contact to discuss its suggestions in more detail.*
- **Executive summary**: When everything else is complete and agreed upon, we can write an executive summary. An effective summary is should include:
    - Brief and a good challenge is to aim for a maximum of two pages of well-spaced text.
    - Starts with a compelling statement or phrase designed to grab the reader's attention.
    - Uses strong verbs and an active voice to make our writing more engaging and our arguments more persuasive.
    - Includes numbers to quantify the benefits of our proposed solution whenever possible is helpful.
- **Cover page**: An attractive cover page is essential. To reflect our highest standards of professionalism, we should use high-quality images and a consistent colour scheme that aligns with our brand identity. Using a graphic artist to help with the front and back pages is beneficial. These can be standardised and reused with suitable customisation for different proposals.
- **Visuals**: Basic, sloppy, or poorly drawn diagrams and images undermine our professionalism as much as poorly written text. Again, using a skilled graphic artist to emphasise the messages in our text will reinforce them with our prospective clients.
- **Completing the proposal**: In larger consultancies, drafting different parts of the proposal is often delegated to various individuals, and some elements are built using pre-prepared text and images. This means there is a coordinating and management role to ensure the proposal elements can be assembled on time. It also means it may need to be edited to ensure they adhere to a standard writing style and format.

- **Quality check**: After the proposal has been drafted, it should be reviewed thoroughly to ensure that it focuses on the client and the client's requirements, is in line with our quality standards, and reflects the highest level of professionalism.[2] It is helpful for the reviewer to assess not only if the principal areas required are covered but also if they can identify coherent answers to the following questions:
  1. Have we included relevant case studies or testimonials from previous clients to demonstrate our firm's expertise and success?
  2. Do we emphasise how our proposal is tailored to the client's needs and challenges?
  3. Are potential risks addressed, and are the strategies we will implement to mitigate them outlined?
  4. Will the client clearly understand the unique value that our firm can provide to them?
  5. Have we demonstrated how our firm's values and culture align with the client's organisation?
  6. If applicable, have we highlighted our firm's commitment to sustainability and how our solution aligns with the client's sustainability goals?
  7. Does our proposal showcase our ability to innovate and adapt to changing market conditions?
  8. Have we shared convincing and relevant stories of previous clients who have achieved significant results through our firm's services?
- **And finally**, always run a good quality spelling and grammar checker against the document and ask an unengaged person to read the proposal from cover to cover to look for any other errors. If the proposal is critical, we should consider engaging a professional copyeditor to review it.

Our proposal and, in the case of tenders, some of the client documentation will usually form the basis of our contract with the client, frequently being bound into the contract in the form of schedules. This means we will be contractually held to what we say in our proposal, which is the final reason why we need to ensure the quality and accuracy of what we submit to the client.

Step 4: Tendering

Tendering is a special case of proposal writing where the client is in total control of the process. It is usual for public sector contracts to be awarded based on a competitive tendering process. In many jurisdictions, national and even international, rules are followed by public bodies to ensure that the tendering process is open, free, and fair. However, even in the best-regulated countries, errors, omissions, or interference can lead to processes not being followed correctly.

Tender content management

Our excellent practices in preparing proposals still apply when responding to tender requests. Traditionally, the client's primary consideration when selecting any supplier was solely cost. The more modern approach to supplier selection has evolved from focusing exclusively on the lowest cost to embracing the Most Economically Advantageous Tender (MEAT) concept, also known as the Best Quality/Price Ratio Method. This methodology evaluates how well our tender meets the client's stated requirements and cost.

This concept is fully described in UK and European public procurement regulations, which provide guidance on selecting tenders. According to these regulations, the Most Economically Advantageous Tender is assessed from the contracting authority's perspective based on the best price (or cost) quality ratio.

Quality is evaluated on various criteria, including qualitative, environmental, or social aspects of the contract's subject matter. Additionally, these regulations mandate that the weightings for each criterion be pre-determined and included in the invitation to tender documentation. This is enormously helpful. Some parts of the tender evaluations will still be subjective assessments by the purchaser. However, analysing these criteria carefully tells us how to structure our proposal, which elements we should emphasise and where we should put in the most effort to convince the client to award the contract to us.

Mandatory requirements

There is another dimension to requirements, as some are listed as mandatory. Ignoring any of these may, and often will, prevent the rest of our proposal from being evaluated at all. Mandatory requirements may relate to the company and be as simple as including our company policy statements on areas such as health and safety, diversity, or modern slavery or evidence of quality accreditations and three years of audited accounts. Other mandatory requirements can be extensive, and some commonly encountered requirements are set out in Table 6.3.

Table 6.3 Typical Mandatory Requirements

Typical Mandatory Requirements	
Requirement	**Comment**
Plan for engagement delivery	A detailed outline of the engagement approach, methodology, timelines, and key milestones Be wary of revealing intellectual property at this point
Team and qualifications	A clear description of the proposed team, including their roles, qualifications, and relevant experience. We frequently include a shortened profile, but clients sometimes require an entire career history for each consultant We should always include a caveat allowing us to substitute team members if needed, usually with the substitute being subject to client acceptance
Risk mitigation	A risk management plan that identifies potential risks, their impact, and our proposed strategies to address them Be wary of revealing intellectual property at this point
Communications	A communication plan outlining how we will interact with the client, including regular updates, meetings, and reporting We may increasingly be required to use specified means of communication, such as a secure portal
Deliverables	The client could mandate submitting a list of specific deliverables with expected delivery dates As good practice, we should have included these in our proposal anyway
Quality	A detailed description of our processes to ensure the quality of our consultancy services and relevant certificates of accreditation
Client testimonials	Provision of client references or case studies demonstrating successful delivery of similar engagements We should brief any clients that we wish to quote as references on the opportunity
Resources	Detailed information on allocating personnel, tools, and technologies to deliver the services and the processes proposed to control and agree on any necessary changes or substitutions during the engagement delivery
Cost transparency	A detailed cost breakdown for the consultancy services, including additional expenses or contingencies and our margins
Financial stability	Proofs required may include, for example, audited accounts for the last three years

Tender time management

When tendering, time is our enemy. First, the calendar and then the clock run down very quickly. Our clients, who are also under time pressure themselves, often do not make this any easier.

Let's take a very brief site visit to hear from Auri, the procurement manager of a national public body, about the time scales for tendering.

We are meeting in Auri's office in the capital city of a European country. There are papers everywhere, and he seems to be under tremendous pressure. But we have been to the next-door coffee shop and brought coffee and biscuits.

"I am not supposed to meet with suppliers at all or accept gifts or hospitality."

Auri bites into a chocolate biscuit.

"Our policy is that everything has to be done in writing; that way, we have full evidence of everything said. As you are not involved in an active procurement exercise, and we are not planning any for consultancy in the next few months, I am happy to give you my views."

Auri attacks a second chocolate biscuit.

"The timing of tender processes can be a logistical nightmare for us. Understand that we are constrained by various rules and laws that set out what tender response periods must be. Sadly, our managers hardly ever think backwards from the end date of when they want something to be in place to understand when we have to start the procurement process. It's particularly exasperating when we find ourselves authorising tender documents for release before major public holidays. Sometimes, they even want tenders back before a holiday period ends. Then, one or more key decision-makers go off and are inaccessible for extended periods, disrupting the entire procurement process."

Auri pauses momentarily to demolish a third chocolate biscuit and drink some coffee.

Refreshed, Auri continues, "Considerate purchasing managers will account for public holiday schedules when sending tenders out and setting receipt deadlines. However, less considerate ones expect suppliers to work through holidays, disregarding their staff's well-being and work-life balance. This creates unnecessary stress and pressure on both sides of the procurement relationship.

There's a stinger for me as well. If the tender documents go out over a holiday period, guess who has to answer suppliers' questions? Me. Whilst everyone else is enjoying their time off, I'm left to explain their requirements to suppliers.

I try to explain to everyone that timing is a recurring challenge. I want to receive the best, most well-crafted proposals possible, and I want every supplier to bring their A-game. This means that it's crucial for all parties to be mindful of the practical timing considerations if we want a smooth and efficient procurement process.

Thanks for the refreshments; I hope what I said helps you."

We leave, taking the evidence of the used coffee cups with us.

Our issue with timing is that before we can submit the bid, we often have to:

1. Review the invitation to tender, do any required research, and evaluate the opportunity.
2. Bring together information from different parts of the business, including that necessary to meet the mandatory information requirements.
3. Get the commercials and financials signed off.
4. Coordinate the writers for the different parts of the bid.
5. Bring the tender together into a cohesive whole which reads properly.
6. Go through final quality checks, including all the pages there; the mandatory requirements are all addressed, and no pages or images are upside down.

Even if we have completed everything before the submission deadline, we are tempted to keep polishing our tender to the last moment to impress the client more and increase our chance of winning the work. This temptation often means that the bid team puts in long days and nights just before the tender is due. We also have to pay attention to potential last-minute submission issues, not least because we often create large documents. Fortunately, our tender documents in management consulting are not as large as those in construction, which can require a forklift to move. Experience suggests that we should prepare to encounter multiple issues when submitting tenders. If we are required to submit a printed copy or copies of our tender, the printer will break down at a critical point (the risk of printer breakdown seems to increase in direct proportion to the reduction in time that you have left to complete the printing). When the document has been finally printed, we will find that the support staff have gone for the evening, and no one is available who actually knows how to work the binder properly and where all the relevant covers, spines, and boards that may be needed are kept.

Even when we have a properly bound document (checked to make sure all pages are in the correct order and none are upside down), we have to deal with delivery issues. Deadlines for receipt of tenders by post will probably not reflect the postal service's delivery deadlines. In the UK, tender submission deadlines are usually set for noon. Even with the highest level of next-day service from the Royal Mail, it is still recommended that we post as early the previous day as possible. This effectively cuts at least a day off our proposal response time. Still, tenders are often submitted electronically, which at least avoids our physical printing and binding problems. Sadly, electronic submission portals have also been known to suffer problems such as breaking down or being slow to upload our massive documents just before the deadline (maybe because our competitors are doing the same thing). We mitigate this by moving our planned submission forward to the previous day,[3] again cutting our preparation time.

Step 5: Contracting

It is impossible to cover the whole scope of contract law and good practice in multiple jurisdictions. Our objective is to achieve a contract that balances our needs and rights with those of our client and provides a sound basis for delivering a well-managed engagement (see Chapter 7). So, this section has one key piece of advice and many areas to consider.

Engaging a local contract expert or lawyer to review and advise on the draft contract is usually worthwhile. This is especially true if the engagement is high value, high risk, or business critical. It is also worthwhile reading the relevant Section 5 of the ISO 20700 guidelines for management consultancy services (International Standards Organisation, 2017). This sets general guidance on the items to be included in a consultancy contract.

We should split our consideration of contracting and contract management into pre- and post-contract areas.

Pre-contract considerations

- **Detailed scope of work**: A clear and comprehensive scope of work is essential to reduce misunderstandings, limit scope creep, and control costs. We should avoid vague or ambiguous language, for example, instead of saying "provide marketing services," specify "develop a comprehensive marketing strategy, which includes planning for the use of social media, email marketing, and content creation." We should also define specific, measurable deliverables and timeframe, for example, "deliver a business plan-led IT hardware and application strategy within three months of commencement." However, we also need to recognise that situations and intentions may change, and we need to allow for controlled flexibility and adjustments to the scope throughout the engagement, as needed, for example, "any changes to the agreed scope of the work will be subject to written agreement by both parties."
- **Performance metrics and key performance indicators (KPIs)**: Measuring our performance is key to ensuring that we meet our client's objectives for the work and that we deliver the engagement's expected outcomes. We need to establish a mechanism for regularly monitoring and reporting KPIs and ensuring that they are aligned with the client's overall business objectives and strategic goals. For example, if we are proposing to prepare an implementation and training strategy for a new service that the client aims to launch in three months, our KPIs could include submitting a draft strategy in two months and monthly review meetings. We may also wish to consider incorporating performance-based incentives or penalties linked to the achievement of KPIs.
- **Payment terms and conditions**: A well-defined payment schedule helps both parties manage cash flow and understand their financial obligations. We should consider structuring payments based on specific consultancy engagement milestones or deliverables, for example, for a two-phase assignment, paying 35% upon consultancy engagement kick-off, 30% upon completion of the first phase, and 35% upon final delivery. If we intend to offer the client discounts for prompt payment, we should set these out. We also need to state the allowable time for a client to pay an invoice and any penalties for late payment.[4]
- **Confidentiality**: Protecting sensitive information and intellectual property is essential for maintaining trust and legal compliance. We should expect to include Non-Disclosure Agreements (NDAs) binding on all parties to protect confidential information. It is helpful to discuss publicity at this stage, covering areas such as the initial award of contract and client references, testimonials, and case studies for use after the engagement has closed.
- **Intellectual property rights**: Arrangements for the ownership of intellectual property that may be created during the engagement, for example, specifying that the client will own all copyrights to any materials we create or IT code that is prepared. We should also agree on any restrictions on using intellectual property by the client or ourselves.
- **Risk management and mitigation**: Identifying and mitigating potential risks help prevent consultancy engagement delays, cost overruns, and quality issues. We should consider undertaking a joint risk assessment with the client to identify potential risks and their impact on the engagement, for example, economic downturns, regulatory changes, or team member turnover. For each identified risk, we should also agree on mitigation measures and who will bear the cost and impact of such risks.
- **Effective communication and collaboration**: Open and transparent communication ensures that all stakeholders are informed and aligned throughout the engagement. We need to consider defining clear communication channels and protocols, such as the responsibility for

organising regular meetings, frequency of reporting, and use of emails and attachments, including any requirement for client-supplier communication portals. We could also include the timing for change notifications and responses on more extensive engagements.

- **Quality assurance and standards**: As in all our work, maintaining our high-quality standards is essential to maintaining our reputation. We should always set out the quality standards that will be applied to our consultancy services generally and to this engagement in particular. For example, our adherence to industry best practices, ISO certifications, or specific quality metrics. We should also set our detailed quality control arrangements, such as reviews, audits, and inspections. A further area for consideration is how responsibilities for quality will be managed where the engagement team is a collaborative one comprising client and consultancy staff.
- **Resource allocation and management**: Proper allocation of resources ensures that the consultancy engagement has the necessary personnel, tools, and technologies to succeed. We should consider how we can be sure that the client provides us with the resources needed, including office accommodation, access to client staff and technology as required. For example, this may require the client to identify a day-to-day contact to make necessary arrangements for us and a senior manager as an escalation path in the event of difficulties. If we are to be working on a day rate contract, to protect our consultants, we need to specify in the contract the hours each day that consultants will be expected to work.[5] We should also agree to any process required to allow us to adjust staffing and team membership. For example, we should identify how tasks can be reallocated or new resources approved if a team member is overloaded or leaves the company.
- **Change management**: To deliver a "no surprises" culture for our client and reduce the opportunities for disputes, we need to set out a well-defined process to manage changes to the engagement scope, timeline, and budget effectively. This should include assessing how proposed changes will impact the consultancy engagement objectives and deliverables, how these will be evaluated and approved, and by whom.
- **Dispute resolution**: A precise dispute resolution mechanism promptly addresses conflicts and helps avoid costly legal battles. To resolve conflicts efficiently, we should include alternative dispute resolution methods, such as mediation or arbitration. We should specify the process for invoking this, including how mediators or arbitrators will be appointed.
- **Contract termination**: Clear termination clauses help manage the end of the consultancy relationship and protect the interests of both parties. We should agree on clear termination clauses in the contract, which specify the conditions under which the contract can be terminated. For example, the clauses should specify grounds for termination, such as breach of contract or unsatisfactory performance. Also included should be notice periods for termination and the consequences of early termination, that is, liquidated damages or retention of funds.

Watch the weasel words

This is a final cautionary note on the use of language in contracts: Be careful, as the following example reveals.

> *One significant public body in the UK claimed to be using a standard form of contract (actually one of the NEC[6] family of contracts). The standard contract had a clause that referred to other supplier duties that the public body might trigger without additional payment. The form of words used by the standard contract created a closed list, that is, the supplier might have to perform any of the five actions listed.*

By inserting one word, "including," the public body claimed that the items on the list were merely examples, and it was, therefore, able to instruct the supplier to perform a much wider range of tasks within the contract scope and price.

Also, we have to be very cautious about which one of the following three terms the client often wants to insert into a contract; they are not interchangeable and are generally considered to have different levels of obligation, although interpretations may vary in different jurisdictions. They are best endeavours, reasonable endeavours, and best reasonable endeavours.

Best endeavours: This requires us to exert our utmost effort and use all legal means to achieve a particular outcome.
Reasonable endeavours: This requires us to use reasonable care, diligence, and skill in pursuing a particular outcome.
Best reasonable endeavours: A combination of the other two. It therefore, provides much room for legal argument.

Finally, if in doubt, always engage with an expert in contract law.

Post-contract considerations

These are generally non-contractual arrangements that we agree with the client to manage the engagement and ensure its smooth operation:

- **Performance evaluation**: Regular performance evaluations allow us to assess our performance with clients, identify improvement areas, and maintain positive relationships. We should agree on arrangements for client feedback to help improve our performance and for formal joint regular performance reviews to assess our adherence to the contract terms and contribution to consultancy engagement objectives.
- **Knowledge transfer**: Ensuring a smooth transition of expertise, knowledge, and deliverables helps the client, and we maintain the engagement's collaborative approach and ensure a smooth end-of-contract transition. We should consider the documentation to be handed over to the client, including methodologies, data, and deliverables. We should also agree on any arrangements for training client staff to ensure they have the knowledge and skills to carry forward work after the end of the consultancy engagement.
- **Lessons learned**: Jointly analysing the consultancy engagement with the client to identify lessons learned helps us improve our processes and deliver even better results in future engagements. It also assists the client by helping them maximise the value they can obtain from future assignments. We should consider how such a post-engagement review will be carried out and how key insights and recommendations will be documented and shared.
- **Ongoing support**: Offering ongoing support demonstrates our commitment to the client's success and can lead to long-term relationships. We could also establish procedures for notifying issues or problems that arise after the consultancy engagement is completed. This last step has the advantage of channelling and controlling any queries and ensuring that we can apply our quality control processes when resolving them.

Reflections

As in the previous chapters, please continue to draw on your experience and current situation or use the theoretical case study.

- Prepare theoretical forward predictions of fee income using your favourite spreadsheet package covering each month over a six-month period as follows:
  1. Analyse contracted fee income by engagement.
  2. Repeat the previous exercise in a separate table, but this time, list the engagement fee income of potential client engagements, with the value of each fee reduced to reflect the likelihood of winning the work.
- Based on your previous analysis, in each of the six months, how much fee-earning capacity do you have to sell to maintain an acceptable level of profitability, and what is your pipeline coverage ratio?
- Please prepare a script for a telephone call. Your aim is to arrange a virtual meeting with a contact following a brief conversation at a networking event. Hint: Remember to include details of potential objections to overcome and arrange any necessary technical information.
- Your telephone call was successful, so please prepare a plan for the virtual meeting. Identify the topics you want to cover in the discussion with the client, the potential wording for each topic, and the sales collateral you may wish to share during or after the meeting.
- Great news – your prospect has invited you on-site to discuss the opportunity in more depth and to let you get a feel of their operations. What information will you need to gather to evaluate the opportunity?
- Now that the client wants a proposal, please outline the areas your proposal will cover.
- Finally, we are now at the stage of agreeing on a contract. What areas would you want to ensure the contract covers? Please suggest suitable solutions in each area that you identified. Your suggestions should aim to achieve a fair and equitable balance between the parties' interests.

Further reading

Yes!: 50 Scientifically Proven Ways to Be Persuasive. Goldstein, Martin and Cialdini, 2009

Great Networking: The art and practice of building authentic professional relationships. Alisa Grafton 2022

Persuasive Business Proposals: Writing to Win More Customers, Clients, and Contracts. Tom Sant 2018

Notes

1 Less scrupulous clients have been known to request detailed proposals and then use the information given to deliver the engagement themselves or with contractors. Shock!

2 I am thinking here of a proposal for engineering advice on rescuing an iconic London landmark (anyone watching the UK nightly news for years would have seen the building in question appearing covered in scaffolding). The proposal was due by noon but was withdrawn at 11:59 am because the writing was so poor and the solution so banal that it would have undermined the firm's professional credibility with a

major client. As just one example of their many childish errors, the writers repeatedly, but incorrectly, spelt their job title "Principle Engineer."

3 Or for one bizarre proposal submitted at 4:00 am for a noon deadline, on the day most of the client staff finished at lunchtime for the Christmas and New Year holidays. I know it was a riveting read, but . . .

4 Discounting usually works better as a motivation for early payment, especially if we talk nicely to the client's accounts payable team – they seem never to like losing discounts.

5 I will only identify the client as M. Our contract used the term "consultant days." A change of deadline by M resulted in staff working 18-hour days. M turned down the change request on the grounds that "There are twenty-four hours in a day!" Future contracts stipulated an 8-hour day.

6 NEC originally stood for New Engineering Contract, but the family of contracts has expanded, and now it just stands for NEC.

Bibliography

International Standards Organisation. (2017). *ISO 20700 Guidelines for Management Consultancy Services 2017-06*. Geneva: International Standards Organisation.

7 Engagement Delivery

What Should We Do to Keep Our Clients Happy?

Aim of this chapter: To introduce the key role of the consultancy engagement manager and consider how they, and the consultant, should operate to ensure that the engagement is successfully delivered.

Learning outcome: To be able to plan and control the delivery of a consultancy engagement that avoids client surprises and builds towards a successful conclusion, including identifying future opportunities and referrals.

International standards

Before looking at the details of two cycles covering how we might deliver and how we might manage the delivery of client engagements, it is worth considering the impact of the ISO 20700 quality standard on how we deliver our work. ISO20700 aims to achieve better engagement outcomes by improving the understanding between ourselves and our clients. Section 6 sets out the general guidelines for controlling the execution of a consultancy engagement. It covers outcomes, refining and implementing the agreed work plan, management and monitoring, governance, resource management, risks and quality, communications, and feedback (International Standards Organisation, 2017).

Strict discipline: document control

As our engagement progresses, we will generate a multitude of documents, from discussion papers, emails, and notes to contracts and research papers, computer models, and reports. We should enforce strict discipline over these documents. The consequences of neglecting such document control include wasted time, miscommunication, different staff working on outdated documents, delays, and even legal disputes. Software systems can assist us, but control over documentation can also be achieved manually. Whatever control solution is chosen, our engagement manager should implement and enforce keeping all engagement documents, including emails, stored in a centrally accessible and secured location which is organised logically and consistently. We should also assign someone to oversee the day-to-day management of the document control system. Finally, as good practice, the status of each document, including dates, versions, and authors, should be easily identifiable from within the document.

The engagement delivery cycle

Chapter 1 introduced the concept of a cycle for all advisory engagements.[1] This cycle is the core rhythm for the daily work of a consultant and applies across different professional disciplines. Figure 7.1 sets out the main steps in the engagement delivery cycle.

DOI: 10.4324/9781003490456-8

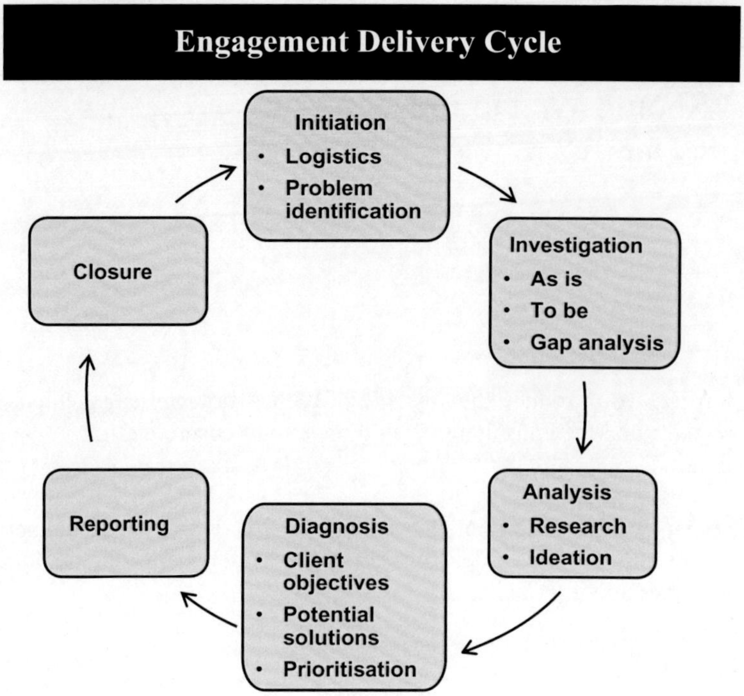

Figure 7.1 Engagement Delivery Cycle.

Initiation

This step is common to all types of engagement. Our first concern in setting up the engagement is our logistics, which centre around the location where the work will be carried out. This should be detailed in our proposal and embedded in our contract. Usually, it will be specified as being somewhere between the extremes of fully remote working and all work carried out solely on a client site or multiple client sites. The location is key to much of our preparation before commencing work. Whilst this preparation is the engagement manager's responsibility, the consultant also needs to be fully aware of the client's expectations and arrangements.

On every engagement where we will need to work at a client site, we should request that the client provide a suitable person to act as a liaison with our engagement manager. This is not our client sponsor, that is, the manager or director to whom we will report, but someone who can arrange resources, marshal attendance at meetings, and fix housekeeping problems for us. If necessary, they should be able to invoke the status of our ultimate sponsor in the client to clear any roadblocks. For example, if a person receives a call from the CEO's assistant, the organisational difficulties we have been experiencing usually melt away quickly.

Without such client liaison, we can burn chargeable time because of problems such as unavailable meeting rooms, promised IT not being made available, key figures failing to attend meetings, or reports and documentation not being available on time.

Remote working often requires less prestart preparation. However, if we are working across time zones, we do need to agree on communication protocols and coordinate contact times.

By contrast, on-site work can require more preparation. We can commonly run into problems which need help from our client liaison person in terms of issues such as follows:

- **Security passes**: If we are to be on-site for any time, staff will need to arrange building passes. Sometimes, this can be a lengthy process that will delay our work. This issue is often encountered on sensitive or secure sites and those requiring health and safety accreditation.
- **Working areas**: We often need to work in an area where our conversations can be confidential. This is difficult to arrange in open-plan offices, or even worse, those with only hot desking. Frequently, the only solution is to use a meeting room for the period of our engagement, but experience shows that these are in short supply and usually booked far in advance. Our client liaison must have the authority or influence to ensure that we have an adequate working space.
- **Technology**: Some clients will be happy for consultants to use the consultancy's IT equipment, while others will require that they use their equipment when on-site. Sometimes, client IT equipment is necessary for us to gain access to client-held information and data. Frequently, IT departments are used to arranging IT equipment on a lead time based on the period it takes to onboard staff and find the quick response required to support a consultancy team challenging.

Time for a site visit. You are back in the hot seat. Remember, in Chapter 1, the PNX partner set you off on a challenge with a difficult client. They said, "The basic issues are that we are halfway through the engagement, we have spent two-thirds of the budget, and the client is close to starting legal action."

The engagement manager briefs you.

"This is one where we are consultants and system developers for a government body. As I see it, the problem is with the client's project manager, who will also be the senior user of the delivered solution. The client sponsor is great, but their PM is at our throats the whole time. At the core, our job is to take a bunch of poorly thought-out requirements that they produced and build a large-scale statistical analysis system for them.

Their PM wanted a customised package as a solution, but we proposed bespoke system development and won the procurement. The trouble is, the more we deliver, the more we find that their original requirements were often vague and sometimes conflicting. We are now facing legal action for non-delivery, and the project manager is bad-mouthing us at every opportunity. It is not doing our wider reputation any good, and if we get sued, we can say goodbye to any more government work."

What would you do?

The initiation phase is also where we, as engagement managers, should work with our client sponsor to review and, if necessary, refine the assessments we made of our client's business challenges or opportunities during the proposal stage. Our output is an updated problem definition that we can use as part of the consultancy team's briefing. While it is always valuable to reaffirm our understanding if there is any gap between completing our research work for the proposal and commencing the assignment, it is critical.

Investigation

This is our main research stage in which we define the current situation, client objectives, and the differences between them as follows:

- **As-is analysis**: We gather relevant data about the client's current situation, including researching industry trends, competitors, and the performance of internal operations and processes and collecting supporting data.
- **To-be vision analysis**: Working collaboratively with client staff, managers, and directors to define desired outcomes and translate their goals into specific, measurable, achievable, relevant, and time-bound (SMART) objectives.
- **Gap analysis**: We identify the discrepancies between the client's current state (called "As-Is") and the desired future state (called "To-Be"), identifying key areas for improvement. At this stage, holding a review session with our client sponsor is often helpful to ensure we understand the main issues they expect us to address.

Analysis

We can break this stage into two key tasks: research and ideation. When we have understood and agreed on the scope of the problems faced by the client, it is often helpful to perform a research scan to identify solutions that others have found beneficial. This stage should apply even when our consultant team considers themselves thoroughly expert and up to date with developments in their field and ensures we use the latest available information. The second part of our research is to set up the processes to gather and analyse the information that we will require; this may range from staff or customer interviews to detailed data analysis; this is very much dependent on the type of engagement. Drawing on the intelligence that the analysed information and the research scan have provided, we move into the ideation phase. In this phase, we explore the full range of possible solutions, often in facilitated sessions with staff and managers (see Chapter 2, Step 3) or in interviews.

Diagnosis

During this stage, we formulate, select, and justify the solution which will form our recommended course of action. The options analysis techniques that we use at this stage are discussed in Chapter 2, Step 4. We use objectives agreed upon with the client to set selection criteria against which we can evaluate potential solutions and identify the most promising approach to recommend to the client. This should enable us to include an evidence-based business justification section in our report. Our solution design is a necessary adjunct to our recommendations. This could consist of preparing items such as strategies and process maps, organisational charts, resource allocation, timelines, and key performance indicators.

Reporting

The most critical stage in our client support is preparing our key documents, our "leave-behinds." It is by these that our work will be judged, and, therefore, they require the closest attention to detail (see Chapter 6, Step 3, for suggestions on how we can ensure we prepare high-quality documents). We should always start with a peer review of the engagement. A consultant with appropriate knowledge and expertise who has not been engaged in the assignment should be asked to critically and meticulously examine our findings, analyses, and recommendations, ensuring they are appropriate, accurate, consistent, and unambiguous.

The next step is a rigorous check of all the data, calculations, spreadsheets, and references we used to reach our conclusions. When this check is complete, we can finalise the draft of our report. Before submitting a discussion draft to the client, a senior consultant from outside the team should scrutinise it for any weaknesses, inconsistencies, or areas requiring further clarification.

We should plan to discuss our draft findings, conclusions, and recommendations with various client stakeholders,[2] but it is advisable to discuss this with our client sponsor.

Such a collaborative approach, coupled with our meticulous review and verification processes, should help ensure the delivery of high-quality insights and recommendations that our clients perceive as being genuinely beneficial.

Closure

Closure is discussed more fully in Step 5 of our engagement delivery management cycle. Assuming that we agreed to it during our post-contract discussions when we reach closure, our team should have shared knowledge and best practices with the client and arranged a documentation handover. By doing so, we help ensure our solution's long-term sustainability.

Other considerations

This engagement delivery cycle provides a clear framework for delivering disparate engagements. However, two additional areas operate across the whole cycle, which we need to consider to ensure that our consultancy team provides value to clients and contributes to the sustainability and success of our business:

- **Meeting client expectations**: Delivering or exceeding client expectations involves all delivery team members and the engagement manager. We should
  - Use active listening, effective questioning, and careful analysis skills to identify the client's goals and challenges.
  - Maintain clear formal and informal communication channels with regular formal meetings, progress reports, and less formal client briefings and discussions.
  - Aim to meet or exceed client expectations regarding accuracy, timeliness, and relevance.
- **Commerciality**: There are several aspects to supporting our commercial objectives while delivering an engagement:
  - Profitable delivery: Aim to deliver an acceptable margin on every engagement or for the engagement to contribute to another commercial objective.
  - Networking: By building relationships with individuals within the client organisation and other stakeholders and recording them, we can multiply our professional network, leading to potential future opportunities.
  - At the right time, we must also proactively seek referrals and client testimonials.

Engagement delivery management

Every consultancy engagement is unique in its scope, the professional skills necessary, and the contracted scope. Figure 7.2 sets out a core process that can be adapted to manage the delivery of any typical advisory consultancy engagement. For other types of engagement, the principles still apply, but the details may need further tailoring to meet specific requirements.

Step 1: The contract and delivery management processes

Our contract is the formal lens through which our relationship with the client is focused. It is the only legal basis for the engagement and outlines our and the client's rights and obligations. The test of a well-written consultancy contract is that it sets clear expectations for all parties, reduces the scope for misunderstandings, and ensures that both sides are aligned on the engagement's objectives (see Chapter 6). The contract and the proposal should sit within the engagement manager's metaphorical (or actual) top drawer and be ready for consultation at any time.

As discussed in Chapter 6, the contract details the scope of our work, deliverables, timelines, and financial terms. It provides a transparent framework for meeting our client's expectations and for our delivery processes, but it must be backed up by implementing effective contract management practices and processes. We should design these to enable us to keep our delivery directly aligned to the contract. This approach will safeguard our profitability, manage our risk, support the successful delivery of our work, and strengthen our relationships with the client.

Managing scope

One of the most critical aspects of delivery contract management is controlling scope. It is imperative to ensure that the scope remains well defined and controlled throughout the engagement to prevent increased costs, delays, and decreased profitability that inevitably arise from scope creep. Scope creep is a pernicious problem and occurs when additional work or requirements are introduced into the engagement. Individually, these changes can be minor to the point of triviality. Still, allowing numbers of even small uncontrolled changes can have an additive effect, leading to issues with meeting contractual requirements and our forecast profitability. Such change can creep in for various reasons, such as changing client priorities, increasing client understanding of the issues, unforeseen challenges, or a lack of clear communication. However, whatever the cause, we should not undertake additional work without acknowledging it and making corresponding adjustments to the contract.

To mitigate any risks of scope creep, from the outset, it is essential to implement robust scope management processes, including the following:

- **Comprehensive scope definition**: As previously discussed, the contract should include a detailed and unambiguous scope statement. Ideally, it will also outline our specific deliverables, their acceptance criteria, and the engagement boundaries. Our proposal and contract should also have included a detailed scoping statement. If this is not the case, the engagement manager should draft one and agree it with the client during the engagement kick-off meeting. Also, as part of our engagement review process, we should conduct reviews throughout the engagement to ensure our work meets and stays within the agreed scope.
- **Change control procedures**: A formal change control process is essential to manage any proposed scope changes properly. As engagement managers, we must log any requested changes, discuss them with the client, and agree on additional work or requirements as

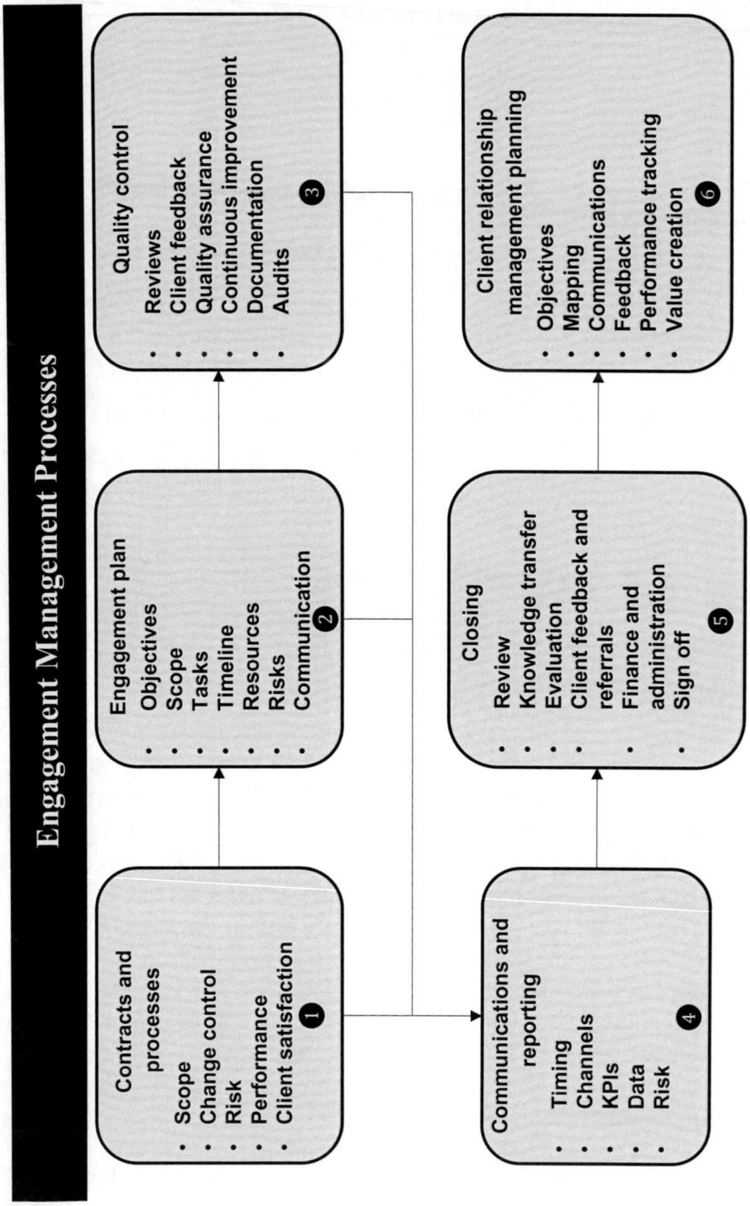

Figure 7.2 Engagement Management Processes.

contract variations. The client representative must be authorised to make these contract variations before commencing work on any requested changes. PNX's change control process is as follows:

PNX Consultancy Services

Engagement Change Control Procedure

Change Request Submission

Only the client's sponsor or PNX's engagement manager may initiate a change to the scope of the engagement. Such a request for change must be prepared in writing and clearly outline the change's nature, rationale, and impacts on the delivery timeline, budget, and deliverables.

Change Evaluation and Assessment

Our engagement manager will review the change request to assess its feasibility, and if necessary, the responsible director will provide guidance.

Impact Analysis

Our engagement manager must also prepare a detailed impact analysis to evaluate potential effects on the engagement's delivery timeline, budget, resources, risks, and deliverables.

Change Authorisation and Approval

- **Internal approval**: The engagement manager may authorise an increase in the engagement's value by up to 5% unless the change materially alters the engagement's objectives or forecast profitability. All other change requests must be passed to the responsible director for review and approval before submission to the client.
- **Presentation to the client**: The engagement manager shall present the internally approved change request and shall explain the impact analysis to the client.
- **Negotiation**: Any required negotiations take place with the engagement manager to address any concerns or questions from the client.
- **Authorisation**: No action may be taken until the client has provided formal authorisation for the change. This must be in writing in the form of a signed contract variation order. On some engagements, client authorisation may require the variation to be approved through the same processes as the original contract.
- **Internal notification**: The engagement manager will notify the administration team of the change notification, and they will update the PNX contract register, CRM system, and revenue forecasts.

Change Implementation and Monitoring

- **Integration**: After receiving client approval, the engagement manager will reflect the impact of the approved change in the engagement plan, including updating the timeline, budget, and resource allocation.

- **Communication**: Depending on the size and impact of the change, the engagement manager informs all relevant stakeholders of the approved change and its implications immediately or as part of ongoing progress reporting.
- **Monitoring**: The engagement manager closely monitors and reports on the change's implementation to ensure it is executed as planned and that any unforeseen issues are addressed promptly.
- **Documentation**: The signed change request and supporting documentation are passed to the administration team for retention on the contract file.

Other contract management processes

Other contract and delivery management processes are required for the management of risk, performance metrics, and gauging customer satisfaction. Control of risk is about forecasting future events and determining actions that are needed either now or in future to lessen their probability or to reduce their impact. Our engagement manager should prepare and keep updated a comprehensive risk management plan, which should be reviewed with the client. This should identify each possible threat to the delivery of engagement and identify strategies to address them, for example, the risk of losing a team member whose specialist skills we were relying upon to deliver a task on our critical path. We could mitigate this by ensuring their work is fully documented and that another team member works in tandem with them. Ideally, this should be openly discussed at progress meetings with the client.

We should have set out all performance metrics in the contract, and the engagement manager needs to set up mechanisms to track progress against them to ensure that our work is on track and that we are delivering value to the client. Processes to ensure that we are maintaining a positive client experience are also crucial for long-term consultancy business success. Consequently, throughout the engagement, the engagement manager must work proactively with the client to seek their regular feedback on our progress and take action to improve our performance where difficulties arise. This includes identifying a clear escalation pathway to deal with any issues arising promptly.

Step 2: Engagement plan

Our contract and engagement delivery processes are effective only when we start with a clearly defined delivery plan. This delivery plan is the cornerstone of every successful consultancy engagement and is much more than a simple timeline or Gantt chart. It should communicate not only how we will deliver the engagement but also how each task will be performed. It should contain the following key features:

- **Clear engagement objectives**: As with previous documents, not everyone reading our plan will be aware of other documentation and the details of our contract, so we should start by clearly rearticulating the engagement's goals and outcomes. We should also show how these fit with the client's business strategy.
- **Scope definition**: Following the engagement's objectives, we should set out the contracted scope, which may include tasks, deliverables, and resources. This ensures a common understanding of the assignment and mitigates against unwitting scope creep (as discussed earlier).
- **Task descriptions**: Every task that we have identified should be detailed in a task description that identifies its objectives, the resources needed, the timeframe within which it must be delivered, and the person responsible for its delivery.

- **Timeline and milestones**: These are usually set out in a detailed Gantt chart or similar, which should include key milestones and deadlines and show the engagement's critical path. This helps us ensure that we can keep the engagement on track and mitigate the impact of any delays in delivering an individual task.
- **Resource allocation**: Our plan should identify the necessary resources to support engagement execution, including personnel, equipment, and budget, from ourselves and the client. This helps ensure that the engagement has the resources it needs to succeed when it needs them.
- **Communication plan**: This outlines what, how, when, and with whom we will share information about the engagement. It helps ensure that we communicate appropriate information to different types of stakeholders and that we can address their issues or concerns promptly.

A well-known example of a consultancy engagement that failed due to a lack of a comprehensive delivery plan is the implementation of the USA Healthcare.gov website in 2013.

The website project was designed to facilitate enrolment in the Affordable Care Act. It included several large consultancy companies engaged to use their experience and expertise in managing large-scale IT projects plagued by technical issues and delays.

Healthcare.gov was subject to substantial public criticism and financial losses. Reports into its problems indicated that a lack of coordination between companies and comprehensive planning contributed to the significant issues during the website's launch.

Step 3: Quality control

ISO 20700 is a solid foundation on which management consultancies can build a quality control strategy that addresses professionalism, client satisfaction, and continuous improvement. Adhering to its guidelines allows us to enhance our reputation and deliver more effective engagements.

To achieve this, our quality strategy must address the following elements:

- **Independent periodic reviews**: The principal features of this process are separation from the engagement, relevant skills, comprehensiveness, and timeliness. The person assigned to lead the review process does not need to be a senior manager. Still, they do need relevant experience and be available to conduct reviews of our work during the engagement. This means that we will identify potential issues as early as possible and can take any action necessary to improve our performance. The first task of the reviewer is to set out the criteria that will be used to evaluate the work's quality, including its accuracy, completeness, relevance, adherence to best practices, and alignment with client objectives. It is helpful if reviews are scheduled before key engagement milestones so that the quality of work can be assessed prior to passing deliverables to the client.
- **Continuing quality assessment**: We should develop a culture where our team members are encouraged to provide feedback on each other's work. This type of peer review can help flag potential issues or areas for improvement very early. However, for peer reviews to be effective, we need to prepare clear guidelines, including evaluation criteria and our expectations for constructive feedback.
- **Client feedback**: Asking for feedback from clients throughout the engagement and after provides valuable insights into the work's quality and helps identify areas for improvement. We should use client satisfaction surveys to gather quantitative and qualitative data or conduct in-depth interviews with key client stakeholders.

- **Quality assurance checks**: Conducting regular quality assurance checks to ensure our work meets established standards and procedures will involve a separate independent assessment of key deliverables before they are shared with the client, for example, a review of documents, verification of calculations, and an audit of spreadsheets. We can streamline these checks by using quality assurance tools like standardised checklists, templates, or software. We also need to provide appropriate training for our team members in quality assurance best practices and using tools and processes relevant to the specific engagement.
- **Continuous improvement**: This only arises through carefully thought-out and monitored processes. We should assess the results of all quality control reviews for areas where the firm can improve its processes and practices and ensure that they are shared so that they can be included in our consultancy's broader continuous improvement process.
- **Documentation and record keeping**: This is not an adjunct to our quality control processes but a core part of them. Central to our record keeping is a detailed quality control log in which we document all reviews, findings, and the corrective actions which were taken. This log needs to reference evidence that we collect to support the quality of the work, such as client feedback, project documentation, and review results. Where possible, we also must analyse the data collected through quality control processes to identify trends and patterns that can inform future improvements.
- **External audits**: On longer engagements, we should consider commissioning periodic external audits to independently assess our quality control practices and ensure our compliance with industry standards and best practices, for example, ISO 9001 and ISO 20700:2017 [E].

Table 7.1 suggests a format for recording quality reviews that ties into the engagement management and monitoring approach required by ISO 20700:2017 [E].

Step 4: Communications and reporting to clients

All service elements, including reporting, fall within ISO 20700's general framework for management consultancy services. Consequently, we should always provide accurate and truthful information about our engagement's progress, including any challenges or setbacks we have encountered.

When setting up our reporting processes and arrangements, we need to take into account several requirements:

- **Timeliness**: All reporting follows a cycle based on the availability of supporting information, the engagement's complexity, our client's expectations, and our contractual obligations. By striking a balance between providing timely updates and overwhelming the client, we will establish a reporting timeline that supports effective communication and collaboration. Tying our reporting timelines to the client's availability is useful whenever possible; for example, we should always check on the workload and schedules for any meeting to which we have to report. For example, we should avoid a main deliverable being presented to a meeting that usually has a heavy workload, such as a main board meeting that reviews annual budgets. We should also make sure that we know the closure deadline for documents for any meeting to which we are reporting.
- **Channels**: When selecting the ways in which our reporting is to be communicated with the client, we must consider their preferences and the type of information being shared. For example, if our report contains sensitive or confidential data, we should select a secure, encrypted email or ask for a face-to-face meeting.
  Never leave a copy of any report on a client's printer or copies on an unattended desk.
- **Key performance indicators**: KPIs are indispensable tools for measuring progress and demonstrating value to the client. They should be directly aligned with the engagement's objectives and the client's expectations. These metrics should be quantifiable, trackable, and

Table 7.1 Engagement Quality Review Record

Engagement Quality Review Record			
Client			
Engagement name			
Engagement manager(s)			
Review date		**Reviewer(s)**	
Reviewer's summary assessment			
Deliverables reviewed			
Deliverable	**Finding**		**Status**
1			Acceptable/Improvement needed
2			Acceptable/Improvement needed
3			Acceptable/Improvement needed
4			Acceptable/Improvement needed
Other findings			
Area	**Finding**		**Status**
Engagement governance			Acceptable/Improvement needed
Engagement management approach			Acceptable/Improvement needed
Resource management			Acceptable/Improvement needed
Commitment of resources			Acceptable/Improvement needed
Progress monitoring			Acceptable/Improvement needed
Change control			Acceptable/Improvement needed
Risk management			Acceptable/Improvement needed
Client communication			Acceptable/Improvement needed
Evaluation and feedback			Acceptable/Improvement needed
Summary			
Areas of strength			
Areas for improvement			
Corrective actions required			
Action		**Responsibility**	**Target completion date**
1			
2			
3			
4			
Completed by (signature)		**Date**	

relevant to the engagement goals. KPIs let us provide clients with evidence of our progress and identify areas where we need to make adjustments before they become significant issues.

- **Performance data collection and analysis**: Creating a comprehensive and informative progress report requires meticulously gathering relevant progress data from our different sources, sometimes our own and sometimes the client's. These sources may include engagement documentation, including the contract, feedback from team members and clients, and information systems. We always have to be aware of data collection and reporting cycles and make adjustments so that data such as finance and time spent are current and use the same time frames, for example, if we have to prepare a weekly progress report on a Friday and timesheet information for this week is not available until Monday we may have to collect it from consultants manually.[3]
- **Risks**: We have already identified that formal logging, analysing, and mitigating engagement risks are essential to managing our engagement. We should include our current risk evaluation in our progress report.
- **Progress reports**: A well-structured progress report is essential for effectively communicating our progress to the client. Our report should be clear and concise and include an executive summary, engagement overview, progress against KPIs, key achievements, risks and mitigation strategies, and next steps.
- **Language and presentation**: To ensure that our report is easy to understand, we should always use plain language and avoid technical jargon. Visuals such as charts, graphs, or diagrams can also make our report more engaging, and our messages more explicit. However, these and the language used must be selected carefully to reflect the needs of the report's readers.
- **No surprises**: Just submitting a report to a meeting or circulating it to stakeholders is not appropriate where any changes are being requested or difficulties are being discussed. We should make an effort to discuss our preliminary thinking with key stakeholders before we finalise our reports or presentations. We need to be able to assess their reactions to negative information or controversial conclusions on a one-to-one basis. We can use their thoughts to review and possibly refine the report to ensure a smoother reception of the final document.
- **Internal review**: Our quality strategy (see earlier) should require that we complete a quality review before submitting a key deliverable. This review should verify the report's accuracy and completeness. Only after the report has passed, this quality review should be passed to the client sponsor as a "draft for discussion." We should consider and address any questions or concerns they have and make any needed revisions, provided that they are in accordance with our professional judgement.
- **Distribution and follow-up**: After the client sponsor has approved a report, it needs to be promptly distributed. This may be our responsibility or the client's. For example, we may need to send a copy only to the board secretary for it to reach all board members. It can also be useful to have follow-up meetings or calls with leading stakeholders to discuss any of their remaining questions or concerns.
- **Continuous improvement**: In our reporting, as elsewhere, it is helpful to seek client feedback and identify improvement areas. Immediately after submission, it is worth checking to see whether we can refine our reporting process to meet their needs more closely. We could, for example, change the frequency of progress reports or modify the way we present deliverables by increasing or decreasing the use of visuals.

Step 5: Closing an engagement

Closing an engagement comes after we have prepared all of our main deliverables. During this step, we must maintain open communications with the client sponsor. We should respond promptly to inquiries and their concerns and provide ongoing support as needed. As before, our closing process should align with ISO 20700's requirements as the best example of accepted good practice. These requirements include closing several topics, including administrative issues, for example, fees, outstanding legal or contractual matters, a final evaluation, communication, and intellectual property rights. Bearing these in mind, we need to undertake a number of tasks as part of the safe closure of an engagement, including the following:

- **Review deliverables**: We should review all deliverables and verify that they meet the agreed-upon quality standards and our contractual requirements. We should obtain formal client acceptance that this is the case. Think of it as a consultancy equivalent of a goods received note (GRN) for physical goods purchased. Just like a GRN, we may need to obtain written sign-offs or certifications from the client. If they raise any outstanding issues or discrepancies, we should promptly address them and ensure that we receive the sign-off.
- **Documentation and knowledge transfer**: In addition to our final reports, we should hand over engagement documentation supporting our key findings, recommendations, and lessons learned. This is a valuable resource for the client's implementation team and can be used to inform their future work. We may have been required to follow a knowledge transfer process to ensure that the client's team fully understands the engagement's implications and can support our recommended solution. We should check that this has been completed satisfactorily and discuss with the client whether there is scope for a contract extension for longer-term support through more training sessions, one-on-one support, or creating new instructional materials. We also should complete our internal processes for archiving engagement-related documents, including contracts, reports, presentations, meeting notes, and correspondence, for future reference.
- **Evaluate our performance**: We should conduct a post-engagement evaluation separately from any post-engagement review with the client. This evaluation should compare our outcomes against our original objectives and our key performance indicators (KPIs). For example, did we meet our profitability targets and deliver the engagement within the contracted terms?
- **Obtain client feedback**: While our internal performance evaluation is useful, client feedback is essential. We should always conduct a client satisfaction survey to deepen our understanding of the client's satisfaction and identify areas for improvement. This survey should cover the overall quality of our services, engagement outcomes, and the performance of our team members. We should commit to actively addressing any concerns or areas for improvement raised by the client, thereby demonstrating our commitment to their satisfaction. After completing a survey, it is an ideal time to seek referrals and testimonials from satisfied clients to support expanding our network.
- **Settle financial and other commercial matters**: Before closing the engagement, we must verify that all invoices have been issued and payments received according to the agreed-upon terms. This will require reviewing our financial records and reconciling any outstanding balances, which may be straightforward but can be complex if we have received a number of contract variations. Sometimes clients will have disputed invoices, asked for refunds, or not paid us within agreed timescales. We should see that these are dealt with quickly, even if it involves negotiating with the client. Once these financial matters have been resolved, we can close the engagement's financial records and reconcile any outstanding balances. Other matters, including returning building access passes, closing access rights to systems, and returning any equipment used by the team, can then be settled.
- **Formalise engagement closure**: To close the engagement, we should always obtain the client's formal confirmation of engagement closure, acknowledging that all deliverables have been accepted, final payments have been made, and equipment returned. This confirmation will serve as official documentation of the engagement's completion. Finally, we must update our engagement management system with the engagement closure status and relevant documentation.

Step 6: Manage client relationships for the long term

Our secondary commercial objective of delivering engagement is to build our relationships with the client and client staff. This will support the continuing development of our network and open future opportunities. With an existing network, including new contacts encountered during an engagement, we can take a more organic and personalised approach to networking. For example, we might track and support all existing contacts as they move, either elsewhere in the client or are promoted. This will significantly expedite our relationship-building process and open new opportunities. For instance, a consulting firm working with a client for several years can leverage existing knowledge to introduce new team members or propose additional services. The established rapport enables them to navigate the client's organisational structure more effectively and anticipate their needs. Beware, however, the comment like this:

> *"You guys are like the wire coat hangers in my wardrobe – every time I open the door, you seem to have doubled in number"*

In contrast, when we start working for a new client, especially one where we had limited access to the client during the tender process, we will require a more proactive and structured approach to widening our contact base. This should echo our processes for developing our prospecting information.

Building trust and credibility across key stakeholders in the client from the outset is paramount. As we have few or no existing relationships, stakeholder mapping is crucial to identify key individuals and understand their organisational roles. For example, suppose we are in the situation of having won a contract via a tender process. In that case, we must invest significant time and effort in refining our understanding of the new client's structure, culture, and pain points. If we undertake a detailed stakeholder analysis, we can identify key players and expand our network to support the successful delivery of the current engagement and lasting relationships.

There are some differences in emphasis between expanding a contact network within an existing client and building one in a new client. In an established relationship, we can concentrate on deepening existing connections and exploring expansion opportunities directly with them. For example, we might ask for a meeting with the client's finance director to discuss how we could improve the performance of a poorly performing finance system. In contrast, a limited network requires a more concerted effort to build trust and credibility, often involving frequent check-ins and highly tailored communications.

Client relationship plan

In all cases, we need to separate tasks relating to managing the current engagement with managing the client relationship. Building strong long-term relationships with a client or a prospective client requires a planned approach tailored to each client that considers the specific context and the stage of the relationship. This is much wider than managing the current engagement, and effective client relationship management requires a comprehensive plan for nurturing and growing relationships across our client organisations. Our plan should outline tailored strategies and tactics to ensure client satisfaction, loyalty, and advocacy.

Key components of a client relationship plan include the following:

- **Clear objectives**: We should set specific goals for client relationships, such as increasing customer lifetime value and proposing opportunities.
- **Relationship mapping**: We need to expand the way in which we map relationships beyond understanding the key stakeholders within the client organisation. We also need to know who within our organisation has the best relationship with them and tailor our communication and engagement strategies accordingly. We should, however, always nominate a client relationship manager and allocate time for them to undertake the task.
- **Communication plan**: This now involves both the client recipient of communications and our identified best contact with them. We can then select the most effective communication channels and their frequency. This can include regular account meetings, engagement in conferences and exhibitions, and collaboration in preparing thought leadership papers, podcasts, and videos.
- **Feedback mechanisms**: We should have developed systems for gathering and analysing feedback from all clients on our relationships with them. These should be referenced in the plan and responsibilities assigned to a nominated individual.
- **Performance tracking**: We should also have developed systems for analysing data to measure the effectiveness of our client relationship management efforts. These should also be referenced in the plan and assigned to a nominated individual.
- **Value creation initiatives**: Strategies to provide exceptional client value, such as offering customised services, exclusive benefits, or thought leadership.

Reflections

Once again, please draw on your personal experience or your current situation for the case study or use the theoretical case study.

- List five client expectations for your case study.
- Based on your case study, set out the scope of the client engagement and a comprehensive plan for delivering it, including scope, resourcing, timing, deliverables, and quality standards.
- Did you remember to include the reporting cycle in your plan? If not, please include it now.
- Imagine that you are about 40%of the way through the engagement. Please prepare a progress report highlighting the main features of the work completed, any issues encountered, and an assessment of the delivery status against the contract.
- Draft a survey form to elicit client feedback on the engagement performance.

Notes

1 As mentioned in Chapter 1, there is another delivery cycle. The second one is essentially a project management cycle concerned with implementation support. Obviously, you should read Project Management Bootcamp A Step-by-Step Guide to help deliver any engagement moving into implementation support.
2 The most salutary lesson about why we need continuing communication during an engagement was having a chief executive physically tear a final report in half because they felt that staff "lied to you" during our research.
3 And of course, check it on Tuesday in case someone has dumped time on to your job code!

Bibliography

International Standards Organisation. (2017). *ISO 20700 Guidelines for Management Consultancy Services 2017-06*. Geneva: International Standards Organisation.

8 Consultancy Practice Management

How Should We Organise Ourselves?

Aim of this chapter: To consider the benefits and drawbacks of different ways of operating and delivering consultancy services.

Learning outcome: To be able to evaluate the different needs of a consultancy organisation for structure and support, including identifying how meeting these needs changes as the scale of the operation changes.

Solo consultant or corporate career?

Deciding on a solo management consultancy venture or joining an established corporate firm presents a strategic career choice for any experienced professional with refined skills; individual career aspirations, risk tolerance, and personal preferences deeply influence this decision.

A solo management consultancy is attractive because of its unparalleled autonomy and flexibility. As solo consultants, we dictate our schedules, select projects that interest us, and set fee rates. The financial upside is also attractive, as we retain all profits. Such a choice is often reinforced by the perceived opportunities for building our personal brand, cultivating a loyal client base, and avoiding the constraints of corporate bureaucracy.

Yet, our path as a solo consultant is not without its challenges. Building an initial client base can be time consuming and requires effective networking and marketing strategies. Income can be unpredictable, especially for new entrants, as workflow will vary. Experience shows that frequently, there is a need to undertake business development work to obtain future engagements at precisely the same time as existing client work, which is at peak effort. Additionally, we must manage all aspects of our business, including administrative tasks, accounting, and business development, which can be overwhelming. Without the support of a team of consultants, handling complex projects and accessing the diverse expertise required for some client assignments can also be challenging.

There are many advantages to joining a corporate consultancy instead of taking the solo option. Established firms typically have a steady stream of clients and a reputable brand. They have established consultancy teams and invest in developing and testing new working methods. Many will find working in such a team environment that fosters collaboration, idea exchange, and innovative solutions stimulating. Equally, new consultants may find the extensive training programmes and mentoring available in a larger firm extremely attractive.

DOI: 10.4324/9781003490456-9

A corporate consultancy route also has limitations, for example, rigid hierarchies, siloed operations, and limited autonomy. Sometimes, corporate policies on established methodologies and protocols stifle our creativity and innovation. Also, some consultancies have been shown to have a long-hours, high-pressure culture, leading to burnout and work–life balance issues. While income may be more stable, consultants often receive a fixed salary with limited control over their earnings, as a significant portion of the revenue generated goes to the firm. Finally, advancement up the corporate pyramid may be difficult as there is intense competition for limited opportunities, and some consultancies will operate an "up or out" policy.

Ultimately, our decision on which career path we choose to follow depends on our individual preferences, career stage, aspirations, and risk tolerance. A decision between being a solopreneur and joining a corporate consultancy is not necessarily a one-time choice. As consultants gain experience and their career goals evolve, they may transition between corporate and solo roles. Some consultants even combine the best of both worlds by establishing a consulting practice while working as part-time consultants for a corporate firm.

Ownership and management structures

Professional business consultancy organisations employ a variety of business and financial operating models to structure their operations, manage costs, and allocate responsibilities for profit and loss. When setting up or developing a consultancy organisation, it is always advisable to take expert advice on the operating model that will best meet our needs and fit within the business legislation of the jurisdictions where we intend to operate. The following section explores several distinct models, including sole ownership, partnerships, limited liability partnerships, and limited and public companies:

- **Sole proprietorships** are the simplest form of business organisation, where a single individual owns and operates the business. The proprietor may be a solo consultant or run a small firm with employed consultants and support staff. As the business owner, we have complete control of all aspects of the business, but our assets are at risk if the business fails. This makes it a high-risk, high-reward model. Many small consultancy firms start as sole proprietorships. For instance, a freelance business consultant might operate as a sole proprietor, managing all aspects of their business independently. In many jurisdictions, sole proprietors can create a simple form of a limited company, which may give their assets some protection.
- **Partnerships** are one of the oldest forms of business organisation. In a partnership, two or more individuals share ownership of the business and each share in its profits and losses. Partnerships set out the allocation of costs and responsibilities between the partners in a partnership agreement. Partnerships have shared risk, which means that partners are jointly liable for the business's debts. This can be a significant drawback because each partner's assets are at risk if the company incurs debt. This model allows for a high degree of collaboration and shared responsibility among senior consultants. The number of equity partners in the top ten echelon of consulting firms varies substantially, with many having another role of non-equity partner or director. McKinsey & Company operates as a partnership, with 2,700 partners sharing profits and losses and controlling the firm's strategic direction. The personal risk of such arrangements was revealed by the agreement of McKinsey in January 2025 to pay $650 million to resolve criminal and civil investigations regarding its consulting work with opioid manufacturers.
- **Limited Liability Partnerships (LLPs)** combine elements of partnerships with limited liability companies. They are not recognised in all jurisdictions and operate under regulations

varying between countries. Partners' liability is limited to their investment in the LLP, and costs and responsibilities are allocated based on a partnership agreement tailored to the firm's situation. For example, Deloitte operates as an LLP in many countries while limiting individual partners' liability for the firm's debts.

- **Limited and public companies** are separate legal entities from their owners. This means the company can own property, incur debt, and be sued. The owners (shareholders) have limited liability, meaning they are only responsible for the company's debts up to the amount they have invested. This model is advantageous because, like the LLP, it protects shareholders' personal assets. Costs and division of profits are clearly understood and are typically allocated based on the number of shares each shareholder owns. However, private limited companies must meet regulatory requirements, which vary by location. Public companies are similar to limited companies, with shares traded on public stock exchanges, and they can raise capital by selling shares. Capgemini is a public company listed on the Euronext Paris stock exchange, allowing it to access a broad base of investors and raise significant capital for expansion and development.
- **Cooperatives** are formal collaborations owned by their members and operated for mutual benefit. Each member has equal input to decisions, but profits are typically shared based on each member's participation. While this promotes democratic decision-making, it is challenging to manage because a consensus among members must be reached. The cooperative bylaws usually also set out how costs and responsibilities are shared. Examples of consultancies operating as cooperatives are relatively rare.
- **Franchises** allow individuals to operate a consultancy business under an established company's brand and business model. The franchisee pays an initial fee, which may be substantial. The franchisee usually also pays continuing fees for the right to use the brand. This model gives the franchisee a proven business model and brand recognition, reducing the risk of failure. ERA (previously Expense Reduction Analysts) has over 1,000 specialist consultants operating in 50 countries.
- **Hybrid models** combine elements of different structures to meet the business's specific needs. For example, a consultancy firm might operate as one or more limited companies but use a partnership model for particular service areas, collaborations, or international operations. This approach allows the firm to benefit from the liability protection of a limited company while maintaining the ownership, flexibility, and shared responsibility of a partnership. Hybrid models can be complex to manage but offer the advantage of tailoring the business structure to the firm's unique requirements. Costs and responsibilities are allocated based on the specific agreements governing each aspect of the business. PricewaterhouseCoopers, for example, operates as a network of firms, each a separate legal entity. This hybrid model allows them to operate globally while maintaining flexibility and local responsiveness.

Support teams

Creating effective support teams to provide essential services enables consultants to focus on delivering high-quality advice and solutions to clients. Their contribution is often overlooked but is critical to our overall success. They contribute directly to our clients' satisfaction, mitigate risks that could impact our success, and preserve, develop, and share our intellectual capital. While support teams are frequently found in larger consultancies, replicating them to ensure that consulting skills are focused on winning and delivering client engagements is essential for small firms and even solo consultants. We can do this by insourcing support from specialist providers, for example, virtual personal assistants, IT support, or graphic designers.

Typical support areas that we need to consider developing include at least the following:

- **Administrative support**: Our support teams handle various administrative tasks, including recruiting, onboarding, managing employee records, processing invoices, managing payroll, and handling financial reporting. They maintain office space, equipment, and supplies. They may also book travel and accommodations for consultants on client engagements and process and reimburse consultant expenses, ensuring timely reimbursements and facilitating smooth financial operations for consultants. Even a small firm may employ "back-office" staff to provide many of these functions. In contrast, a solo consultant may buy services from outside sources such as accounting, a virtual assistant, and travel booking.
- **Technology and infrastructure**: IT support teams are responsible for maintaining the firm's complex digital infrastructure, protecting sensitive client data, and complying with relevant data protection regulations. They have the difficult task of assisting widely dispersed consultants by ensuring they have access to the necessary tools and resources, which are kept updated and secure. There seems to be an inflexible rule of IT support that the more remote the client site, the more frequent the issues with the consultants' IT and phones.
- **Proposal development**: Writing compelling proposals requires a specific set of skills that is different from preparing consultancy reports. These skills include organisational, writing, graphic, and subject knowledge skills. Consequently, many consultancies have a dedicated support team for proposal development and bring in consultants as subject matter experts for a specific proposal. The support team also handles quality reviews and proposal submissions, including managing procurement deadlines and following up on client questions or concerns.
- **Research and analysis**: Larger consultancy firms may employ dedicated teams to research, collect, and organise vast amounts of data from various sources. These data may include industry reports, financial statements, market surveys, and internal company records. The data they organise are a foundation for their consultants' analysis and recommendations. Smaller firms can find replicating this approach challenging, but a data research analyst role can be attractive to recent graduates looking to develop a consultancy career. The competitive intelligence unit in one major consultancy routinely analyses industry trends, regulations, and economic factors to provide context for consultants' recommendations.
- **Financial modelling and analysis**: Many consultants develop financial models to forecast the potential impact of different strategic decisions, such as mergers, acquisitions, or cost-cutting measures. Still, there are inherent dangers in developing models outside strict controls and review protocols. Consequently, one major firm has used specialist teams to build financial models to guide companies through large-scale mergers. Scenarios are developed to evaluate the potential costs, benefits, and risks of different courses of action.
- **Engagement management and coordination**: Support teams often create and manage engagement plans, timelines, and resource allocation. Engagement managers (called project managers in some firms) are key to keeping our engagement on track and reporting progress to clients and within the consultancy. Although consultants sometimes act as engagement managers, they may equally be dedicated staff, particularly on more significant engagements. Their role is to coordinate the efforts of consultants, subject matter experts, and other stakeholders to ensure that engagements are delivered on time, to agreed quality standards and within budget. They also identify and mitigate potential risks that could impact engagement success.
- **Knowledge management and sharing**: In many larger consultancies, dedicated teams develop and maintain a repository of project documents, templates, and best practices. These teams aim to facilitate knowledge sharing to enhance efficiency and effectiveness. They may also support consultants' professional development through training programmes and mentorship initiatives.

Not all consultancies have this range of support teams. However, the areas of work they cover must be addressed as part of the fundamentals for maintaining a successful consultancy operation.

Continuing professional development

All management consultancies face increasing pressure to deliver innovative and practical solutions to their clients driven by a rapidly evolving business landscape. This requires that all consultants stay current with the latest industry trends, methodologies, and technological advancements. This requires us to invest in a process of planned continuous learning. This should include activities such as training programmes, gaining new certifications, and attending conferences and workshops. In this way, we acquire the new specialist skills and knowledge that enable us to continue to provide our clients with the most informed and valuable advice.

Not all training is painless, as we will see in a quick visit to consultant Jac's home. The partners in Jac's firm had a long-established practice of bringing their information security specialists together annually. This represented a significant investment for the firm in direct costs, staff and partner time, and lost fee income. However, ensuring that consultants' specialist skills were kept current was a key company policy, and the annual training conference also helped maintain a uniform culture and cross-team collaboration.

Jac has raised the issue of the annual training course.

"Jac, you are not planning on missing my birthday, again?"

It was a question with a sting. Jac had missed the last three birthdays because of the same annual course.

"It's not my fault; it's a combined course for all the firm's information security specialists across Europe. It's an update on industry developments and our evolving methods. It is just about mandatory. They always run it for a full week in June. For some reason, the firm's partners have agreed that the last week is best. I suppose it avoids peak holiday periods just about everywhere. So, I will have to suffer another week away from you."

"Suffer another week in some resort hotel with great food, sunshine and a pool!"

"But sunshine isn't guaranteed, and I promise we work hard all week."

"Just don't come back with a suntan, and I expect you to make it up to me – again!"

Why train consultants?

The argument for investing time and resources in training is that well-trained consultants are more likely to be efficient, effective, and saleable. On a personal level, developing our consulting skills should improve our problem-solving abilities, enhance our project management capabilities, and strengthen our written and verbal communication. A consistently high level of skill and expertise should visibly differentiate us from our competitors, help us attract more high-quality clients, and secure more high-value projects. Also, offering opportunities for professional development is an effective way to attract and retain the high-quality talent we need. It shows our commitment to our consultants, and when they feel valued and emotionally invested, our turnover rates are reduced, creating a more stable and productive work environment.

How much time should we invest "off the clock" in training and development? This varies between consultancies, with some setting aside a specific percentage of each consultant's time for training and development, perhaps 10–20%. Others may opt for dedicated training weeks, as in our last site visit. These immersive experiences allow consultants to focus exclusively on their development without the distractions of client or sales work. As in our site visit, some firms organise annual or bi-annual training weeks offering comprehensive programmes covering a wide range of topics, from new methodologies and technologies to industry trends and best practices.

Other firms follow a more flexible approach to personal development, often relying on ongoing learning alongside client work. This includes access to online courses, certifications, and attending industry conferences. Encouraging consultants to learn at their own pace and in relevant areas that interest them helps improve the results of such training. Many firms have adopted a mix-and-match approach, where a consultant's professional development may include various types of learning at different times.

Whatever approaches to professional development are adopted, ensuring that all professional development activities are relevant to our staff's current roles or are prepared for future ones, is essential.

Impact of profit and loss responsibility on operations

When creating or expanding a consultancy, it is essential to consider responsibility for profit and loss, which can be a significant factor in influencing behaviour. Except in the solo consultant situation, consultancies are competitive organisations internally, and the systems we design and how we measure individual senior managers influence their behaviours.

Let's drop in on a few conversations drawn from real-life large consultancies to see the way that profit and loss responsibilities can impact behaviours:

First, to Jac, a consultant in a consultancy linked to an accountancy partnership. Although employed by a regional partnership, Jac is currently working on a long-term engagement led by the London headquarters. The senior consultancy partner from their home regional office is calling Jac.

"Jac, you have been working on the London office client site for the best part of a year now."

"Yes, and I'll probably be there another year. It means a huge amount of commuting and very long days, but obviously, it's been marvellous for the company – high profile in the industry. I have expanded the work massively, and now we have a team drawn from the London office working for me. Not only am I booking all my time, but they would take me at weekends too if they could, and my fee rate is fantastic."

"It's that last piece that I want to talk to you about. The trouble is that we, the local partners, only get the value of your basic rate, and the London client is paying more than double that. So, we have agreed with London to split the added value between us. The only way to make this transfer happen is through the time booking system. This means that on the 1st of July, I want you to book 192 chargeable hours to the client."

"I am on leave that day."

"Book that as well."

Jac knew better than to ask if any funds this curious arrangement was transferring were coming their way. Perhaps during the next promotion round. . .

Second, a call between two senior managers, Jay and Kai, who work for a large quoted company that delivers consultancy services to public sector bodies. In this company, every team is charged with managing its profit and loss account and maximising profit. Jay leads a department that owns a framework contract and is trying to get consultants from Kai, the team director of a specialist team whose skills are required to support delivering a significant assignment.

Jay: "Kai, we have a fabulous opportunity to bid on the government framework to provide management and design staff to lead a major refurbishment project for an iconic building. The whole contract will be around 500 days, and it looks like over 50 days work initially for your team. We are likely to at least double that as I think the work will be far more complex than the client imagines. It will be high profile for us, and if we can clinch this one, there will be some other huge projects coming down the track from them, and we will be in a prime position to win them. Usual framework rates apply for principals, seniors, and consultants and as before, we will share the margin equally to reflect our contract management and framework sales costs."

Despite Jay's enthusiasm, Kai is not sold on the idea:

"I am sorry, Jay. It might seem a bit abrupt of me, but I cannot help you out on this one. I have to make my target margins, and the framework contract rates are too low for me even to consider sharing any margin with you. Frankly, it's better for me to let my team do my own practice development and drink coffee all day, waiting for higher-value work."

It will take senior director-level involvement to ensure Kai engages with the bidding process.

Third, two senior managers in a global consultancy have a policy that profits sit centrally in the company, not in individual teams.

"Hello, is that Dee? I am Bea, a group director from the London office. Dee, it has been suggested that one of your senior system security specialists in Seattle could provide some advice and support for a couple of weeks to a job I am leading from the UK for a client in the Middle East. It can be done remotely, so no worries about travel arrangements."

Dee, without hesitation: "Thanks for thinking of us. Sure, I can provide someone. When would you like them to start?"

These examples show different aspects of the problems that can arise when cross-team work meets accounting and management systems.

In the first case, sharing staff between offices was the norm, but the creaking accounting systems could not cope with reallocating staff at anything other than a single cost-based transfer rate, and even that required a degree of creative manipulation of the timesheet system.

In the second case, staff sharing was not routine, and although the accounting systems supported cross-team working, the lack of rules or processes led to the managers' argument.

Our last example involved a major consulting firm. Although its annual global turnover exceeds $14 billion, it operates a single profit and loss account. This approach supports its use of seamless staffing arrangements as a market differentiator.

Before proceeding, please take a few moments to consider the goals a multi-team consultancy should set for its financial systems and processes.

The first and second conversations in our micro-site visits are typical of consultancy organisations operating in multiple departmental or geographic business silos. Here each team operates essentially as a mini-business. Our third conversation was more unusual as the company operated a very different model of a single global profit and loss account. The choice between these models depends on each consultancy's strategic objectives, operational needs, and any client requirements.

Siloed business units can have significant advantages, foremost of which is that maintaining separate profit and loss accounts at the business unit level allows us to track their financial performance precisely. This enhances accountability, as each team or department manager is responsible for their financial outcomes. Also, when our business units operate as individual profit centres, they can develop deep specialisation in their respective areas. This leads to higher levels of expertise and more tailored services for clients. In addition, managers and employees can be more motivated to achieve financial targets when their performance visibly impacts profitability. Business units often also have greater autonomy in making decisions, which can lead to a more entrepreneurial culture within the organisation.

There are, however, also disadvantages, as we saw in our first and second examples, where the companies had failed to set up internal transfer pricing mechanisms to support cross-team working and to allocate costs and revenues between different business units. These mechanisms must be effective to ensure that the locus of cost remains in alignment with the locus of fee earning. We also saw that local considerations over profit levels can run counter to the interest of the firm as a whole. In the second conversation, the firm could not bid for a valuable 500-day contract with significant benefits across the firm because of one manager's narrow focus on rates for 50 days. Another issue is that siloing business units may lead to overlaps in skills, where teams prefer to build their own local talent pool rather than bring in staff from specialist teams, which would impact their profitability.

By contract running with a single profit and loss account allows consultancies to centralise resources, streamlining financial management and reducing administrative overhead. They can allocate expertise and skills where they are most needed, regardless of geographic location or the team within which they work. This ensures that client engagements benefit from the best available talent and knowledge, enhancing the quality of service provided to clients. It improves client outcomes by enabling the most appropriate consultants to be allocated to an engagement. It also means that the firm is flexible and agile and is able to respond to new client needs and changing market conditions quickly. In the firm in our third example, a single profit and loss account fosters a culture that enhances collaboration and communication. This supports clients' perception that they are dealing with a unified entity rather than a collaboration of semi-independent teams.

Monitoring and control – the importance of indicators

Consultancy is a data-rich business. Our business processes accumulate data on sales, staff, client engagements, and financial performance. At an organisational level, we need to establish data-led management processes and systems to ensure that we meet our current targets and are predicted to meet future targets. These monitoring and control processes have a single purpose: to enable us to adjust our actions and change our ways of doing things where we need to meet our goals, whether they are a utilisation rate of Z%, a turnover of $Y million, or a gross profit margin of X%.

Leading and lagging indicators

We can and do identify many indicators to keep us informed about the health of our consultancy business. Our problem is that many indicators, such as traditional financial reports, tell us where we have been. This is because a time lag exists between actual events and data about them appearing in reports. Take a consultant's time for the first week of a month. Typically, time data is built up during the month in a timesheet system. At month end, this data is transferred to the accounting system, valued for each job, reported in the accounting system, and invoiced to the client at some point. Consequently, we can expect a minimum delay in reporting week 1 activity in an accounting system of around four weeks and longer if month-end processing takes several days (or even weeks). Therefore, to manage our business, we also need other indicators to help us assess our current state and predict our future performance. These are typically derived from assessments of the progress of current engagements, sales predictions, and utilisation forecasting (much more on that later). This is because to control our business, we need to understand where we are varying from our expected performance as early as possible so that we can take action. First, we need to identify our key indicators and set our targets for each of them. Table 8.1 includes a list of possible indicators that we could include in a performance dashboard.

Table 8.1 Potential Performance Dashboard Components

Potential Performance Dashboard Components				
	Component	**Detail**	**Type**	**Source**
Sales	**Weighted sales forecast**	Projected revenue for the next quarter	Leading	Sales pipeline data
Sales	**Win rate**	Percentage of sales closed as won	Leading	Sales pipeline data
Sales	**Average deal size**	Average revenue per closed sale	Leading	Sales pipeline data
Sales	**Sales cycle length**	Average time taken to close a sale	Leading	Sales pipeline data
Engagement Progress	**Milestone completion**	Percentage of milestones completed on time	Leading	Monthly engagement reviews
Engagement Progress	**Milestone delay**	Number of days behind schedule for each milestone	Leading	Monthly engagement reviews
Engagement Progress	**Revenue recognition**	Actual revenue recognised versus budgeted revenue	Leading	Monthly engagement reviews
Engagement Progress	**Revenue recognition percentage**	Percentage of revenue contracted recognised to date	Leading	Monthly engagement reviews
Engagement Progress	**Client satisfaction**	Client satisfaction ratings (e.g. Net Promoter Score, Customer Satisfaction Score)	Leading	Client satisfaction surveys
Engagement Progress	**Client complaints**	Number of client escalations or complaints	Leading	Monthly engagement reviews
Engagement Progress	**Engagement budgets**	Actual engagement costs versus budgeted costs	Leading	Monthly engagement reviews
Engagement Progress	**Billings**	Actual billings to date versus planned billings	Lagging	Monthly engagement reviews
Engagement Progress	**Change in unbilled work**	Increase/decrease in unbilled work this period (value of work in progress)	Lagging	Monthly engagement reviews Accounting system

(Continued)

Table 8.1 (Continued)

Potential Performance Dashboard Components				
	Component	**Detail**	**Type**	**Source**
Utilisation	**Planned utilisation**	The timeline showing percentage resource utilisation by week is planned over the next period for current engagements	Leading	Monthly engagement reviews
	Actual utilisation	Timeline showing percentage resource utilisation by week over the previous period	Lagging	Consultant timesheets
	Utilisation forecast	Timeline showing percentage resource utilisation by week planned over the next period for current and forecast engagements	Leading	Monthly engagement reviews Weighted sales forecast
Financials	**Revenue year to date**	Actual revenues year to date	Lagging	Accounting system
	Revenue forecast	Forecast of revenue for the next quarter	Leading	
	Cost year to date	Actual costs year to date	Lagging	Accounting system
	Cost forecast	Forecast of operating costs, including labour costs, overhead, and other expenses	Leading	
	Profit and loss (P&L) year to date	Company's P&L statement, including revenue, cost of goods sold, operating expenses, and net income year to date	Lagging	Accounting system
	Profit and loss (P&L) forecast	Forecast of the company's P&L statement at year end, including revenue, cost of goods sold, operating expenses, and net income	Leading	Accounting system Monthly engagement reviews Sales pipeline data Budgeting system
	EBITDA year to date	Earnings before interest, taxes, depreciation, and amortisation year to date	Lagging	Accounting system
	EBITDA forecast	Forecast of earnings before interest, taxes, depreciation, and amortisation	Leading	Accounting system Monthly engagement reviews Sales pipeline data Budgeting system
	Cash flow forecast	Forecast of cash inflows and outflows	Leading	Monthly engagement reviews Sales pipeline data Budgeting system
Debt	**Levels of debtors**	A report detailing the total amount owed by clients	Lagging	Accounts receivable system
	Debt ageing	Breakdown of outstanding invoices by age, showing how long each invoice has been overdue	Lagging	Accounts receivable system

It is essential that alongside the data selected for our dashboard, we add variations from our expected level of performance for each one. So, in an oversimplified example, if our monthly revenue expectations are set to our annual revenue target divided by 12, that is, 8.33%, we need to know if there are any variations from that figure. We also need to be able to drill down into the underlying data to understand why such differences are arising and consider if and where actions need to be taken. Supporting a dashboard with exception reports where the underlying data deviates significantly from expectations is a valuable way to highlight issues where action may be required. In our simple example, if we have lower than planned revenue, a list of engagements where billings are less than anticipated may reveal issues such as follows:

1. *The engagement manager missed the cut-off date for a monthly billing cycle.*
2. *The engagement is progressing more slowly than planned.*
3. *The client has withdrawn from the contract.*

Goal or target setting

It is worth noting that some companies have a track record of repeatedly setting higher goals or targets without identifying plans to reach them. Typically, these are in the form of a statement such as:

> *This year, you achieved a total revenue of $X. Therefore, next year, your target is $X+10%.*

Instead, our ideal target-setting process should be different, and we should at least first ask the question:

> *What would you need to change to achieve a target of $X+10%?*

Setting a pathway of activities to meet a new higher target means that our monitoring and control processes can move from a post-event consideration of performance, that is, the review of lagging indicators, to the proactive evaluation of both activities against a plan and the output from those activities shown in our leading indicators. This type of early cycle review allows time for corrective action to be taken; for example, considering the value at each stage of a sales pipeline rather than merely considering closed sales gives us additional time to flex our actions to increase our pipeline value or increase resources to meet the potential workload.

We need to recognise that monitoring and control are two aspects of the same process and should be carried out on an established cyclical basis. Monitoring should be a data-led activity that generates management control actions to adjust performance. In most consultancies, this will be on a monthly cycle, balancing the management time and effort required with the need to intervene and take timely action. Figure 8.1 shows the complexity of the data sources we could use to include in a consolidated dashboard.

> *Ideally, monitoring data will be generated from and integrated with the consultancy's operating systems and processes, as Figure 8.1 suggests. However, this is not always the case.*
>
> *Consider the example of a multibillion-pound major UK consultancy and broader business services company. This FTSE 100 company insisted on using a cumbersome*

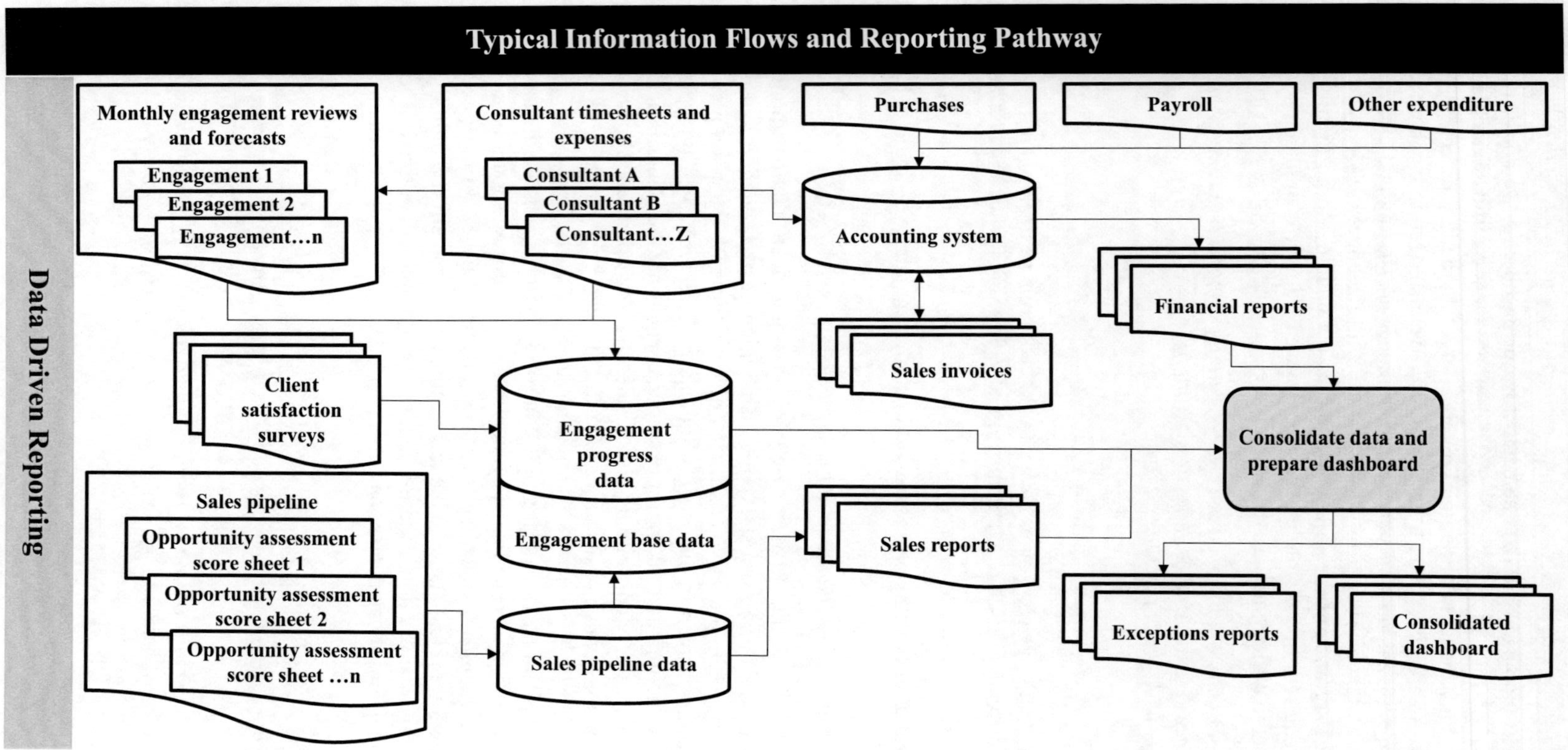

Figure 8.1 Typical Information Flows and Reporting Pathway.

spreadsheet-based monthly analysis of the financial performance of all of its areas of activity. From mid-month onwards, many senior managers' time was dedicated to detailed projections of the monthly income of all projects and future sales, each of which was discussed with a more senior manager. These projections were balanced against budgeted costs and then aggregated through a many-level hierarchy with variances from previous projections and variations between data held by different systems having to be justified at every level. Although the spreadsheet was loaded from the accounting system, it was totally divorced from the sales management system to which it had to be reconciled. It was also divorced from the usual month-end review of engagements.

These factors increased workloads and reduced managers' time available for sales or engagement management and control.

Please take a moment to list five ways such a process could be improved to make data more readily available to both team managers and the company board.

Professional services automation

Adopting an integrated professional services automation software package that removes or heavily reduces the need for the detailed data manipulation and transformation required in the example is desirable, even for a small company. When selecting an integrated professional services automation software package, we should consider the following functional features and other non-functional factors:

- **Functional features**: Some of these may be mandatory requirements, and others may be desirable. We can use the simple MoSCoW prioritisation of each one to help us select a suitable solution. MoSCoW stands for "Must have," "Could have," and "Would like to have."
  - Engagement management, including engagement planning and tracking, task management, milestone tracking, Gantt charts.
  - Resource management, including resource allocation and scheduling, utilisation tracking, capacity planning, skill-based resource management.
  - Financial management, including budgeting and forecasting, expense tracking, invoicing, and billing, profitability analysis, revenue recognition.
  - Time tracking including billable and non-billable hours tracking, timesheet management, real-time time tracking.
  - Client management, including customer relationship management (CRM), client communication tools, client portal access.
  - Collaboration tools, including team communication platforms, document sharing and management, real-time collaboration features.
  - Reporting and analytics including customisable dashboards and KPI tracking, financial reports, utilisation reports, project performance reports.
  - Automation and workflow, including automated billing and invoicing, workflow automation, notifications, and alerts.
  - Security and compliance, including data security measures, access controls, and permissions, compliance with national legislation and industry standards.
  - Mobile access for mobile time tracking and expense reporting.

- **Non-functional factors**: These are areas for us to consider rather than direct features of the proposed software:
  - Ensure the chosen solution can accommodate both current company size and planned growth.
  - Consider the operational service levels that the system will require and how the supplier will support these. For cloud-based solutions, this should be expressed as a percentage system availability; 99.99% is not unreasonable. Where software is being installed in-house, we need to consider fault fix times and the level of maintenance that the system will need, which requires the system to be taken offline.
  - It is always desirable to be able to easily customise the software to fit specific business processes and reporting. However, remember that our current business processes and reporting evolved based on previous systems, and consider amending them to take full advantage of the software's capabilities.
  - It is critical to avoid the problems in our last example and ensure compatibility with other tools and systems, such as customer relations management and accounting systems. If a package cannot provide full and seamless data integration, it will not yield maximum benefits.
  - Both initially and as the use of the software develops, excellent and accessible local support and resources will be essential. This includes the provision of onboarding support for the firm, user training, and customer support services.
  - Access to a customer-focused knowledge base and online documentation.
  - Total cost of ownership, including hardware, operating system, and other facilitating software, communications, insurance, maintenance, backup systems and staff, or cloud or other service provision arrangements.

Key performance indicators (1) revenue and utilisation

Certain key performance indicators in Table 8.1 are fundamental to demonstrating the health of any consultancy operation, and revenue and utilisation are at the top of the list.

Revenue projection – stay away from the cliff edge

The truth is that management consultants work on a short lead time, and clients usually want our help as soon as possible and for as short a time as possible. After that, there is a cliff edge beyond which we have no work arranged. Sometimes, the cliff edge is closer to us than others, and sometimes, it is far too close for comfort. The concept of the cliff edge is even more stark when, as the leader of a consultancy team, we plot a chart of contracted revenue. Each team member always has a cliff edge, after which they become available for work. We can translate this as:

> *After which they will generate no income while still generating cost.*

During our site visit in Chapter 1, the partner said,

> *"I have a forward looking weekly timeline representing chargeable time booked, non-chargeable time allocated – that's holidays, training, sales and so on, and the balance of time available. It really is that last one that I have to be concerned about, it is the "stock" that I still have to sell."*

Table 8.2 shows the impact of the partner's weekly timeline on the consultancy team's finances, with its income rapidly declining over the following 13 weeks.

Table 8.2 Forward Financial Projection – Contracted Work

Forward Financial Projection – Contracted Work													
Name	**Week 1**	**Week 2**	**Week 3**	**Week 4**	**Week 5**	**Week 6**	**Week 7**	**Week 8**	**Week 9**	**Week 10**	**Week 11**	**Week 12**	**Week 13**
Alex	6,000	6,000	6,000	6,000	6,000	6,000	4,800	3,600					
Avery	4,500	4,500	3,600	3,600									
Casey	5,000	5,000	5,000	5,000	5,000	5,000		5,000	5,000				
Jordan	4,250	4,250	3,400										
Kai	3,750	3,750	3,750	3,750									
Kris	6,000	6,000	6,000	6,000	6,000	6,000	6,000						
Lacey	4,950	4,950	4,950	1,650	1,650	1,650			1,650				
Morgan	4,500	4,500	1,800	1,800	900	900	900	900					
Phoenix	5,400	5,400	5,400	5,400	4,050	4,050	4,050	4,050	4,050	4,050	1,350	1,350	
Riley	3,750	3,750	3,750	3,750	3,750	3,750				3,750	3,750	3,750	3,750
Sage	4,250	4,250	4,250	4,250	4,250								
Taylor	4,950	4,950	3,300	3,300	3,300	3,300	3,300						
Zephyr	5,600	5,600	5,600	5,600	4,200	4,200			1,400	1,400	1,400	1,400	
Total	**62,900**	**62,900**	**56,800**	**50,100**	**39,100**	**34,850**	**19,050**	**13,550**	**12,100**	**9,200**	**6,500**	**6,500**	**3,750**
Fixed Costs	**56,610**	**56,610**	**56,610**	**56,610**	**56,610**	**56,610**	**56,610**	**56,610**	**56,610**	**56,610**	**56,610**	**56,610**	**56,610**
Margin	**6,290**	**6,290**	**190**	**-6,510**	**-17,510**	**-21,760**	**-37,560**	**-43,060**	**-44,510**	**-47,410**	**-50,110**	**-50,110**	**-52,860**

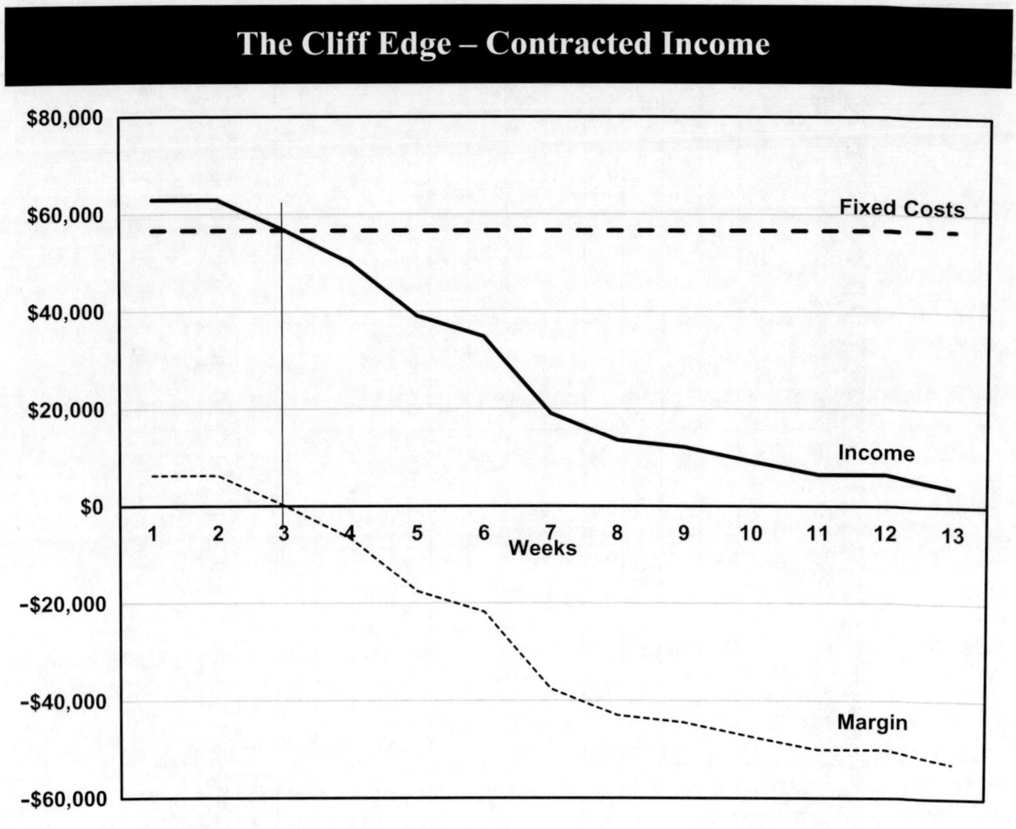

Figure 8.2 The Cliff Edge – Contracted Income.

The revenue cliff edge effect is shown even more starkly when the income projection is plotted as a graph. Figure 8.2 clearly shows that the team starts running at a loss as early as week 3 and is running out of almost all income by the end of the period:

Our management and control objective, as is that of the partner in the example, is both to push the cliff edge as far into the future as possible and to try and answer that question:

> *"And what happens to us then?"*

Utilisation – the key to success

Before moving on, it is worth considering an aspect of the partner's words: "the balance of time available." The metric they were concerned about was utilisation, perhaps the crucial leading indicator of efficiency and profitability. Utilisation rates measure how effectively resources are being employed within a professional services organisation.

A high utilisation rate generally indicates efficient resource management and good productivity. In contrast, a low rate may suggest underutilisation and the suggestion that perhaps we need to close more business more quickly. The downside is that excessively high utilisation rates over more extended periods are problematic. They can lead to burnout, decreased quality of work, and difficulty freeing up time for sales-related work, training, and holidays, as well as, in the long run, attracting and retaining talent.

The utilisation rate is calculated as follows:

$$Utilisation\ Rate = \frac{No.\ of\ Hours\ Billed}{Total\ Billable\ Hours} \times 100$$

When comparing utilisation rates between firms, it is worth noting that some firms will include all possible contracted working hours in their definition of total billable hours, for example, 52 weeks and 1 day × 40 hours per week = 2,088, or 2,096 in a leap year. Consequently, their utilisation rates should be lower than those of other firms that exclude contracted non-billable time, such as public holidays and vacations, from their calculations.

Accurate time tracking is crucial for calculating utilisation rates and for accurately billing consultant time-based engagements. It may also be a legal requirement in some jurisdictions, for example, to ensure that the total time worked does not exceed legal maximums.

We should also understand that fluctuations in client demand can impact resource utilisation, particularly where consultants are highly specialised and lack the flexibility to work across several types of engagement. Other individual consultant-related factors such as motivation, skill level, and location flexibility can also influence utilisation.

Taking our previous example (Figure 8.2) and stripping out the impact of different charging rates demonstrates the approaching cliff edge even more starkly. Figure 8.3 shows how the average staff utilisation rate drops rapidly over the same 13-week period.

Monitoring planned utilisation rates will identify areas for improvement and allocate resources. Consider the following hypothetical example:

1. A consultancy aims to make a profit margin of 10% across all of its activities.
2. An individual consultant is charged out at $2,000 per day for a planned 20 chargeable days, generating $40,000 in revenue with a margin of $4,000.

Due to poor coordination between engagement managers, the consultant is only chargeable for 18 days. Losing two days equals a $4,000 revenue loss, cancelling out the planned profit for the month.

We can improve utilisation rates by focusing on engagement management practices, optimising staffing levels, enhancing billing procedures, and better utilising technology. Simple actions such as scheduling training and holidays during otherwise quiet periods can significantly impact utilisation rates and improve profitability.

Key performance indicators (2) looking beyond the revenue cliff edge

Table 8.2 shows known costs and contracted revenue, which is fine but only part of our future income. To better understand the future, we must look beyond our contracted work's cliff edge. Estimating the value of our future sales, that is, our sales pipeline in addition to contracted work, is crucial for accurately forecasting revenue, setting realistic sales targets, and effectively allocating resources.

Putting you in the case study hot seat again. You are about to receive a call from the partner. The timing is not ideal, as it is late on a Friday afternoon, and Monday is a public holiday. You were about to take the whole long weekend off for a family celebration.

Your phone rings and the partner's name comes up. Looking at your watch, you grimace; you were about to leave a little early to avoid the worst of the homeward rush.

"Ah [insert your name here]. I'm glad I caught you. Are you still in the office?"

"Yes, I was just finishing a few things before the weekend."

"I have been in a partner's meeting all day, and they have been looking at the firm's sales pipeline measurement."

You need to say something to fill in the pause. "Er, yes?"

"They have asked me – by which we mean you – to prepare an overview of different techniques we could use. We do not need a major piece of work, just a few lines on each so that when we continue on Tuesday, we can have something to focus our discussion around."

"What time on Tuesday do you want it?"

"We are not meeting until noon, so would 11:00 be a good time for you to lead me through what you have prepared?"

You think, "Ah, so I am giving you a training course before you have to explain this to the other partners," but you say,

"OK, I am sure that I can do that."

"Thanks very much. I'm sorry it's short notice, but I knew you could handle it. Have a great weekend."

You put the phone down, smiling. Having just come back from a sales management course, you know this one is easy to handle, and your weekend is saved. Pulling out your course notes, you put together the following briefing note. You could send the it to the partner now, but perhaps an email with a delayed send until, say, midnight on Sunday. . .

Now you can catch that early train home.

PNX Consultancy Services

Briefing Note: Sales Pipeline Indicators

By [Insert your name here] DD/MMM/YYYY

Data from our pipeline can be analysed using several different methods, which can give us valuable insights into our potential revenue stream.

Weighted pipeline: This is a very commonly used metric. It requires that we assign a probability of closing a potential sale based on its stage in the sales process. This involves evaluating where each stands in our sales pyramid and estimating the likelihood of our closing the sale. Potential sales on the lower steps have a lower probability, while those in the final negotiation stages might have a higher one. We multiply the value of each sale by its probability of closing and sum the results to determine the total pipeline value.

Example: A sale worth $100,000 is judged to have a 50% probability of closing successfully; its weighted value is, therefore, $100,000 × 50% = $50,000.

We then predict the months in which the revenue will be earned to give us a view of our forward revenue stream. The advantage of this approach is that it provides a more realistic forecast because it considers the likelihood of each sale being achieved individually.

Historical conversion rates: Using our sales pyramid again, we ask a simple question: Historically, what are the average conversion rates at different steps on the pyramid? We apply these conversion rates to our current pipeline to estimate our expected revenue. This method is quicker than the weighted pipeline as it looks at groups of sales proposals. As it relies on past performance to predict future outcomes, it is helpful for businesses with consistent sales processes.

Example: If 20% of leads at the proposal stage historically convert to sales, and we have $500,000 worth of deals, we can expect $100,000 in revenue from these deals. We add similar calculations based on data about prospects at different steps in our pyramid to give future sales values.

Sales velocity: We calculate sales velocity to measure how quickly deals move through our sales pipeline and how much revenue they generate on average.

Sales velocity is a technique in which we combine several factors, the number of opportunities, our average deal size, expected win rate, and our sales cycle length, to provide a comprehensive view of our sales efficiency. The formula is:

$$Sales\ Velocity = \frac{No:of\ \ Opportunities \times Average\ Deal\ Size \times Win\ Rate}{Sales\ Cycle\ Length}$$

This method helps us understand the efficiency of our sales process and predict future revenue based on current pipeline dynamics.

Example: If we have 50 opportunities, an average deal size of $100,000, a win rate of 20%, and a sales cycle length of 30 days, our sales velocity would be:

$$Sales\ Velocity = \frac{50 \times 100,000 \times 0:2}{30} = \$33,333:33$$

This will generate approximately $33,333.33 per day from our sales pipeline.

Pipeline coverage ratio: Our pipeline coverage ratio is worked out by comparing the value of our sales pipeline to our sales target. In the interpretation of results, a higher ratio indicates a healthier pipeline, suggesting more potential deals than needed to meet our targets. The formula is:

$$Pipeline\,Coverage\ Ratio = \frac{Total\ Pipeline\,Value}{Sales\,Target}$$

Example: If our sales target for the quarter is $2,000,000 and our total pipeline value is $5,000,000, our pipeline coverage ratio would be:

$$Pipeline\ Coverage\ Ratio = \frac{\$5,000,000}{\$2,000,000} = 2.5$$

This means we have 2.5 times the pipeline value needed to meet our sales target.

Weighted lead scoring: We assign values to leads based on various criteria such as client engagement level, the fit of the client with our ideal customer profile and our past interactions with the clients. We also weight these criteria according to our assessment of their importance. This method helps us prioritise leads that are more likely to convert, providing a more accurate forecast of future sales. The formula is:

$$\textit{Total Lead Score} = \textit{Engagement Score} \times \textit{Engagement Weight} + \textit{Fit Score} \times \textit{Fit Weight} + \textit{Past Interaction Score} \times \textit{Past Interaction Weight}$$

Engagement Score = points assigned based on how the prospect has interacted with us to date for this opportunity, for example, by issuing a tender, holding preliminary sales meetings, and responding to outreach marketing.

Fit Score = points assigned based on how well the lead matches your ideal customer profile (job title, company size, industry, etc.).

Past Interaction Score = points assigned based on previous interactions with your company (attended webinars, requested demos, etc.).

Weights = allow us to flex the relative importance of each factor in our calculations. A higher weight means that it is more influential in the overall score.

However, to calculate our potential revenue, we also have to take into account our historical conversion rate and the average value of each sale.

Example: The table shows the various factors and values used in calculating the potential revenue of an opportunity.

Factor	*Score*	*Weight*	*Weighted Score*
Engagement	40	0.40	16.00
Fit	35	0.50	17.50
Past interaction	5	0.10	0.50
Total lead score			34.00
Max possible score			100.00
Historical conversion rate			0.70
Average sale value			100,000.00

Our calculation of potential revenue is as follows:

$$\text{Estimated potential Revenue} = \left(\frac{34}{100}\right) \times 0.7 \times \$100{,}000 = \$23{,}800$$

By using these methods singly or in combination, we can comprehensively understand our sales pipeline and make informed decisions to drive revenue growth.

Extending our previous example, Figure 8.3 shows potential income from different perspective engagements using the weighted pipeline method. We can now add this projected value of future sales to our known contracted income to give a more balanced view of our future revenue.

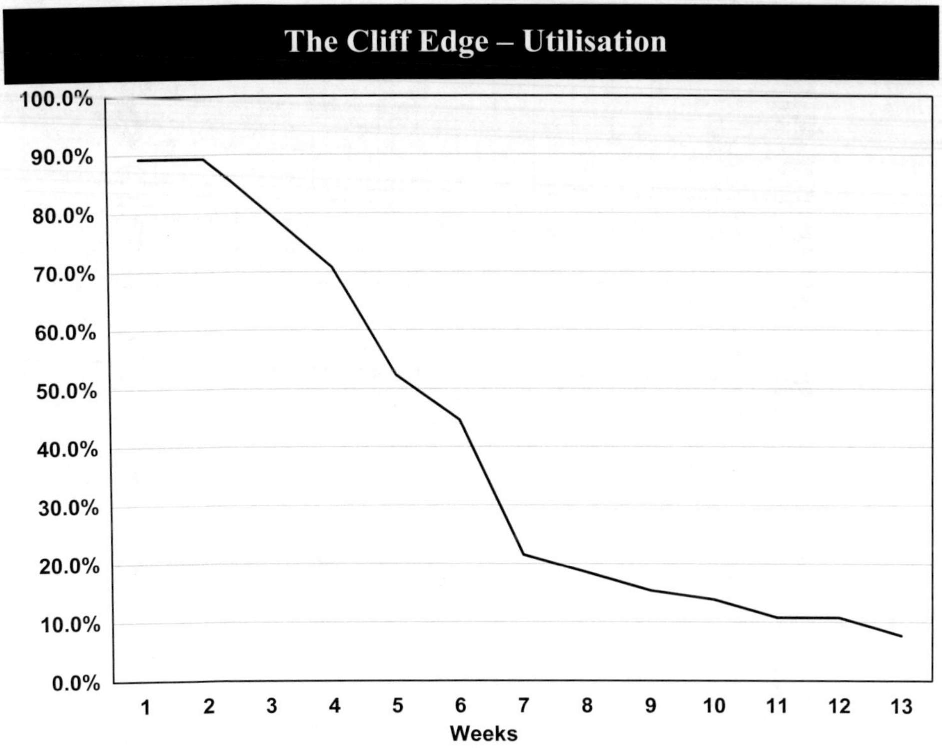

Figure 8.3 The Cliff Edge – Utilisation.

This potential income is again shown by week as we are commonly interested in the valuation of possible future sales and their delivery timing. In consultancy, we must always introduce another dimension to our income projections: resource availability. We are interested in forecasting not only revenue based on client needs but also actual hours that may be delivered. This is because staff contracted hours are reduced by holidays, sickness, and training. If needed, we may increase our forecast in the shorter term to include agency staff or contractors (remembering that the margins will be different) and in the longer term to include additional recruitment.

Table 8.3 shows that by including the weighted sales pipeline values, we may have an additional six weeks before we meet our cliff edge. Figure 8.4 plots these values and again underlines that although the cliff edge moves further away, it never disappears!

In summary, setting realistic and achievable revenue and utilisation targets, monitoring progress against them, and taking early action when differences arise are the bedrock of controlling the performance of any consultancy. Many of the other leading indicators help us understand how each of the processes we need to help us reach our overall objectives is currently performing. The lagging indicators allow us to compare recent performance with past periods. Again, investigating variances from expected performance can help us understand which areas we need to concentrate on to improve overall performance.

Table 8.3 Forward Financial Projection – Sales Pipeline

Forward Financial Projection – Sales Pipeline														
Client	**Weight (%)**	**Week 1**	**Week 2**	**Week 3**	**Week 4**	**Week 5**	**Week 6**	**Week 7**	**Week 8**	**Week 9**	**Week 10**	**Week 11**	**Week 12**	**Week 13**
Aardvark Apps	**80%**	–	–	4,000	4,000	4,000	4,000	4,000	4,000	–	–	–	–	–
Badger Bytes	**70%**	–	–	–	4,400	4,400	4,400	4,400	–	–	–	–	–	–
Cactus Creations	**50%**	–	–	–	–	–	–	3,600	3,600	3,600	3,600	3,600	3,600	3,600
Dolphin Designs	**60%**	–	–	–	–	–	–	–	–	–	–	4,000	4,000	4,000
Eagle Enterprises	**30%**	–	–	–	–	4,000	4,000	4,000	4,000	4,000	4,000	4,000	4,000	4,000
Fox Finance	**70%**	–	–	3,200	3,200	3,200	3,200	3,200	3,200	3,200	–	–	–	–
Gecko Games	**30%**	–	–	–	–	2,400	2,400	2,400	2,400	2,400	800	800	–	–
Hippo Health	**90%**	–	4,000	4,000	3,200	3,200	3,200	3,200	3,200	3,200	800	–	–	–
Iguana Innovations	**90%**	–	–	–	–	2,400	2,400	2,400	2,400	2,400	2,400	800	800	800
Jaguar Jets	**70%**	–	–	–	–	–	–	–	–	4,000	4,000	4,000	4,000	4,000
Kangaroo Kids	**20%**	–	–	–	–	2,400	2,400	2,400	1,600	–	–	–	–	–
Lemur Labs	**20%**	–	–	–	–	–	–	–	2,400	1,600	1,600	1,600	4,000	4,000
Monkey Media	**20%**	–	–	–	–	–	–	–	3,200	3,200	3,200	2,400	2,400	4,000
Total		**–**	**4,000**	**11,200**	**14,800**	**26,000**	**26,000**	**29,600**	**30,000**	**27,600**	**20,400**	**21,200**	**22,800**	**24,400**

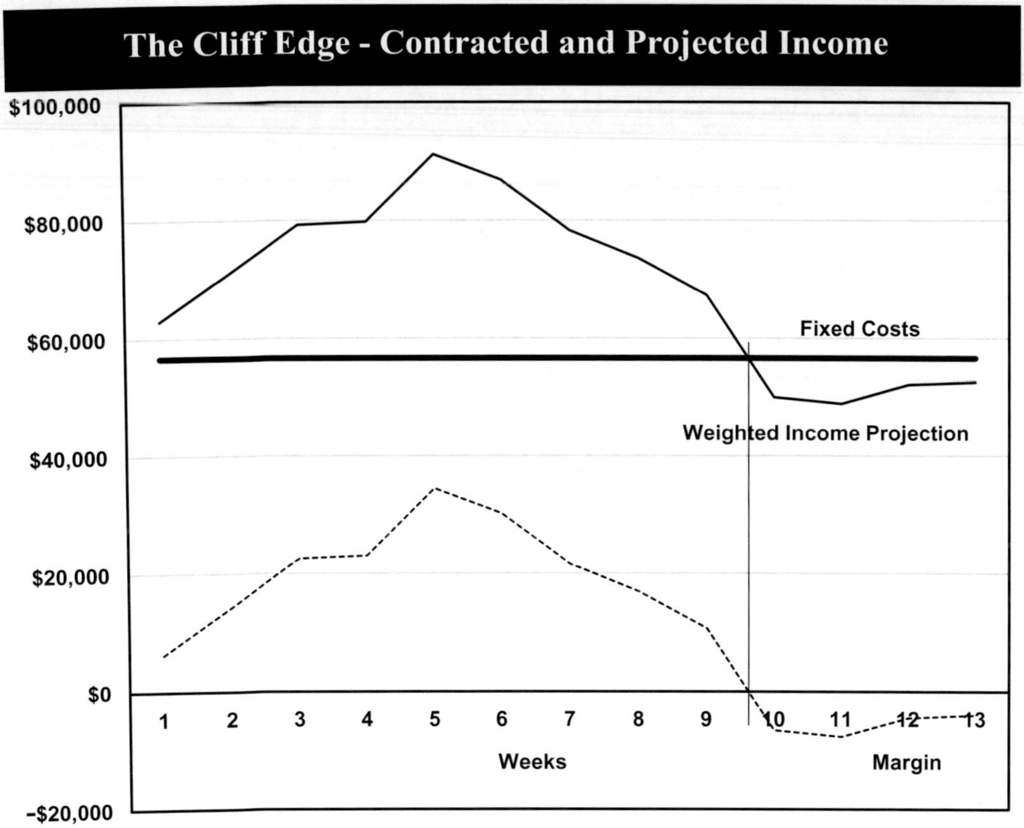

Figure 8.4 The Cliff Edge – Contracted and Projected Income.

Reflections

As always, please draw on your experience and current situation or use your imagination to help fill in your answers from the theoretical case study.

- Please highlight the key functions and support staff requirements for your consultants. If you are basing your answers on a small consultancy or solopreneur situation, please formulate these needs as work packages for a supplier to quote against. For larger consultancies, please create a series of short role descriptions.
- For smaller consultancy and solopreneur examples, please design an effective reward structure for a collaborative marketing and delivery arrangement. For larger consultancy examples, please create a manager's incentive programme based on team performance, which aims to foster cooperation between managers of different teams.

9 Methodologies and Tools

Whose Thinking Should We Use?

Aim of this chapter: To identify different areas in which fast-evolving methodologies, techniques, and tools can often be used to increase the effectiveness of delivering consultancy or reduce its cost, including employing artificial intelligence as a support tool. Such thinking and analysis tools expressly include PESTLE.

Learning outcome: Understand and apply the basic principles of evaluating different methodologies and tools.

In this chapter, we are concerned with tools to support our engagement delivery.

In delivering a consultancy assignment for a client, we can use multiple approaches and tools, which are developing continuously. There are tools, aids, and methodologies that we can employ during the principal stages of any advisory assignment. As always, not all of our engagements will follow this classic advisory pattern, and some specific types of engagement will require more specialist tools. Figure 9.1 introduces tools that could assist in our key engagement stages of information gathering, analysis, problem resolution, and reporting. As before, these stages are often iterative processes that overlap, and we will revisit different tools and techniques multiple times during the assignment. A full description of each of the tools identified is beyond the scope of this book, and a consultant wishing to use one is advised to research further details. Some of the tools also have accreditation requirements.

Step 1: Problem investigation and information gathering

You are back in the hot seat again in your role as the new soon-to-be director of the consultancy service aimed at sharing financial services expertise and solutions across other sectors.

Your phone rings, and it's your partner's executive assistant.

"Hi [insert your name here]. It's Dee. I was wondering if you could help this client. I am afraid it's a bit left field for you, but as you know, there is a major partner conference on . . . Briefly, this is a very important client-we have a call-off contract with them, which gives us 5% of our turnover, and we always give them the highest priority. I have Jay, their CEO, on the phone. Jay is a personal friend of our international board chair. Please will you take it. I have nowhere else to turn."

Dee is the person who holds all of the unofficial power in your part of the organisation. Not only does Dee control access to the partner, but also sits on various staff committees

DOI: 10.4324/9781003490456-10

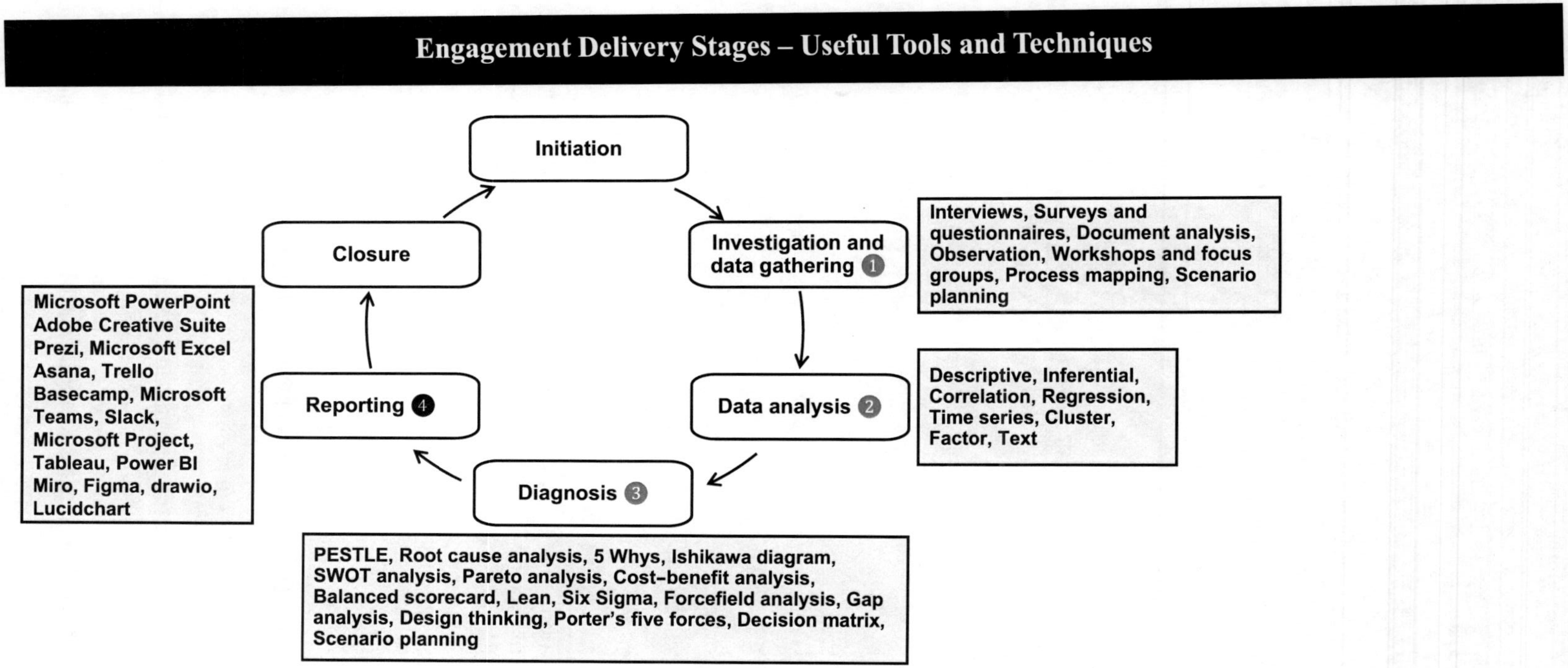

Figure 9.1 Engagement Delivery Stages – Useful Tools and Techniques.

with main board members. Dee reputedly runs a shadowy organisation of all executive assistants.

So, of course, you say.

"Yes, Dee, put them on. I'll see what I can do."

A moment or two later

"Hello, this is Jay of XFX Company. I am so glad to talk to an expert who may be able to help us out."

You wonder what Dee has actually told him.

"What is it that is worrying you?"

"I suppose it's a simple problem, but our team can't find an acceptable answer, and time is getting short. Dee says you could come in tomorrow and discuss the way forward with us. We can call off your time from the standing contract, probably take a week and then come back and let me know what you think."

You still have no idea what Jay is worried about. So, you say.

"That's fine. I can get to you at about 9:30. I need to describe this in our time booking system. What should I put down?"

"Oh yes, I hadn't said that our problem is we need to introduce a new product labelling and numbering design that meets international standards but can cope with the tiny size of some of our product packaging. Ask for me at reception, and I will see you get looked after."

"Your first thought was, Dee, you must have been desperate to pass this on to me."

"Your second thought was, What do I do now?"

What would you do?

When we select the information-gathering techniques we wish to use in an engagement, we should be sensitive to various factors. These include our research questions, the target population, our available resources, the timescale, and the desired level of detail to be collected. During our site visit, before meeting the client, you may have had the opportunity to do background reading on the company, its products, international labelling and design standards, and a little else.

When planning an information-gathering exercise, the available approaches include the following:

- **Interviews** are a primary foundation of our qualitative research, especially where we are not collecting information from large numbers of people. Provided we adequately prepare for each one, they provide a rich primary data source. There are three approaches to interviews that we should understand:
  - Structured interviews have pre-determined questions to ensure consistency across a large sample. Often, these interviews are an in-person way of collecting survey data, which can also be obtained by other means. They are particularly useful for quantitative analysis. If, for example, we are assessing customer satisfaction, a structured interview might ask a

series of Likert-scale questions about various aspects of our services or products. Typically, we might ask respondents to rate their satisfaction on a scale of one to five, where one is "very dissatisfied" and five is "very satisfied."

- Unstructured interviews give us maximum flexibility due to their open conversation format. We may utilise them for exploratory inquiries or when the subject is complex. For example, we could conduct an unstructured interview to discover the underlying causes of a drop in client satisfaction. It is beneficial to conclude interviews with the unstructured question, "Is there anything else we should have covered?" or with a more structured approach, "Are there three things that a solution should avoid?" Next: "If we are to be judged successful, are there three things we should do well?" Asking the questions in this order ensures that the interview closes on a favourable note.
- Semi-structured interviews allow us to balance structured questions and flexibility. We follow a general guide but can adapt our questions based on the interviewee's answers. We can also pursue any issues that emerge with them, generating unexpected insights and leading to new lines of questioning. We may also use these responses as potential lines of inquiry in later interviews.

- **Surveys and questionnaires** are extremely powerful means of collecting quantitative data from samples of larger target populations. Frequent methods used to gather information on attitudes, opinions, and behaviours include the following:
  - Likert scales, where respondents are asked to quantify the intensity of their views using a numeric scale, often zero to five.
  - Semantic differential scales are similar to Likert scales, with the added refinement that respondents are asked to respond based on their position on a continuum between two adjectives, such as between happy and sad or expensive and cheap. For example, a question might ask respondents to give a brand a position on a scale ranging from "weak" to "strong."
  - Open-ended questions are helpful when we need to gather qualitative data. We ask respondents to describe their views in their own words; for example, we might ask our respondents to briefly describe their experiences with a product, company, or service.
- **Document analysis** gives us insights into a client's performance, challenges, and opportunities by systematically reviewing various documents such as emails, finance and other reports, web pages, and social media posts, and extracting and summarising relevant information. Automating such reviews using AI can speed up our work enormously and allow us to focus on higher-level analysis. The danger, as ever, is that the selection and summarising processes may obscure data sources, and inappropriate or unbalanced analysis may result from including documents of doubtful accuracy or origin. The Garbage in, Garbage out rule applies to AI's suggestions.
- **Observation** allows us to gain first-hand insights into organisational behaviour and processes. Participant observation involves immersing ourselves in the setting, while non-participant observation involves observing from a distance. Taking observation to the next level, a quantitative technique, time-motion studies, can be used to measure the time taken to complete specific tasks. This was the core of the Charles Bedaux method (see Chapter 1), with the Bedaux's man (usually) pictured as hiding behind a pillar with a clipboard. Analysing the data collected can allow the identification of differences between groups of similar workers and help to identify best practices to replicate or inefficiencies requiring improvement. For

example, a famous observation study of a hand-built sports car manufacturer revealed the following:

- Engines were being fitted early rather than late in the process, thereby increasing the cost of stock holding without adding any value.
- Reorganising the manufacturing process on the factory's sloping site would enable production to flow only downhill, reducing the effort required to move partially completed vehicles.

- **Workshops and focus groups** are interactive methods that facilitate collaborative problem-solving and idea generation. They also have an edge on interviews in that we can engage with multiple people simultaneously, saving time and allowing engagement with a much wider range than we would probably interview. The interaction between individuals also generates information and ideas that may not have been discovered otherwise. Many techniques can be used to utilise groups, such as follows:

  - Open discussion, which can have limitations when we wish to ensure that all views are heard, such as some participants being reticent to express their views, others attempting to dominate a discussion and deference to senior managers present.
  - Structured discussion, which is facilitated to ensure that the views of all participants are heard and valued equally.
  - Brainstorming, which is also facilitated and is a common technique, which encourages participants to generate a large number of ideas without judgement.

  Other tools include starbursting and mind mapping, which are visual tools for organising information and identifying relationships between different concepts (see Chapter 3).
- **Process mapping** is a visual representation of a process, and there are multiple different ways of mapping processes from very simple to highly complex and sophisticated. For example, swim lane diagrams, which plot different activities against different roles in the process, can be very useful for the consultant, and are easily understood by clients. Identifying the existing flow of work allows us to spot bottlenecks and inefficiencies and be able to recommend improvements to streamline operations and reduce costs. If, for example, we map a customer service process, we could reveal where some steps or delays could be eliminated. As this is a visual tool, it can be of enormous value when engaging with workshops or focus groups where the participants can be facilitated to define current and improved processes and to identify the barriers to and the facilitators of change. All we need is a wall, a roll of brown paper, a felt marker, and a pad of sticky notes[1]
- **Scenario planning** is a tool that allows us to gain an understanding of our client's often complex operating environments and the uncertainties that they face. Based on a range of assumptions about the uncertain future, it involves developing multiple plausible future scenarios with the client and exploring potential risks and opportunities in each. For example, a scenario planning exercise might involve developing multiple scenarios by varying economic, technological, or political factors. Running scenario planning as a specialised workshop is helpful, usually with attendees drawn from across the affected areas of the client's business. However, it may also be beneficial to include key stakeholders and other people with specialised knowledge.

Often, we use a combination of methods to triangulate information and ensure a comprehensive understanding of issues by ourselves and the client. For example, we might use surveys or structured interviews to collect quantitative data and analyse areas where workshops are required to explore specific topics in depth. We then give feedback on the workshop outputs to key stakeholders in unstructured interviews.

Step 2: Data analysis – getting a handle on the numbers

By transforming raw data into insights and forecasts, we provide the evidence on which to base our recommendations, whether they concern strategic direction or operational improvements. AI tools, big data derived from continuous process monitoring, and integrating data from different sources are transforming how we can access and analyse data, making data analysis an ever-more-powerful tool. Even when AI is employed to speed up the analysis, if we understand common data analysis techniques, we can select the most appropriate ones for the current engagement.

The most common data analysis techniques include the following:

- **Descriptive analysis** makes raw data more comprehensible by summarising and organising it, often with basic statistical tools such as the arithmetic mean, median, mode, and standard deviation.[2] This gives us a view of the data that lets us identify patterns, trends, and anomalies. Spreadsheet software such as Excel has many built-in statistical functions, which are often extremely useful. Tools such as histograms and scatter plots allow us to visualise data distributions, which helps us quickly identify trends, anomalies, and potential areas for improvement. For example, if we need to analyse sales data for a retail customer, we might use Excel to create a scatter graph of sales figures over time against marketing spend. The visual insight this gives may then prompt us to investigate the effectiveness of different marketing strategies.
- **Inferential analysis** allows us to derive inferences about a wider population from a sample of data. This goes beyond simply reporting the data and will enable us to make predictions and test hypotheses. An essential feature of inferential analysis is our ability to extrapolate results obtained from a sample to a larger population. This lets us test our hypotheses to assess whether the differences or connections in the sample are statistically significant or due to chance. How we select our sample can impact our results, but ideally, a genuinely random sample will be chosen. Our results should always be expressed within a confidence interval; 95% is the level usually quoted. This means that we are 95% confident that our sample result will reflect the larger population. Generally speaking, the larger our sample size, the greater the level of confidence that we can have in our result.
- **Correlation analysis** is used to indicate relationships between variables. It helps us comprehend and explain the strength and direction of these linkages, for example, understanding the relationship between marketing spending and sales revenue. The following tools can help check the correlation between variables:

  - Pearson's correlation coefficient is used to measure linear correlations between variables.
  - Spearman rank correlation examines associations that show a consistent directional trend between variables but are not necessarily linear.

  Correlation does not imply causality. A classic illustration of this is the correlation between the level of ice cream sales and the number of shark attacks in the USA. Both increase during the summer months. However, this does not mean eating ice cream causes shark attacks or vice versa, but there is a link. The common factor is warm weather, which leads to more people buying ice cream and swimming in the ocean, increasing the likelihood of shark attacks.

- **Regression analysis** is another powerful statistical tool for predicting outcomes and understanding the relationships between variables. It entails investigating the effects of one or more independent variables on a dependent variable. Regression analysis is helpful when we want to predict future trends and optimise processes. Regression analysis, like all other statistical methods, has limits, and the accuracy of our forecasts is always determined by the quality of our data and the suitability of the models we have chosen to use.
- **Time series analysis** allows us to understand trends, seasonality, and cyclical patterns in data collected over time. Various tools, such as Autoregressive Integrated Moving Average (ARIMA), seasonal ARIMA (SARIMA), Holt-Winters Exponential Smoothing, Error, Trend, and Seasonal (ETS), allow us to forecast future values and identify underlying trends. For example, we could predict future demand for a product by analysing historical sales data and helping the client to optimise their manufacturing and inventory levels.
- **Cluster analysis**, as the name suggests, is an effective statistical way of identifying groups within a dataset. This means we can obtain more profound insights and make better judgements by categorising related items or individuals based on particular qualities. Perhaps the best-known example of cluster analysis was a spatial cluster analysis of victims of London's 1854 cholera epidemic in Soho. By analysing the distribution of the victims' addresses, Dr John Snow showed that the source of the epidemic was a single water pump. Cluster analysis examines the similarities and contrasts between data points and groups them into clusters. Each cluster has data points that are more comparable to one another than to those in other clusters. For example, consider an engagement for an online retailer wishing to target their marketing more closely to customers' needs. We could use cluster analysis to segment customers based on their previous purchasing behaviour, demographics, and any expressed preferences. This type of segmentation would allow us to identify where targeted campaigns for each customer group could increase the effectiveness of our client's marketing efforts and increase their sales.
- **Factor analysis** identifies underlying factors in datasets that explain the correlations between the variables that we can observe and measure. The idea is that simplifying the complexity of a dataset enables us to pinpoint the most significant factors driving a particular phenomenon, for example, the warm weather driving both ice cream sales and shark attacks. Factor analysis is particularly valuable when numerous interrelated variables make it challenging to discern the primary influences. Using AI tools to support factor analysis can help us handle complex data, improve data accuracy, and identify additional underlying factors. We could use factor analysis, for example, to understand customer survey data to enhance customer loyalty for a retail client. This analysis could be based on key data such as the frequency of each customer's shopping visits, the content, and the value of their shopping basket. Factors significantly influencing the loyalty of their customers could then be determined, which could include the quality of our client's products, perception of their brand, and their service to customers. We then have the evidence to back recommendations for prioritising improvements in these areas.

Step 3: Diagnosing the problem

Fortunately, we have a multiplicity of tools to help us. We have already used some in the early stages of the project. We are now refining them to help us identify the solution or solutions most applicable to our client's situation. In many cases, we will use multiple tools to identify different aspects of the client's issues. The tools we use evolve continuously, and radical new tools also emerge. However, the following are frequently used:

- **PESTLE** analysis is used to understand the external environment in which a client operates. It stands for:
  - **Political**: Government policies at local, regional, and national levels, including political stability, tax policy, trade regulations, and political risk.
  - **Economic**: Economic trends, including economic growth, interest rates, exchange rates, inflation rates, and disposable income levels.
  - **Sociocultural**: Cultural norms, values, demographic changes, population growth rates, age distribution, and career attitudes.
  - **Technological**: Technological advancements, rate of technological change, and level of innovation.
  - **Legal**: Employment laws, consumer laws, health and safety laws, and environmental regulations.
  - **Environmental**: Environmental regulations, climate change, and natural disasters.

Table 9.1 is an example of a completed high-level PESTLE analysis.

Table 9.1 XYZ Exotic Furniture Manufacturer: Example PESTLE Analysis

XYZ Exotic Furniture Manufacturer Example PESTLE Analysis		
Factor	**Potential Impact**	**Strategic Implications**
Political	Changes in import/export tariffs, subsidies, and trade agreements affecting tropical hardwoods	Monitor global trade policies, diversify sourcing, and explore alternative materials to mitigate potential supply chain disruptions
Economic	Economic fluctuations impacting consumer spending on luxury goods Exchange rate volatility	Adjust pricing strategies and target niche markets Optimise production to balance costs and quality
Sociocultural	Changing consumer preferences towards sustainable and ethical products Increasing demand for bespoke furniture	Emphasise sustainable sourcing, offer customisation options, and communicate brand values to attract discerning customers
Technological	Advancements in woodworking machinery, design software, and digital marketing	Invest in modern technology to improve efficiency, precision, and product design capabilities Utilise digital platforms to reach a global customer base
Legal	Stricter environmental regulations on deforestation and timber sourcing, labour laws, and consumer protection laws	Ensure compliance with international timber certification standards, invest in sustainable forestry practices, and prioritise fair labour practices
Environmental	Climate change impacting timber supply Increasing awareness of deforestation and resource depletion	Source timber from responsibly managed forests Explore alternative sustainable materials Implement better cutting and waste reduction strategies

PESTLE analysis is a core component of the Common Body of Knowledge of the USA Institute of Management Consultants and has several significant strengths. Most importantly, it provides a comprehensive overview of the external environment, which informs strategic decision-making by identifying opportunities and threats. It also enhances market understanding by prompting us to evaluate market dynamics and consumer behaviour. Finally, PESTLE is industry and sector-neutral and can be applied to virtually all clients.

Equally, PESTLE has some limitations and weaknesses, which we need to consider and address in the other analysis tools we choose to use. One major criticism is that external factors can be over-emphasised at the expense of internal capabilities, strengths, and weaknesses. Also, an external environment that is constantly changing makes it challenging to keep a PESTLE analysis up to date. The different external factors that PESTLE analyses have complex and multiple relationships, making using this approach challenging. In terms of delivering a consultancy engagement, PESTLE analyses depend upon how we interpret the information collected. Consequently, as different analysts may have different perspectives and biases, it is recognised that this may lead to varying conclusions. Finally, preparing a PESTLE analysis for a client can require significant time and resources, which we must allow for in our engagement plan.

- **Root cause analysis (RCA)** delves beyond surface-level symptoms to uncover the underlying causes of issues. RCA is a systematic, investigative technique used to identify the root causes of problems, whether internal or external to the client organisation. We drill down to identify the underlying issue so that we can recommend carefully targeted resolutions. For example, in a factory experiencing frequent equipment failures, we might use RCA to uncover multiple causes, such as poor maintenance practices, inadequate training, or poor component quality.

  There are several benefits to using RCA to support an engagement, including focusing on identifying the root causes of problems rather than their presenting effects. This leads to us being able to recommend practical solutions that prevent the recurrence of the client's issues. It is also seen as a very effective way of identifying inefficiencies, allowing us to recommend where clients could streamline processes and reduce waste. It also helps investigate areas such as quality, health and safety, and customer satisfaction.

  Like PESTLE, RCA also has several disadvantages, including being time consuming, resource intensive, and subject to bias. Additionally, incomplete or inaccurate data can hinder our analysis. We should involve key stakeholders with relevant expertise and knowledge to overcome these limitations and ensure a comprehensive and accurate analysis. Using a structured RCA approach, such as the 5 Whys or Ishikawa (Fishbone) diagram, will help ensure that our analysis is systematic. We should also use data analytics and other tools to identify trends and patterns and support the RCA process.
- **The 5 Whys** technique is a variation of RCA and involves repeatedly asking "why" when a respondent answers our previous question. For example, if a machine frequently breaks down, using the 5 Whys might lead to us asking a chain of questions:

  Q1: Why did the machine break down?
  A: Because it overheated.

  Q2: Why did it overheat?
  A: Because the coolant pump failed.

  Q3: Why did the coolant pump fail?
  A: Because the bearings seized.

Q4: Why did the bearings seize?
A: Because they weren't appropriately lubricated.

Q5: Why weren't they lubricated properly?
A: Because the maintenance schedule wasn't followed.

Using 5 Whys with groups of client staff helps develop a shared understanding of the problem and encourages them to generate and own innovative solutions. It also helps assists us in breaking down silo working between client teams and improving their internal communications, facilitating the adoption of the identified solutions. However, the 5 Whys technique has limitations. The degree of subject knowledge, personal perspectives, and agendas of the individuals we engage with will influence its effectiveness. Again, there is a level of subjectivity in 5 Whys, and different people may arrive at different root causes, potentially leading to varying solutions. The other major issue we should be aware of is that complex problems often have multiple underlying causes. The 5 Whys might oversimplify this by focusing on a single root cause.

- **SWOT Analysis** (Strengths, Weaknesses, Opportunities, and Threats) is an easy-to-understand tool which enables us to prepare and present a structured view of the client's internal and external landscape. We can then pursue opportunities where they can implement changes to capitalise on their opportunities, mitigate threats and weaknesses, and leverage their strengths. For example, we could work with a restaurant that requires to improve its profitability and is considering extending its opening hours. Using our information-gathering tools (outlined earlier), we can prepare an SWOT analysis for the proposal extension of hours and, equally, any other comparable profit improvement programmes which we might identify. Table 9.2 is an example of what a SWOT analysis might look like.
- **Ishikawa or fishbone diagram** allows us to prepare a visual representation that helps identify potential multiple root causes of a problem. The main problem is represented as the head of the fish, and the bones represent the possible causes. These are divided into categories (e.g. workforce, machinery, materials, methods, environment). For example, a hospital experiencing high patient wait times might use a fishbone diagram to identify potential causes such as inadequate staffing, inefficient scheduling, poor facility layout, and outdated IT systems. Figure 9.2 shows a high-level fishbone diagram illustrating this high wait time problem. Figure 9.3 delves more deeply into one of the problem areas shown in Figure 9.2. It demonstrates how a picture of the underlying causes of one issue may be uncovered. Our investigation of the problem's deeper roots may involve utilising the 5 Whys technique or, possibly more usefully, the star bursting technique (see Chapter 2) and employing our full range of questions starting with How, Who, Why, Where, What, When, and Who (and not forgetting How Much).
- **Pareto analysis** is based on the simple concept that 80% of outcome effects arise from 20% of input causes. For example, a manufacturing company with quality control issues might use Pareto analysis to determine the top 20% of types of defect that account for 80% of its product quality issues. Consequently, Pareto analysis is used to help resolve issues by focusing efforts on the most significant factors. The premise is that we can improve outcomes with the least effort by identifying the few input factors contributing to most of the problem. It is a powerful tool for identifying key change drivers and where our clients should concentrate their actions.

  We should use Pareto analysis judiciously as it is based on observations in specific contexts, such as economics, business, and quality control, which may not hold in all situations or industries. Also, it is a rule of thumb rather than a scientific law and provides a general guideline but doesn't guarantee exact ratios. Consequently, when considering complex issues with many variables, we should question whether the distribution of causes and effects

Table 9.2 Restaurant L'XYZ – Profit Improvement Programme: Example SWOT Analysis

	Restaurant L'XYZ – Profit Improvement Programme: Example SWOT Analysis	
	Proposal: Increase opening hours from 8:00 am to 10:00 pm, providing additional use of premises for breakfasts and afternoon tea	
	Positive	**Negative**
INTERNAL	**Strengths**	**Weaknesses**
	1. **Unique cuisine**: The restaurant offers a distinctive menu that sets it apart from competitors	1. **Outdated facilities**: The restaurant's infrastructure may need modernisation to meet increased demand
	2. **Loyal customer base**: A strong, dedicated customer following ensures consistent patronage	2. **Limited menu**: A narrow range of offerings might not cater to diverse customer preferences
	3. **Prime location**: Situated in a high-traffic area, attracting both regulars and new customers	3. **High operating costs**: Extended hours could lead to increased expenses for staffing, utilities, and maintenance
	4. **Experienced staff**: Skilled and knowledgeable employees contribute to high-quality service	4. **Inconsistent quality control**: Variability in food and service quality could affect customer satisfaction
	5. **Strong brand reputation**: Established brand recognition and positive reviews enhance credibility	5. **Limited marketing efforts**: Insufficient promotional activities may hinder the restaurant's visibility and growth
EXTERNAL	**Opportunities**	**Threats**
	1. **Afternoon teashop**: The town has an expanding tourism market, and opening from 2:00 pm to 5:00 pm can attract a new customer base	1. **Increased competition**: New restaurants opening in the area could attract potential customers away
	2. **Breakfast services**: Nearby commuter area means providing eat-in or takeaway coffee and breakfast goods will attract existing lunchtime and new customers	2. **Rising food costs**: Fluctuations in ingredient prices can impact profitability
	3. **Partnerships with local businesses**: Drive mutual growth and customer referrals	3. **Economic downturns**: Economic instability may reduce discretionary spending on dining out
	4. **Seasonal menu additions**: Introducing seasonal dishes can attract repeat customers and keep the menu fresh	4. **Health and safety regulations**: Stricter regulations could require costly compliance measures
	5. **Loyalty programmes**: Implementing such programmes can enhance retention and encourage repeat visits	5. **Changing consumer preferences**: Shifts in dining trends and preferences could affect customer demand

follows the 80/20 pattern in reality. For example, a few causes might account for nearly all effects in some cases, or the distribution might be more even in others. We must, therefore, be wary of neglecting essential factors that don't fit the 80/20 pattern. We also need to consider if the factors contributing to outcomes can shift in rapidly changing environments, making the Pareto Principle even less reliable.

- **Cost–benefit analysis (CBA)** is widely used (and abused) in assessing the potential costs and benefits of different solutions so that we can make informed recommendations. For

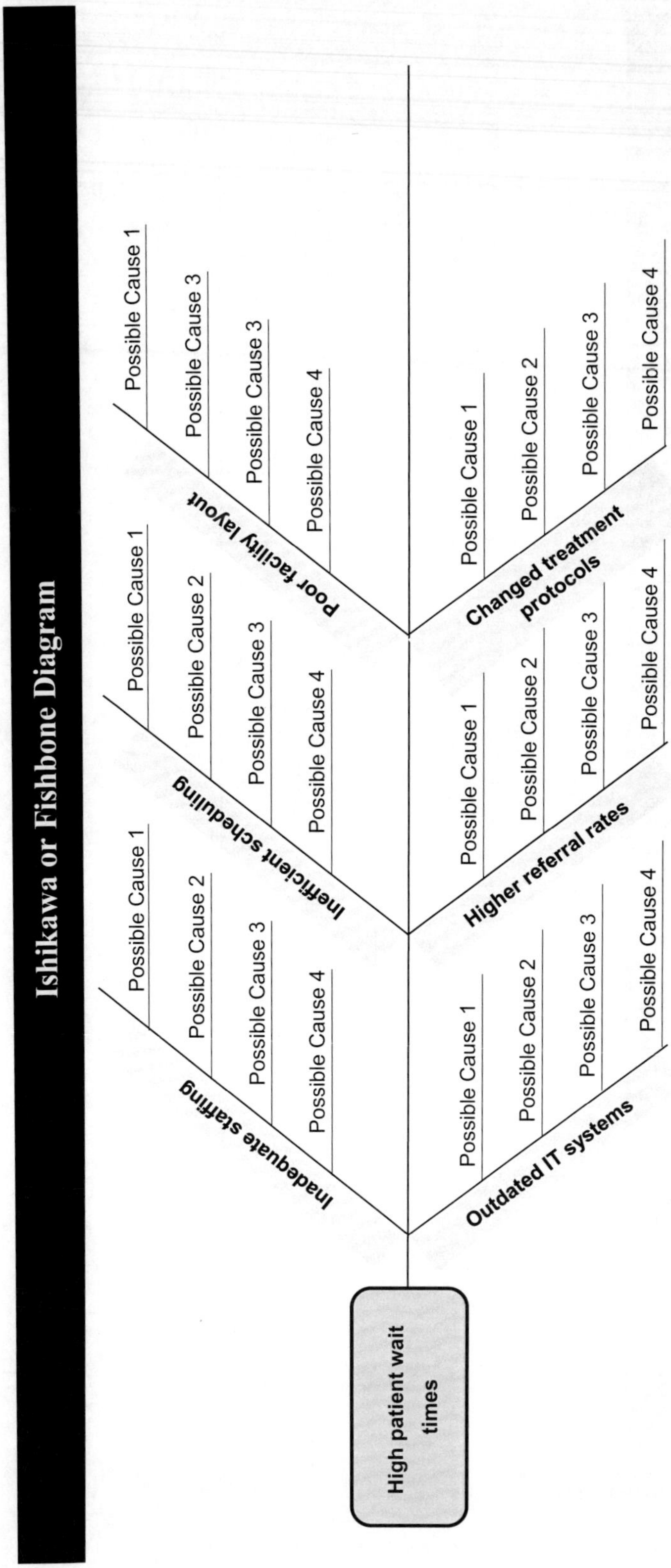

Figure 9.2 Ishikawa or Fishbone Diagram.

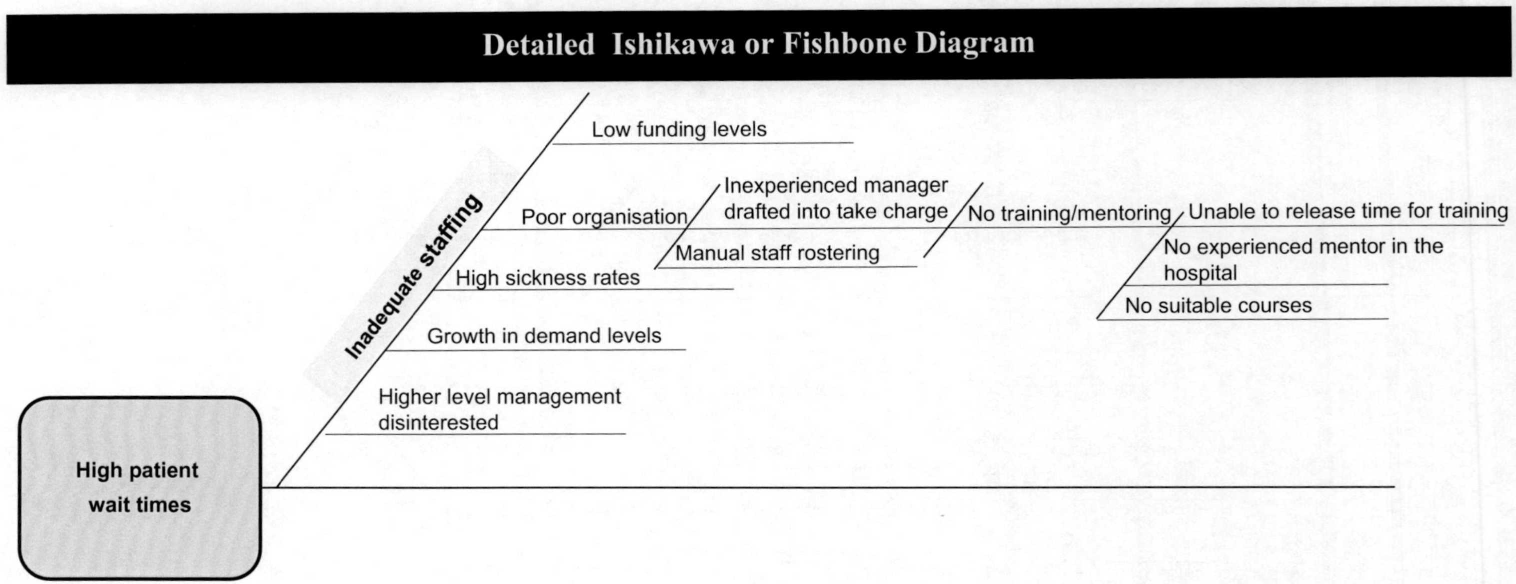

Figure 9.3 Detailed Ishikawa or Fishbone Diagram.

example, a government agency considering a new infrastructure project might ask us to use CBA to evaluate the various impacts of alternative solutions. It is a valuable tool that we should employ but with caution. CBA results can be sensitive to small changes, so we should clearly state our assumptions, data sources, and methodologies from the outset. Ideally, we should get our client to sign off on these assumptions before populating our analysis to avoid any suggestion of bias or manipulation in our work. This is because the CBA approach has been manipulated many times to give skewed results and false conclusions. This manipulation has taken many forms, including inflating benefits, underestimating costs, and ignoring opportunity costs. Many projects have been criticised for including intangible and non-cash-releasing benefits, selecting biased data, and making overly optimistic assumptions as part of their justification. These problems may not be the result of deliberate manipulation but can also arise from unconscious bias and over-optimism. The UK's High-Speed Rail 2 project was accused of manipulating assumptions where the data used for benefits calculations, such as the saving of time by business people, were challenged and costs shown to be massively underestimated, Not to be outdone the costs for Germany's new high-speed rail hub in Stuttgart were massively underestimated at €4.1 billion, by 2024 the running total had risen to €11.45 billion.

We should also be aware that issues can arise with valuing costs and benefits over time. CBA assumes that future costs and benefits are valued less than current ones and achieves this through a discount rate. For example, a discount rate of 7% would mean that a $100 benefit this year is valued at $93 next year. As costs tend to occur in the initial stages of a project and benefits often come over an extended period, increasing the discount rate reduces the value of future benefits with less impact on costs, making a project appear less attractive. If we decrease the discount rate, the reverse happens, and we inflate future benefits, making the project seem more appealing. Guidance on rates to be used varies over time and sometimes between projects; for example, on government projects in the USA and Australia, 7% is the rate generally advised; in the UK, it's 3.5%; in the EU, it is 3%; and in India, it's 12%. The same $100 benefit would be valued against costs as $97 on an EU project, $96.50 in the UK, $94 in the USA and Australia, and $88 in India.

The time horizon used in the CBA can also significantly influence the results. Taking our government infrastructure project, typically, most costs occur sooner due to construction, and benefits come later from using the new asset. A shorter period will, therefore, make a solution look less attractive. The situation is even more complex when different areas of expenditure have markedly different useful asset lives. Consider the advice that we might have to give on the time horizon of the investment required for a railway development project. As an example of useful asset life, we could examine the London to Bristol mainline in the UK. It currently runs multiple express trains per hour. The line opened in 1841, and the original bridges, tunnelling, and groundworks are still delivering benefits today. However, the track and signalling systems have probably been replaced many times.

- **Balanced scorecard (BSC)** Consultants Robert Kaplan and David Norton designed the BSC to provide a comprehensive overview of an organisation's performance and doesn't rely on financial data alone as in other methods of analysing organisational performance. To the traditional financial metrics, BSC adds non-financial measures. For each measure, we can document and evaluate specific objectives, measures, and targets. BSC's perspectives are as follows:

    1. Financial measures financial performance in terms of variables such as revenue growth, profitability (EBITDA), and return on investment. For example, a client might set a target to grow annual revenue by 10% and profit by 12% and track its progress through quarterly financial reports.

2. Customer measures include satisfaction, loyalty, and market share. A retail company might track its in-store customer satisfaction scores through regular surveys and set a target to improve these by 10% by enhancing customer service, product quality, and availability.
3. Internal process measures operational efficiency, quality, and innovation. For example, a manufacturing company might monitor production cycle times and defect rates, aiming to reduce to improve both overall efficiency and product quality.
4. Learning and growth measures employee skills, knowledge, and motivation. A company might focus on increasing the number of training hours per employee and track the impact of this training on employee performance and satisfaction.

Table 9.3 is an example of a balanced scorecard for a retail company, showing how it will measure and target improvement in each of the four areas.

Table 9.3 XYZ Retail: Example Balanced Scorecard

XYZ RETAIL Example Balanced Scorecard				
	Objective	**Measure**	**Target**	**Initiative**
Financial	Increase profitability	Gross profit margin	5% increase	Implement cost-cutting measures Optimise inventory management
	Improve cash flow	Days sales outstanding	Reduce by ten days	Implement stricter credit policies Improve collection processes
	Enhance shareholder value	Return on equity	Increase by 2%	Invest in growth opportunities Optimise capital allocation
Customer	Enhance customer satisfaction	Customer satisfaction score	15% increase	Conduct regular customer surveys Improve customer service training
	Increase customer retention	Customer retention rate	10% increase	Implement loyalty programmes Personalise customer experiences
	Expand market share	Market share	5% increase	Launch new product lines Additional marketing campaigns
Internal Process	Improve operational efficiency	Order processing time	20% reduction	Automate order processing Streamline the supply chain
	Enhance product quality	Defect rate	Reduce by 15%	Improve quality control measures Improve manufacturing processes
	Increase supply chain agility	Supplier delivery performance	95% on-time delivery	Improve supplier relationships Optimise logistics
Learning and Growth	Develop employee skills	Training hours per employee	40 hours	New employee training programmes Provide opportunities for professional development
	Improve employee engagement	Employee satisfaction score	10% increase	New employee recognition programmes Improve work–life balance
	Foster innovation	Number of new product ideas	Increase by 20%	Encourage employee creativity Establish innovation teams

We can use the BSC to show how our client can align activities with strategic goals by using the balanced scorecard to monitor progress across multiple dimensions and ensure a balanced approach to achieving long-term success. However, the BSC approach has significant challenges, not least because creating a BSC to support a consultancy engagement can be resource intensive and require considerable time, effort, and expertise to set up the necessary data gathering, cleansing, and analysis. Once again, there is a risk of subjectivity in selecting and defining measures, which would introduce bias and inconsistency in performance assessments. This includes the possibility of overemphasising quantitative metrics, potentially neglecting qualitative factors crucial for long-term success.

When using the BSC as part of an engagement, overcoming these challenges requires us to engage key stakeholders from across the client to ensure buy-in and ownership of the BSC. We should also focus our attention on a limited number of critical measures to avoid information overload, which helps ensure that monitoring will be effective and practical. These critical measures should combine quantitative and qualitative measures to provide a more complete picture of performance. Where the client is to adopt the BSC for ongoing use, we should identify how they may streamline the BSC process by using technology to automate data collection, cleansing, analysis, and reporting. In addition, we should always recommend that the client regularly reviews and updates the BSC to ensure that it stays aligned with their strategy and priorities.

- **Lean** is a methodology centred around continuous improvement and offers a potent toolkit for us to diagnose operational inefficiencies and develop practical solutions. Lean can be used for diagnosis and solution development, and we can include some of the tools we previously encountered. Lean's diagnosis tools include the following:

  - Value stream mapping: Visually mapping out the entire process to identify areas of waste (non-value-adding activities) and bottlenecks. This provides a clear picture of the current state and helps pinpoint areas for improvement.
  - 5S methodology: Assessing the organisation's workspace and identifying areas for improvement regarding organisation, tidiness, cleanliness, standardisation, and discipline (see earlier).
  - Root cause analysis: By understanding the root causes, consultants can develop targeted solutions that address the underlying issues (see earlier).

  Lean's solution development tools include the following:

  - Kaizen events: These short, structured, intensive team workshops are most effective when tackling specific, well-defined problems. They follow a specific methodology and facilitate rapid, focused improvement projects. They encourage employee involvement and can lead to quick wins and significant improvements.
  - Standardised work: These are meticulously documented, detailed systems designed to eliminate variation and inconsistency, making processes more predictable, reducing error rates, and providing a foundation for continuous improvement. The current best way is documented to create the baseline against which we can measure future improvements.
  - Visual management: Our objective in using visual management is to help make data transparent and allow teams to react quickly to deviations from targets. Visual tools like Kanban boards and cords make information readily accessible and processes transparent. This facilitates problem-solving, helps us identify bottlenecks, and makes data-driven recommendations.

- Poka-Yoke: This is a way of error-proofing systems, and we can identify and recommend techniques to prevent mistakes or, as a secondary goal, to identify them quickly, significantly reduce defects, and improve product quality. These may be quite simple, such as designing a part to be asymmetric so it cannot be fitted incorrectly, or a complex multistage process with visual and automated quality prevention and immediate detection controls at each stage, for example, a computerised detector which immediately rejects a defective component.

When used in a consultancy engagement, Lean's clear visualisation techniques help us pinpoint and communicate areas for improvement. Lean's focus on customer value means that because we understand the needs and expectations of our client's customers, we can recommend processes to deliver products or services that meet those needs. We can also promote adopting Lean's continuous improvement culture, which empowers client teams to identify and implement improvements by involving employees in problem-solving and decision-making. However, like all methodologies, Lean has limitations and may be more appropriate in some environments than others. We should take into account that Lean is effective in manufacturing environments but could be less effective in service industries, which may have less defined processes. When recommending that a client implement Lean, we should recognise that its implementation can be time consuming, complex, and require significant organisational change. The client may also require a significant upfront investment in training and resources.

- **Six Sigma** is another approach we may use to help clients achieve "operational excellence." It is often seen as complementary to Lean. It aims to improve product and service quality, which enhances customer satisfaction, increases efficiency, and reduces costs. Six Sigma is divided into the following stages:

  1. Define: We identify the client's issues, set goals, and define the scope of the work required.
  2. Measure: We gather the necessary data to understand the client process being reviewed and measure its performance.
  3. Analysis: We analyse the collected data to identify the causes of inefficiencies or defects in the process.
  4. Improve: We develop possible solutions to overcome the issues we identified during the analysis stage. We may also help the client implement them.
  5. Control: We define controls so the client can monitor the changed process and maintain its improvements over time.

  Six Sigma has several advantages in supporting our work, including a track record of success in improving quality, for example, reducing defects and increasing reliability. It also encourages collaboration and client staff engagement in problem identification and resolution. Based on data evidence, it relies on statistical analyses to support informed choices. Like Lean, it also promotes a culture of continual improvement. When using Six Sigma, our scope needs to be carefully defined to ensure we cover all relevant areas, including organisational ones. As it focuses on selected quantitative data, we need to be aware that it may not adequately account for qualitative issues such as staff morale or creativity. We also need to ensure that affected client staff understand and engage with the process.

- **Force field analysis** enables us to understand the dynamics of change within a client. It allows us to identify and analyse the driving and restraining forces influencing a change initiative, giving a clear overview of our client's challenges and opportunities. Starting with defining the change initiative and its goals, we identify the driving forces for the change and the restraining or hindering forces that oppose it. These are mapped out on a diagram that helps identify areas where restraining forces outweigh driving forces and where intervention may need to be focused. For example, a company seeking to implement new production processes might be driven by a desire to increase efficiency and reduce unit costs but face employee resistance and high initial costs. Force field analysis is a valuable tool, but its results can be unreliable because of its inherent subjectivity. The identification and assessment of forces always rely on individual's perceptions and consequently will also reflect their possible biases and prejudices. Another problem is that it may not account for unexpected external factors influencing the change process.

- **Gap analysis**: We use a gap analysis to compare a client's current state to its desired future state, enabling us to recommend areas for improvement and develop highly targeted improvement plans for our clients. For example, if we performed a gap analysis in a financial services company aiming to enhance its customer service and found that it did not have a reliable and impartial customer feedback system, we could recommend a suitable system and implementation plan. Gap analysis has advantages in that it provides a clear framework for identifying areas of improvement and developing targeted strategies. It also ensures alignment with strategic goals and allows us to recommend areas of improvement on which our client should focus its resources. However, we should recognise that a gap analysis can be time consuming, which may be a factor when planning and costing an engagement. It also requires accurate data, which may be challenging on some engagements, and we may have to budget for extra time for data cleansing. Finally, it may not identify all possible external factors that could impact the desired outcomes.
- **Design thinking** is described as being human-centric, and it is very useful when we need to concentrate on users' needs and experiences in developing practical and desirable solutions. Design thinking is divided into five stages:

  1. Empathise: During this stage, we develop a deep understanding of the users and their needs. This involves observing, engaging, and empathising with people to understand their experiences and motivations.
  2. Define: Our insights from the empathise stage are used to define the client's core problem(s). We reflect this in an unambiguous problem statement concentrating on users' needs and challenges.
  3. Ideate: We foster a creative environment where unconventional solutions can emerge. We can use brainstorming sessions, mind mapping, or other creative techniques to encourage free thinking and innovation to explore as many ideas as possible without judgement.
  4. Prototype: We turn the most promising solutions from the Ideate stage into tangible prototypes, for example, simple sketches, models, or interactive simulations, that is, we create a physical representation of the ideas to test and refine them.
  5. Test: Our testing and gathering feedback on how the potential solutions work in practice helps us identify areas where improvement is needed to refine the solution.

  Consider a healthcare provider aiming to improve patient experience. During the empathise stage, we would interview patients to understand their issues. We identify that long waiting times are the core problem in the define stage. During ideation, we brainstorm solutions such as a mobile app for appointment scheduling or informing "walk-in" patients about current wait times. We would then prototype the app, test it with patients, and gather feedback to refine the design. Design thinking supports creativity and innovative solutions. Its benefit is that it primarily focuses on users' needs, and its use of iterative prototyping and development should result in practical and user-friendly solutions. However, it also has limitations when used during a consultancy engagement, as it can be resource intensive and time consuming. It also requires us to develop an in-depth understanding of user needs and create an effective stakeholder collaboration process.

- **Porter's five forces analysis** helps us work with clients to assess their competitive landscape and identify potential improved business strategies. As the name suggests, we use this tool to analyse five key forces identified by Porter as being:

  1. Intensity of competitive rivalry.
  2. Power of suppliers.
  3. Power of buyers.
  4. Threat of new entrants.
  5. Threat of substitute products.

  We could use Porter's approach to identify the key external forces acting on a pharmaceutical company facing combined threats of global competition for the supply of generic drugs, increasing reluctance or ability of buyers to pay premium prices for branded drugs, new entrants to the therapeutic market developing non-drug therapies, or repurposing existing generic drugs. Porter's Five Forces provides a structure that gives us a comprehensive view of our clients' competitive landscape. It also identifies key factors influencing profitability in our client's industry and provides evidence to support our strategic recommendations. However, we also have to consider the potential for oversimplifying complex market dynamics. As with the PESTLE approach, we primarily consider external factors, which may lead us to overlook internal ones or dismiss them as having no significant impact. Lastly, we must be aware of issues arising from rapid changes, such as in technology or regulation.
- **Decision matrix**: This tool provides a structured approach to evaluating multiple options against a set of criteria. We have already used this tool in our service options selection (see Chapter 2). As a refresher, weights are assigned to each criterion based on importance, and each option is scored accordingly. We then calculate the weighted scores to identify the most preferred option. A decision matrix offers a clear and, on the surface, objective method for comparing options provided that all relevant criteria are considered and facilitating informed decision-making. However, the weights, the criteria chosen, and some scores will be subjective. It may also be time consuming and require detailed information about each option and the engagement of a wide team of client staff to ensure that the process's results are fully accepted.
- **Scenario planning**: This technique is a collaborative effort with our clients that allows us to analyse uncertainty in client situations by exploring multiple possible futures. It enables us to evaluate the potential impacts of changes on the client of numerous internal and external factors. We identify and vary the principal drivers of change to construct various scenarios, each representing a different potential future. Our next step is to analyse the implications of each scenario on our client's strategic goals, market position, and operations. For example, when working with a financial services company, we could use scenario planning to prepare them for economic uncertainty. Our scenarios could evaluate different levels of recession or growth in various markets and different types of technological disruption. Working from these scenarios, we could identify risks for the client to consider and the mitigation strategies that may be required, like the need for diversified investments.

  Using scenario planning techniques during an engagement has significant client benefits. These benefits stem from enhancing the client's preparedness by anticipating future challenges and opportunities. This means the client will gain strategic flexibility because different potential futures will have been analysed and understood. In addition, we can enhance the client's risk management because we will have identified significant risks and considered how they can be mitigated, especially those emerging in multiple scenarios.

Like any other tool, scenario planning has drawbacks when we use it to support a consultancy engagement. These include being time consuming and resource intensive. Subjectivity and bias can also be issues when developing scenarios. However, we can mitigate this by using diverse teams, structured brainstorming, and sensitivity analysis. Data completeness and robustness are always issues, but we can mitigate these problems by using various data analysis techniques first, followed by scenario planning. Developing effective and acceptable strategies for action based on our insights can also be problematic due to conflicting scenarios, difficulty in prioritising actions, and resistance to change within the client organisation. Our biggest issue, however, regards the variables and assumptions we make about them regarding the uncertain future that we use to develop scenarios. These can be incomplete or inaccurate, undermining the value of any strategies that we recommend.

In reality, on many assignments, we may use a mix of tools and techniques to ensure that we have fully understood the client's problems, gathered the relevant information, analysed it appropriately and have an evidence base to support our recommendations.

Step 4: Reporting – convincing the client

Back to our virtual case study.

You are approaching the end of your first major client engagement.

You've been back at PNX HQ for a few days going through documents, and now you're considering how to prepare your report when you bump into Chris at the coffee station. Chris is not formally recognised as your mentor – yet.

Chris: "How are things going? Are you getting more comfortable with your joint role as salesman and consultancy expert?"

You: "It's not going too badly. I am now planning the report for the end of the first assignment. We have been working with a staid government agency, trying to drag their systems into the current millennium."

Chris: "Why don't we take our coffee somewhere quiet? I have a tale to tell about a lesson I learned the hard way about client reports. I use it on junior consultant training courses now, but I depersonalise it and don't admit to them that I was the team leader and the one who carries the scars."

A few moments later, Chris starts to explain.

"We were to present our final report to a governing board, all of whom were academics except the Director of Finance, our client sponsor. They were all frighteningly clever people. We had already cleared the report with the Director of Finance, who had discussed it in broad outline with their colleagues on the board.

We had developed five options for a new customer relations software package. Each carefully costed and supported by cost–benefit analyses, SWOTs and implementation timelines. I had had all the figures and calculations independently checked. The report was prepared in good time and sent out with the board papers. There were no spreadsheet howlers, grammatical faux pas, or typos, and it had an excellent executive summary. Our visual communications team had created a cracking set of slides for my presentation. Every box in 'How to prepare a persuasive report' had been ticked, yet it was about to fail dismally.

We were kept waiting for an interminable period whilst the Board had deep discussions on some topic or other. When we were called in, I launched straight into explaining the five different options and running my slide pack. I said something like the most expensive option is the one that a highly comparable but smaller agency has just installed. The software industry calls this software the Rolls Royce solution. Following the same theme, we have called the other options the BMW, the Volvo, the Ford and so on, each reflecting different levels of sophistication and costs. I powered on for a full ten minutes and paused to absolute silence

The board chair then said simply, 'Thank you, Chris and your team, for coming today, but the Board has decided to reject your report. Will you all please leave us. Now?'

The next day, in a telephone call, the Director of Finance said, 'I'm sorry, Chris, I couldn't believe it. The report was robust, and I had prepared every member for it. They could not relate to the way the options had been named using car brands. It just was not clear to them what we meant. I suppose to them, cars are just things with four wheels. Anyway, I was really embarrassed, but the chair insisted that only they would speak. They want your report rewritten and presented at their next meeting.'

To end the story, I did a quick edit and changed the option names to ABCDE, and at the next meeting, they loved the paper, accepted our recommendations, and gave approval to proceed. Sadly, by then, the project had lost a month, all impetus had gone, and I had had to disperse the team onto work for other clients.

So, my moral for you to take away is don't assume that you and your audience have anything in common. Always communicate using language in a way that makes sense to them and research this in advance. Just imagine trying to convey a complex message using examples of British tea brands to Americans or American supermarkets to an international audience. Please always put your audience first because failure to do so can significantly impact the acceptability of what is being said. In this case, I obviously didn't pay attention to this or really listen to the warning from the most junior consultant, and the project has suffered. I have not made the same mistake again."

The task of a report or presentation is not merely to document our findings, conclusions, and recommendations but to present a persuasive set of arguments as to the actions our clients should take and why. However diligent we have been in the earlier stages of the assignment, failing to understand that we need this final stage of our work to convince our client will result in our failure to meet their expectations. One of the keys to being persuasive is presenting our recommendations in a way the client can readily accept. Our last case study visit shows that understanding how clients prefer to receive information is crucial for effective communication and successful consultancy engagements.

Clients have different preferences for reporting (and prejudices[3]). These are based on their experience, their roles, the nature of the information we will be presenting, and the context in which we will be presenting it. Tailoring our reports and presentations to meet client preferences is key to ensuring our insights and recommendations are well-received. During our site visit, we saw a dramatic consequence of not recognising these preferences. Once again:

*It's not about **US**. It's about **YOU**.*

When we focus on what matters most to the client, we will ensure that the information we present is relevant and actionable. However, this may mean that we need to prepare multiple deliverables, each aimed at a different audience within the client, for example, a simple information sheet for staff, a briefing document for managers, and a comprehensive report detailing all findings, conclusions, and recommendations, with supporting data analysis for the main board. Areas to consider that may increase the impact of our reporting with each client include the following:

- **Storytelling**: A well-written narrative can help our clients understand and recall the details of complex data and analysis. We can use examples to frame our information and recommendations within a relevant story to convey the significance of our insights and recommendations.
- **Visual communication**: Including high-quality visuals, such as charts, graphs, and infographics, is a very powerful way to illustrate our key points and enhance client understanding and retention. This may include harnessing AI tools to transform complex data into easy-to-understand charts and graphs. However, if our visuals are poorly designed or executed, they will undermine the credibility of our report and may harm future client relationships.
- **Check, edit, and verify everything**: It is worth repeating; it is easy to destroy the validity of our report by failing to spot even an insignificant factual error, a glaring typo, or a poor visual. We should always hold a peer review in which a suitable consultant from outside the team is tasked with reviewing and critiquing the draft report, including checking and verifying all figures presented and underlying calculations.

Reports vary immensely according to client needs and preferences, and it is helpful to always discuss the contents of the final report as early as possible in the engagement. Perhaps three different types of generic reports can be identified based on the nature of the target audience and the work undertaken. These are strategic, tactical, or operational level reports:

- Strategic reports:
  - Audience: Senior executives and board members focused on long-term goals and overall direction.
  - Format: Concise, high-level, and focused on strategic insights and recommendations. The head of one UK manufacturing company famously used to insist on reports at this level being no more than half a page in length!
  - Content: Executive summary, key findings, strategic recommendations, and visual representations of data to support the analysis.
- Tactical reports:
  - Audience: Middle management and project teams responsible for implementing specific projects and achieving medium-term objectives.
  - Format: Comprehensive and includes actionable recommendations on detailed decision-making and project implementation.
  - Content: Detailed objectives, tactics, timelines, budget allocation, and performance metrics, along with visual aids to track progress
- Operational reports:
  - Audience: Frontline managers and staff focused on day-to-day activities and operational efficiency.
  - Format: Specific, data-driven, and focused on immediate actions

- Content: Detailed performance data, recommended process improvements, and key performance indicators. The report would include sections on delivery metrics, quality assurance results, and process improvements supported by detailed data tables and charts.

Table 9.4 lists several tools that might be helpful in preparing high-quality reports and presentations at different levels; each has strengths and limitations. However, many tools may be helpful in various types of reports, and as each requires time to learn how to use them effectively, it is not suggested that every consultant master them all. Preparing a final report or presentation can often be helped by engaging creative design and other software package experts to help produce high-quality output to ensure that our key messages are presented

Table 9.4 Suggested Tools to Support Report Preparation

Suggested Tools to Support Report Preparation			
	Tool	**Strengths**	**Limitations**
Strategic	• Microsoft PowerPoint	Versatile, user-friendly, and widely accessible	This can lead to template-heavy, visually monotonous presentations if not used creatively
Strategic	• Adobe Creative Suite	Unparalleled control over design elements, ideal for pixel-perfect visuals	The steep learning curve is time consuming for complex designs and requires advanced design skills
Strategic	• Prezi	Non-linear storytelling format, visually engaging, and memorable	It can be overwhelming for complex topics, requires careful planning and design, and may not be suitable for all audiences
Tactical	• Microsoft Excel	Versatile, powerful data analysis capabilities and automation features	It can be complex for large datasets and requires technical skills. Poorly controlled spreadsheets can hide errors
Tactical	• Asana • Trello • Basecamp	Project management, task tracking, and team collaboration	They can be overwhelming for large-scale projects and may require significant setup and configuration
Tactical	• Microsoft Teams • Slack	Real-time communication, file sharing, and video conferencing capabilities	Too many notifications can be overwhelming and lead to information overload
Tactical	• Microsoft Project	Powerful project management tool for planning, scheduling, and tracking projects	It can be complex to learn and use and unsuitable for small, simple projects
Operational	• Tableau • Power BI	Powerful data visualisation capabilities, interactive dashboards, and easy-to-use drag-and-drop interface	They can be complex for large datasets, require some technical knowledge, and may have a steep learning curve for beginners
Operational	• Miro • Figma	Collaborative whiteboarding, real-time collaboration, and versatility for various design and brainstorming activities	They can be complex to learn and use and require a stable internet connection for optimal performance
Operational	• draw.io • Lucidchart	User-friendly interface, a wide range of shapes and templates, and the ability to collaborate in real time	While they offer robust features, they may not be as powerful as specialised software like Microsoft Visio

clearly and gain the client's attention. A cost-effective way to use these experts is for them to create a series of report and presentation templates, which can be used as a standard format for all client reports.

When using reporting tools, there are perhaps three main rules to observe. First, we should tailor our toolbox. We should consider the specific needs of the types of engagements that we deliver, the complexity of our reports or other deliverables, and, above all, our clients' typical requirements. We can then determine the range of tools we might need to make our reports engaging and persuasive and invest in the technical skills to use them to the maximum effect. Second, we need to use a combination of tools: When we create comprehensive and impactful reports, we will be able to draw from our toolbox and combine the functionality of several different tools to produce a deliverable that meets each client's specific requirements. For example, we might use Microsoft Excel to display the data we have analysed,[4] Microsoft Project to plan and track project implementation, and draw.io to visualise processes. The final rule is to stay updated. The landscape of tools and technologies is constantly evolving. It is essential to invest time updating our knowledge of developments and changing best practices regarding our chosen tools.

Development of proprietary methods of operation

Developing our proprietary tools, methods, and databases can be a strategic move, allowing us to differentiate ourselves from competitors, improve efficiency, and create valuable intellectual property. Standardising approaches using our in-house toolset elevates the quality of our work, mitigates risks associated with key personnel departures, and potentially opens up new revenue streams through licensing, training, or specialised consulting services. For example, one consultancy built up a database of information on the performance of local authority IT systems. This created a virtuous circle in which engagements were undertaken to benchmark operational performance, and each engagement generated more data for the database, making the service even more attractive to other clients. This example shows how creating intellectual property can reinforce our market position and attract new clients.

Developing and maintaining proprietary tools may require significant investment at the outset, and further funds may be required to ensure that they are updated and relevant in a rapidly evolving market. The second major issue is that relying too much on these tools may make our approach to client issues overly rigid, where flexibility and adaptability are often required.

Striking the right balance between maximising the return on our intellectual property and maintaining our agility is crucial to our long-term success. Once again, we can turn our consultancy tools inwards on ourselves to provide the structured approach essential to maintaining this balance, including the following:

- **Analyse:** Identify areas where new methods or tools may increase our effectiveness or attractiveness to the market.

    1. **Define:** Clearly outline the proposed method or tool's goals, scope, and intended users.
    2. **Research:** Review internal and external best practices and identify potential gaps our new method or tool could fill.
    3. **Design and prototype:** Create a specification for the new method or tool and refine it using prototyping and iterative development.
    4. **Pilot:** Test on a smaller-scale engagement, perhaps even selecting a previous engagement and comparing the results where feasible. Gather feedback and further refine the solution.

5. **Implement:** Including preparing documentation and providing appropriate consultant and support staff training.
6. **Communicate:** Integrate the solution into marketing and sales, stressing the client benefits.
7. **Monitor:** Track the performance of engagements that use the solution. Gather user and client feedback on its effectiveness and areas for improvement, and consider a programme to update it as needed.

By effectively implementing and managing proprietary tools and methods, consultancy firms can position themselves as leaders in their industry, delivering exceptional value to clients and driving sustainable growth.

Reflections

Please use your personal experience, current situation, or imagination to help fill in your answers from the theoretical case study.

Case study update: The client is a small central government agency that has not reviewed its systems or processes for over a decade. Many were already nearing the end of life then and are now supplemented by workarounds and manual systems.

- Design an internal information-gathering process to establish the current situation in the client and to define (and agree) a set of mandatory and desirable features of the solution you will propose.
- Please propose the tools for analysing the data you collect and prepare a short paper listing the features and benefits of each for the client to consider.
- Prepare a comprehensive list of the tools to be used in the problem diagnosis stage, including a justification of why you have chosen each one to persuade your manager or partner that this is the best approach.
- Suggest a format for your final report, including how and where graphics and data visualisations may help the audience understand what you recommend and why.

Further reading

Data Science for Business: What You Need to Know about Data Mining and Data-Analytic Thinking by Anil Maheshwari.

The Balanced Scorecard by Robert S. Kaplan and David P. Norton

Velocity: "Combining Lean, Six Sigma and the Theory of Constraints to Achieve Breakthrough Performance – A Business Novel" by Dee Jacob, Suzan Bergland, and Jeff Cox

Notes

1 A word of advice – check that the felt tip does not bleed through the paper onto the client's boardroom (or other) wall. If it does, it is guaranteed that your popularity will not be increased.

2 I never really understood why one group of statisticians wanted to use averages of averages rather than using a straight arithmetic mean.

3 On a very technical IT security assignment, the client sponsor took me to one side, removed a copy of The Complete Plain Words by Ernest Gower, and pointedly handed it to me!

4 Always check your data as closely as your text. In one case, a vast Excel table extending to 12 pages that was supposed to be used internally by the project team was bound to the final report and handed to the client sponsor. I hope that the British Prime Minister did not take exception to every entry in the first line of the table on every page reading #DIV/0!

10 The Future Market for Consultancy

How Is Client Motivation for Buying Consultancy Changing?

Aim of this chapter: To identify the implications of why clients really buy consultancy services and to consider the factors that may affect the development of the consultancy market in the future

Learning outcome: To understand what, when, and how key technologies and market shifts will likely impact our delivery of consultancy services in coming years.

Let's start by being frank: Management consultancy is often a distress purchase, that is, one made out of necessity rather than pleasure. In Chapter 5, where we considered client motivation in detail, a partner from a large consultancy firm told us that:

"Our clients buy from us based only on five factors: fear, uncertainty, doubt, greed, and envy."

The implication is that many of our clients avoid purchasing our services except when absolutely necessary. This, coupled with a range of changes covering all areas of PESTLE,[1] results in a dynamic market with new pressures on us and where we continually need to respond to increase our perceived value to the client.

The second frank admission is that given the rate of change, the usefulness of any prediction about the development of management consultancy and its markets is likely to age very quickly. Consequently, we need to allow time to keep up to date with the latest thinking coming from academic research and reviewing publications produced by global consultancies about their practice and surveys of their clients' attitudes. We can, however, project some current trends forward.

Creation of internal management consultancy teams in large organisations

The trend for establishing internal management consultancy teams (IMCTs) within large organisations is not new. It may be seen as a threat to external consultancies and an additional career opportunity for individual consultants. However, even in large corporates such as Coca-Cola and Disney, IMCTs may be small compared to management consultancies. Some have consultancy teams of only around 20 consultants, although others may run teams of over 100 and operate globally.

The trend of creating such teams is not, however, one way. The UK government announced in 2020 that it was developing a consulting hub. In 2021, a 60-strong team was proposed to provide in-house consultancy services to UK government departments to reduce reliance on external consultants, drive down costs, and improve efficiency. The hub closed at the end of January 2023,

DOI: 10.4324/9781003490456-11

with a senior civil servant acknowledging that delivery was challenging, partly because the government's wide range of activities is hard to service with a small consultancy team.

The key drivers for the increasing adoption of IMCTs by larger organisations include the following:

- **Savings**: If the organisation has sufficient demand for consultants with particular knowledge and skills, creating an internal consulting team can lead to cost savings over external consultants. This was a driver in the UK government example; however, having abandoned this policy, it moved on to one of containing the costs of external consultants.
- **Efficiency**: IMCTs overcome one of the external consultants' drawbacks by having an in-depth understanding of their organisation's culture, personalities, systems, and processes. This allows them to create more targeted information-gathering processes and complete assignments more quickly.
- **Learning and growth**: IMCTs score highly on this dimension of the balanced scorecard as they help the organisation retain valuable learning, knowledge, and expertise. By contrast, external consultants may struggle with effective knowledge transfer to client staff.

In addition to the challenges it presents to external consulting organisations, large companies adopting IMCTs offer us a new range of opportunities. To remain competitive, external consultancies need to ask a set of key questions:

1. *What highly specialised areas can we identify where IMCTs may lack expertise?*
2. *How can we collaborate with IMCTs on a partnership basis to extend the range of services or capacities they can offer their clients?*
3. *Where can we provide value-added services to IMCTs through thought leadership, staff training, research, and sharing innovative solutions from other clients?*
4. *Who can we build stronger relationships with at a senior level to create opportunities even when the client has an incumbent IMCT?*
5. *What are the opportunities for us to leverage technology and operating methods to improve our efficiency, lower client costs, and deliver innovative solutions that may not be available to an IMCT?*

Changing client behaviour

Like many knowledge-based industries, management consultancy is seeing a period of rapid transformation, partly driven by evolving client expectations. These impact both the type of engagement we deliver and, now, increasingly, how we work together with the client. Clients expect us to be at the forefront of the trends to which they have to respond, including the following:

- **Client business cycles** are accelerating; they now expect faster responses and turnaround times from consultants. This means that we are increasingly expected to be agile and able to deliver complex assignments rapidly, often within weeks (or even days) rather than months.
- **Data-led decision-making is becoming the norm for our clients,** and we need to be analytically skilled and AI adept. We need to increase and keep updated our skill levels to ensure that we can work with "big data" and leverage advanced analytical tools to provide deep insights into client issues and recommend more effective solutions.
- **Seamless working**: Effective collaboration across various functions within a client organisation is increasingly becoming a fundamental feature of their operations. Consequently, in addition to our extensive professional expertise, we have to develop a broad understanding of

our client's business areas, which may be quite diverse. We may also need to supplement our team by bringing in additional expertise. We can then develop recommendations or design solutions that effectively address the needs of multiple teams, departments, or locations.

- **Innovation and revenue growth** are key for many clients, and they require consultants who can help them drive the rapid development of new products and services, enter new markets, and create innovative business models.
- **Outcome-based engagements** can be favoured by clients. Under this type of contract, we are tasked with delivering specific results, and our fees are dependent on our success; sometimes, this is referred to as "shared risk and shared reward." This type of engagement can shift the focus of our work from providing advice to delivering a working solution and measuring and sharing its benefits. Not all clients are interested in this type of pricing, preferring the certainty of the costs they will be paying rather than agreeing to pay the consultancy an indeterminate future income stream.
- **Tailoring solutions** to address our client's unique challenges and opportunities. Cut-and-paste solutions are not acceptable. Our recommendations must be justified by our data analysis and customised to align with the client's objectives.
- **Agile and adaptive solutions**, the ability to respond to dynamic markets where the pace of technological change and innovations is increasing relentlessly, is a principal determination of our clients' long-term success. They require us to provide agile and adaptable solutions to support this responsiveness.
- **Environmental, social, and governance (ESG) and sustainability** are increasingly significant areas of interest for business investors, stakeholders, and customers. This has resulted in a demand for management consultants to assist clients in developing ESG strategies and implementation plans. Consequently, we must ensure that our work supports the development of our client's sustainable policies, processes, and practices.
- **Leveraging technological innovation**: As well as understanding how to leverage new technologies for clients, we also need to leverage them to increase our accuracy and efficiency. In turn, this enables us to focus our attention on those activities that add higher value than mundane, repetitive tasks. There is, as with all investment in consulting services, a question that needs to be answered, which is as follows:

  How do we obtain a return on investing to achieve higher client value outputs when our less sophisticated clients are centred on comparing costs per consultant day?

- **Remote and dispersed working**: Continually improving IT and communications infrastructure was already enabling a slow shift away from the nineteenth-century concept of the office as a central building for undertaking clerical tasks before being accelerated by the COVID-19 pandemic. In parallel, organisations had already been dispersing their operations for decades by moving tasks to lower-cost areas or outsourcing them altogether. These movements continue to provide a range of opportunities for us. We can assist clients to take advantage of the opportunities that these technological changes present, including the following:
  - Understanding the potential advantages and disadvantages of remote and dispersed working in their operations.
  - Adapting the needs of remote and dispersed working changes by creating and implementing digital communications and accommodation strategies.
  - Training leaders to manage remote teams and individuals effectively.
  - Designing robust processes and systems which maintain and increase cybersecurity, ensuring our clients feel secure in their remote operations.

Price pressure

Overall, management consultancy is subject to cyclical economic pressures, which put additional pressure on consultancy fee rates at some points in the cycle. If, in a downturn, our clients decide to invest in change more slowly, the number of consultancy assignments falls, making the competition for those that do progress fiercer, leading inexorably to price discounting. Once price levels have been discounted, client expectations are to be able to continue to achieve the discounted rates even when the economy and, hence, demand for our service have picked up. However, these pressures are not felt equally across management consultancy. In each business cycle, some consultancy areas may not see a slowdown; for example, post-pandemic, AI consultancy is likely to be more dominated by skill shortages than any other factor.

There are proven strategies to help to mitigate downward price pressure:

- **Focusing on value instead of price**: Too often, clients have no concrete evidence of the value we have delivered. While this is always an issue at times of increased price pressure, we need to work very hard to communicate added value in our marketing materials and all interactions with clients prior to and during an engagement. Post-engagement, we should work with the client to identify our actual added value and include this in clear testimonials and exemplar case studies.
- **Moving the focus of services to cost reduction**: It is axiomatic that a client whose primary concern has moved from investment to cost containment or reduction will be more receptive to proposals that will generate cash savings. It is necessary to focus on value, not price, and to demonstrate where previous clients have saved. Adopting proven methodologies can help; Lean is helpful, especially in a manufacturing context, as it focuses on key areas where specialist expertise can help, such as energy, telecoms, or IT costs. A helpful mantra is "doing more with less."
- **Working with existing clients** can lead to a win/win situation. Our existing clients know us and understand how we have helped them, so we should represent a lower-risk option for them than going to the market to find another consultancy. Our relationship should also mean that by leveraging our knowledge of the client, its culture, and its processes, we can reduce the time required to deliver a solution and, hence, our fees. Extending an existing client relationship removes our direct new client acquisition costs and reduces the management time needed to achieve a sale.
- **Using non-time-based payment mechanisms** in a falling market can disguise levels of discounting and prevent setting client expectations for future work. This may be as simple as offering a fixed price for an assignment or could use the outcome-based mechanisms discussed earlier.

Increasing complexity of engagements

The space within which we deliver management consultancy is increasingly more complex and intricate. Again, our old friend, the PESTLE framework, is a valuable tool for analysing this trend towards complexity as it continues to develop. We can also map our response to complexity on four dimensions: technological disruption, global business developments, industrial complexity, and client structural complexity.

- **Technological disruption**: Each previous digital revolution has ushered in a new era of complexity for business and, hence, opportunity for management consultancies. This is because leading-edge technology adoption means that our clients need assistance in areas with which their staff and managers are unfamiliar. Our tactical responses to this change are those that have been proven in past cycles of disruptive technologies, such as partnering with innovative companies and academic institutions, developing cutting-edge solutions, and working to keep abreast of the latest trends. In doing this, it may be necessary to focus on niche areas, including applying a particular technology in a client sector. We can also build an enhanced technology team. As a people-based business, we constantly need to increase organisational learning and development in emerging technologies. Achieving this may be through recruitment, although there will always be a shortage of sufficiently skilled candidates at the leading edge, or by developing existing staff skills. We also need to use emergent technologies, such as AI, to support consultants in delivering engagements.

- **Global business developments**: Business operations within and between companies are becoming increasingly either integrated or interdependent. This presents us and the business with a series of unique challenges. Increasingly frequently, we have to collaborate with clients and their stakeholders, who may come from diverse cultural backgrounds. This necessitates developing strong intercultural communication skills and sensitivity to local customs and business practices. For example, in one single meeting where client staff and lawyers were from a Hungarian local authority, the suppliers were German, although with an American lawyer and a Serbian project manager, and the funding bank representatives were Dutch, British and Romanian.[2] A diverse range of global political events, market shifts, and other adverse occurrences impact the environment in which our clients operate. This requires us to be able to assess and mitigate risks to our clients across multiple geographies. For example, consider the impact on globalised supply chains when, in 2021, the Suez Canal, one of the world's major trading routes, was blocked for six days by the massive container ship Ever Given. This highlighted the vulnerability of global supply chains to single points of failure, giving rise to significant international, multidisciplinary consultancy opportunities. Our response to this challenge could include the following:

  - Building a global expertise client offer through establishing a global network of consultants with diverse professional, cultural, and linguistic skills required through various partnering, subcontracting, or similar arrangements.
  - Developing global delivery models by establishing a presence in different key locations to develop local relationships and access local-based skills to support global clients.
  - Preparing regular geopolitical risk assessments so that we remain informed about geopolitical trends and can assess their potential impact on the operations of both our existing and potential clients.

- **Industry complexity**: The industrial landscape is continually changing, and the boundaries of previously separate industries are blurring due to the rapid pace of technology changes and shifting consumer preferences. Industry convergence is defined as companies from different sectors starting to provide similar products. Technology changes or market opportunities, such as exploiting a brand name, could drive this convergence. Examples include technology companies, which are increasingly entering the healthcare sector with digital health solutions, vehicle manufacturers providing technology services (and vice versa), and online retailers providing IT solutions.[3]

  Convergence presents many opportunities for us where we can leverage our multi-industry expertise to develop unique strategies and approaches that take full advantage of the client's increasing range of capabilities. Offering services that span the industries in which the client operates means that we can differentiate ourselves from our competitors. Our response to such change could include the following:

- Understanding the range of industries our clients are interested in and developing collaborative networks of consultants covering those industries to continue offering clients a comprehensive service.
- Developing the requisite industry experience within our teams through training, recruitment, or employee exchange schemes with clients.
- Promoting collaboration between consultants from different industry teams mirrors our clients. This may include reviewing the ways in which our internal processes and reporting have created siloed operations.
- Monitoring industry trends and keeping current with emerging technologies, for example, through research, attending conferences, and industry publications.

- **Client complexity** is increasingly an issue, and our clients often have intricate and multifaceted structures, each of which presents a unique situation. Such complexities increase as our clients:

  - Cultivate or acquire multiple and disparate business units, each seemingly working in a separate vertical silo with their own goals.
  - Interact with diverse stakeholder groups which have their own agendas.
  - Develop seemingly baroque and time-consuming ways of arriving at decisions.

  Consulting within such complex internal situations necessitates a deeper than usual comprehension of the client's various cultures and dynamics. Achieving this means that a diplomat's ability to bring together diverse parties and seek out their common interests and complementary goals is often necessary! Our responses to complex client operational structures and cultures may include the following:

  - Investment in gaining a comprehensive picture of current and target client organisations, their aims, operations, and culture.
  - Taking a total client approach to customer relationship building and seeking to develop trust and senior-level rapport across all areas of target clients through continuing engagement and open dialogue.
  - Preparing proactive suggestions for engagements aiming to deliver highly customised solutions that will address each client's unique needs and help them to deliver their strategic objectives.

Talent management

As in global sports and the arts, management consultancy succeeds only when it attracts, fosters, and retains top talent. Often represented as a "war for talent," the truth is that good talent is always in short supply, and consultancy is only one of the career options for suitable candidates. Given the nature of the changes in the demand for consultancy services, this shortage of top consulting talent will likely continue to increase. In addition to the global talent shortage, there are regional and local trends which also impact the availability of suitable consultancy talent, including the following:

- **North America**: Rapid technological change means a massive demand for digital skills. IDC, the global technical market intelligence company, surveyed North American IT leaders in 2024, and over 60% reported that their organisation had missed revenue growth objectives, experienced quality problems, and seen a decline in customer satisfaction due to a lack of skills. In particular, there are increasing demands in "hot" technology areas such as cybersecurity, data analytics, and AI, where a survey by the Federal Reserve Bank of Atlanta in 2024 revealed that job postings requiring AI skills had increased by 50% since 2022.

- **Europe**: In addition to similar challenges faced in North America, research by the European Union has revealed further problems in their labour markets, including demographic change: From 2009 to 2023, the EU's working-age population declined by 3.3% and is expected to decline by a further 10.2% by 2050, from 272 million to 263 million, and it is expected to further decline to 236 million by 2050. A linked challenge will be meeting the increasing demand for skilled workers generated by the green and digital transitions, which is difficult because of a current skill shortage in STEM areas (science, technology, engineering, and maths).
- **UK**: Here, there are similar skill shortage problems to those in Europe, including an ageing population, decreasing economic activity levels of working-age people, and mismatches between the education system and industry needs. A 2024 survey of hiring managers by global talent services company Morgan McKinley reported that 76% found recruitment challenging, including a shortage of skilled technical candidates and difficulties competing on pay. These findings were echoed by the Chartered Management Institute, which found that 70% of managers and 78% of small to medium enterprises experienced difficulties recruiting appropriately skilled staff.
- **India**: An employment market characterised by a rapidly growing workforce with significant skill gaps in emerging technologies. There is also a cause for concern in the disparity in the population ageing profile between urban and rural areas. According to India's National Family Health Survey-5, the Total Fertility Rate in urban areas in 2019–2021 was 1.6, which is similar to much of Europe and the USA, but in rural areas, it was 2.1, which is on a par with many developing countries in Africa, Asia, and South America. In 2024, the National Skill Development Corporation (NSDC) released a study identifying a considerable shortage of qualified workers in India. This study estimated a demand for 103 million skilled people, but the existing supply is only 74 million. A significant cause of this gap is the changing profile of the Indian economy with the emergence of multiple rapid growth sectors, including healthcare, semiconductor manufacturing, green jobs, and artificial intelligence.
- **Australia** experiences acute talent shortages across various sectors, including healthcare, education, construction, and logistics. The Australian government's 2024 Occupations Shortage List identified one-third of all occupations as facing national-level labour shortages, rising to 45% for professionals and 50% for technicians and skilled workers.

Given the global and local demands, which are not likely to ease, each consultancy should adopt a strategic approach to talent acquisition and management and prepare detailed talent management plans that reflect their own needs and situation. Each plan should include a consideration of the following:

- **Talent sourcing, development, and progression**: Seeking and retaining the most outstanding people, nurturing existing talent, and ensuring they acquire the latest skills and knowledge are necessary strategies but not sufficient to ensure our continuing business success. We need to supplement this with realistic progression and reward pathways to ensure that our consultancy continues to be resourced to meet the challenges being presented by our clients. This may require reviewing our career progression models to ensure that our experienced consultants are retained for engagement delivery, even where they are not on a management career pathway.

- **Diversity**: When we create diverse and inclusive workplaces, we help promote our reputation among applicants as a first-choice employer and increase our talent pool. This necessitates a policy that addresses diversity, equality, and inclusion (DEI), for example, by
  - Adjusting our working practices to support people with different life commitments or limitations as much as possible.
  - Ensuring equitable recruitment practices, for example, reaching out to the broadest range of educational institutions and providing internship, apprenticeship, and mentorship programmes.
  - Reviewing our policies, procedures, and practices to ensure that the career progression of all our staff, consultants, and support staff is based on merit alone.
- **Exploiting the power of advanced technologies**: If used effectively, these will revolutionise talent management practices, and we can help our clients at two levels, strategically and tactically. At the strategic level, AI-powered tools and data analytics can help us to improve workforce planning, identify skill gaps, and personalise employee experiences. For example, AI-driven platforms streamline recruitment processes and dovetail staff formal training and assignment experience with company strategy recommendations.[4] Tactically, AI can help by improving the matching of consultants with suitable engagements, an area which becomes exponentially more complex as a consultancy team grows and consultants from different areas or offices are less well known to engagement directors.
- **Hybrid teaming**: Linking client site consultants with remote or dispersed team members works particularly well on large-scale engagements or where a wide variety of skills are required. The potential advantages of hybrid teams include the following:
  - Scarce resource sharing, ensuring that the best available talent is assigned to the client irrespective of location.
  - Reduced charges to the client to cover travel and accommodation costs.
  - Ability to access skills internationally that would not be available for travel to the client site due to cost, national employment restrictions, their need for only short or intermittent periods, or personal circumstances.
  - Increased capacity to support on-site teams with external partners and contractors drawn from a global rather than a local talent pool.
  - Increased knowledge-sharing opportunities and broader client experience by consultants across the organisation.
- **Collaboration**: Collaborating with leading academic institutions, technology providers, and industry associations to access a wider talent pool can be highly effective in creating innovative solutions for clients. This approach has further advantages when linked with knowledge and skills transfer to consultants, enabling them to remain at the cutting edge of industry trends and academic thinking.
- **Standing out from the crowd**: High positive visibility helps ensure our attractiveness to talented applicants and supports talent retention. This requires building a respected employer brand and creating a positive experience for all employees. Ways to improve standing out to consider include the following:
  - Providing bonuses for existing employees who introduce successful new staff. Employees are our best advocates, and if a "stand out from the crowd" strategy works effectively, they will promote our consultancy through their physical and social networks and work to attract talented individuals. A reward mechanism for bringing in quality recruits helps cement such activity as a valued part of our culture.

- Investing in branding initiatives focused on potential employees. There are multiple opportunities to stimulate interest in joining a consultancy, such as creating genuinely engaging content for social media platforms to demonstrate a consultancy's culture, values, ethos and career pathways, unique culture, values, and career opportunities. This could include behind-the-scenes videos and employee success stories. This is also an area where showcasing activities underlining a commitment to DEI can be effective.
- Remaining competitive when offering compensation packages. Surprisingly, the Australian Government's 2024 Skills Shortages review reported that in the three years to 2024, less than 1% of employers altered remuneration in response to being unable to fill skilled vacancies. To continue to attract and retain top talent, we should regularly benchmark our remuneration and benefits packages to confirm that they are at least in line with, or ahead of, our competitors and employment opportunities more widely.
- Embracing flexible work arrangements. If we can offer the potential for remote and hybrid working and flexible hours, we will be perceived as a workplace that genuinely recognises the importance of work–life balance.
- Being recognised for a culture of continuous learning by clear career progression paths supported by appropriate training programmes, mentorship opportunities, and coaching.

Impact of business digitisation on management consultancy

Digitisation continues to drive a profound transformation of business operations globally. Whilst the full consideration of these changes is outside the scope of this book, the transformation is continually reshaping how companies are able to operate and compete, including:

- Global reach expansion.
- Supply chain efficiency improvements.
- Customer experience enhancement.
- Innovation in operations supported.
- Data-driven insights available in actual or near real time.
- Remote and hybrid working enabled.
- Range of routine tasks fully automated dramatically increased.

The balance of engagements for which clients seek consultancy support is shifting as they seek more support for their digital revolution. Consultancies have seen a trend towards clients wanting to create technology-driven solutions and develop innovative business models. This trend requires that we continue to evolve our consulting skills in different areas, including the following:

- **Digital transformation**: Our services can guide clients through intricate digital changes to enhance efficiency and foster innovation. We can lead a client's transformation through services ranging from the initial assessment of a client's digital readiness through formulating digital strategies to implementing AI-driven solutions.
- **Cybersecurity**: As businesses increasingly rely on information technology, cybersecurity and resilience become paramount. Engagements in this area typically involve evaluating IT security, documenting weaknesses, and designing robust, interlocking measures to improve security. There is also a high potential for work related to mitigating risks to business resilience arising from our clients' increasing dependence on digital services and systems, many of which are operated outside their direct control, for example, through the use of cloud computing.

- **Data analytics**: The increased availability of data, especially "big data," is spurring demands for data analytics and business intelligence consulting. Engagements in these areas may involve designing and implementing effective data analytics strategies, developing a data governance framework, and using advanced analytics to create new business insights.
- **Customer experience**: Digital transformation has revolutionised customer experience, driving down customer interaction costs and increasing customer expectations. Typical customer experience engagements include developing customer strategies and designing, enhancing, and integrating customer interactions across multiple digital channels. This may require integrating AI and data analytics technologies into CRM and call centre systems and developing personalised customer interactions.
- **Supply chain and logistics**: We can help clients integrate digital technologies to optimise their supply chain operations by improving visibility and increasing efficiency. This may require, for example, assisting clients in implementing the Internet of Things and AI solutions to enable them to improve service levels, integrate with customer-facing systems, and drive down costs.
- **Advanced manufacturing**: Clients are looking for consultancies to assist them in adopting innovative manufacturing technologies like 3D printing, robotics, and advanced materials. Work in this area, for example, could involve identifying where clients might drive down costs and time to market through integrating 3D printing into their manufacturing processes, thereby facilitating rapid prototyping, individual customisation, and low-volume production.

Other emergent disruptive technologies

The technology revolution cycle will continue speeding up as increasingly current generation technologies are used to visualise, develop, and deploy the next-generation technologies. Two things are clear: Detailed predictions as to the impact of change will not be accurate, and the adoption of new processes and changing technology by organisations will follow the well-worn pattern:

- **Pioneers and innovators**: Seeking to derive advantage by working at the leading edge of change and prepared to accept the risk of failure.
- **Early adopters**: Seeking to move ahead of their competitors by adopting change that has been demonstrated to work.
- **Early majority**: Cautious and slow to move but will accept new ideas after a period of careful consideration.
- **Late majority**: Often sceptical and personally resistant to change and are often in a catch-up situation after a change has been widely accepted and shown to be necessary or highly successful.
- **Laggards**: Virtually every consultant will recognise the mantra of the laggard, "but we have always done it this way." They cling to traditional methods, resist change, and may never be willing to accept new ideas or technologies.

There are, however, some emerging technology trends that are or are expected to be disrupting business in different industries. Management consultancy needs to keep these trends under review and consider the impact that they will continue to have on the type of services that we will need to offer and the types of clients to whom we should be marketing our services:

- **Artificial intelligence and machine learning**: These technologies will continue to develop rapidly. They will replace some cognitive work in the same way that mechanisation in agriculture and industry has replaced much manual work, not completely, but where it is more efficient, effective, and economical to do so. They will continue to expand their impacts on an increasingly wide range of business operations. This impact will include automating processes and data-driven decisions. AI chatbots and virtual assistants will become prevalent in customer-facing services. AI developments include continuing to automate some consultancy processes. We need to regularly re-evaluate its potential for supporting our services in the same way as we would for our clients.

- **The internet of things (IoT)**: This technology will continue to connect an ever-growing number of devices and systems, empowering organisations to collect and analyse vast quantities of data. As sensors and communications improve their cost-effectiveness, the technology's immense capability will allow for real-time analysis and decision-making, from street drains reporting that they need emptying to intelligent buildings, connected supply chains ordering parts, and connected vehicles reporting road defects.
- **Augmented reality (AR) and virtual reality (VR)**:[5] These are moving from the gaming world and will transform business interactions with customers and employees. For example, within a consultancy engagement, we could use VR and AR to design and create realistic but flexible simulations and interactive training modules that offer hands-on learning experiences. Such simulations can be particularly useful for industries that require practical training, such as healthcare, manufacturing, and engineering.
- **5G communications technology**: This will deliver higher speed and more robust internet connections, which are essential for the further adoption of bandwidth-intensive technologies such as the IoT, augmented reality, and virtual reality. It will also boost the ability to work from anywhere and facilitate real-time data processing from remote devices and systems.
- **Blockchain technology**: This may disrupt many businesses and services by delivering new transacting methods with enhanced transparency, improved security, and tamper-proof records. Its continued evolution has the power to disrupt various sectors, including finance, healthcare, logistics, legal services, and the delivery of public services.
- **Advanced robotics**: We can expect this technology to reshape the future of many sectors, including manufacturing, logistics, and healthcare. Especially where skills are scarce, expensive, or work is unappealing, robots with enhanced capabilities will perform delicate and complex tasks, leading to increased productivity, reduced costs, and improved safety. For example, one innovation might be its introduction in agriculture to reduce the use of chemicals and labour requirements for field cultivation and to replace hand picking for fruit and vegetables.
- **Renewable energy**: Technologies, including energy storage, are changing the energy sector. Organisations are adopting renewable energy to reduce costs, minimise their carbon footprint, and deliver on sustainability targets. In addition, energy generation is becoming increasingly distributed, requiring new business models by energy suppliers.
- **Edge computing**: Shifts the processing of data closer to its origin. This reduces system time lags (latency), enabling genuine real-time decision-making. A mundane example of edge computing is speeding up the operation of ticket gates in a citywide metro system by validating a ticket holder's account information and balance in the gate rather than in a centralised data centre. Other advanced examples include smart factories where production lines are managed in real-time and the rapidly advancing field of autonomous vehicles.
- **Quantum computing**: Presents the possibility of solving complex problems that traditional computers cannot. While it may revolutionise some industries in the future, its commercial development is behind many other emergent technologies.
- **Biotechnology and genomics**: Developments may deliver significant change and disruption in healthcare and agriculture.

Reflections

Using either your own experience or the case study

- Please prepare a future vision statement for the consultancy that identifies how it will need to respond to the dynamic changes expected to impact the service demand.
- Please review and update the problem statements for three potential consultancy services prepared at the end of Chapter 2, considering the vision statement.
- How would you now amend the tailored consultancy matrix and team structure for your proposed team prepared at the end of Chapter 4?
- Please update the telephone script you prepared at the end of Chapter 6 to cover one of the three new problem areas you have identified.
- Set out the scope of a new client assignment based on one of the problem areas and a comprehensive plan for delivering it, including scope, resourcing, timing, deliverables, and quality standards.

Notes

1 PESTLE = **P**olitical, **E**conomic, **S**ociocultural, **T**echnological, **L**egal, **E**nvironmental (see Chapter 9).
2 Who tended to windmill arms when excited to such an extent as to endanger the life of other attendees.
3 My Caterpillar-branded spectacles and my Liebherr freezer. Both brands are associated with building sites moving vast quantities of earth!
4 I am unsure if AI can be used unfettered for this. In a small consultancy, we had two very experienced chartered accountants, both former financial directors of medium-sized companies. From an engineering background, one was blunt, direct, and very popular with manufacturing clients. The other's background was in service industries and was warm, supportive, empathetic, and loved by clients, including health and service-based companies. Swapping them would not have been disastrous, as both were highly competent professionals. It was felt that the company, the clients, and the consultants benefitted from the current arrangements.
5 However, in the interests of DEI, it is necessary to state that current technology does not cater well to us spectacle wearers. This is a particular problem where headsets are shared.

Bibliography

Australian Government. (2024). *2024 Occupations Shortage List: Key Findings and Insights*. Retrieved from https://www.jobsandskills.gov.au/data/occupation-shortages-analysis

Chartered Management Institute. (2024). *Recruitment Challenges: Skilled Staff Shortages Among Managers and SMEs*. Retrieved from https://www.managers.org.uk

European Commission. (2024, March 20). *Labour and Skills Shortages in the EU: An Action Plan* (COM(2024) 131 final). Brussels: European Commission. Retrieved from https://eur-lex.europa.eu/legal-content/EN/TXT/?uri=CELEX:52024DC0131

FederalReserve Bank of Atlanta. (2024, October 15). *Recent Trends in the Demand for AI Skills*. Retrieved from https://www.atlantafed.org/blogs/macroblog/2024/10/15/recent-trends-in-demand-for-ai-skills

Ministry of Health and Family Welfare. (2024). *India's National Family Health Survey-5 (2019–21): Total Fertility Rate Insights*. Retrieved from https://www.mohfw.gov.in

Morgan McKinley. (2024). *2024 Survey of Hiring Managers: Recruitment Challenges and Skills Shortages*. Retrieved from https://www.morganmckinley.com/uk/article/7-key-recruitment-challenge

National Skill Development Corporation. (2024). *Study on Skilled Workforce Demand and Supply in India*. Retrieved from https://manufacturing.economictimes.indiatimes.com/news/industry/how-india-can-bridge-talent-and-skill-gaps-in-key-emerging-sectors/112585703

Index

Kolibri 360 GmbH
Ferdinand-Jühlke-Straße 7
99095 Erfurt, Deutschland
produktsicherheit@kolibri360.de